D1736256

From the Collection of
Friends of the Columbus
Metropolitan Library

DEAR DR. SPOCK

Dear Dr. Spock

Letters about the Vietnam War to

America's Favorite Baby Doctor

EDITED BY MICHAEL S. FOLEY

NEW YORK UNIVERSITY PRESS
New York and London

NEW YORK UNIVERSITY PRESS
New York and London
www.nyupress.org

© 2005 by New York University
All rights reserved

All letters reprinted by kind permission of the Benjamin Spock
Papers, Syracuse University Library, Special Collections Research
Center.

Library of Congress Cataloging-in-Publication Data
Dear Dr. Spock : letters about the Vietnam War to America's
favorite baby doctor / edited by Michael S. Foley.
p. cm.
Includes bibliographical references and index.
ISBN-13: 978-0-8147-2743-0 (cloth : alk. paper)
ISBN-10: 0-8147-2743-3 (cloth : alk. paper)
1. Vietnamese Conflict, 1961–1975—Public opinion.
2. Publicopinion—United States.   3. Spock, Benjamin, 1903-—
Correspondence.   4. Pediatricians—United States—Correspondence.   I. Foley, Michael S.
DS559.62.U6D425   2005
959.704'3373—dc22   2005014304

New York University Press books are printed on acid-free paper,
and their binding materials are chosen for strength and durability.

Manufactured in the United States of America
10 9 8 7 6 5 4 3 2 1

For my parents,
   Bill and Judy Foley

CONTENTS

ACKNOWLEDGMENTS

To START with the obvious, this book would have been impossible without the incomparable life of Dr. Benjamin Spock. I regret that I did not get to interview him for this project or for my book on draft resistance. When I began research on the antiwar movement I thought of him primarily as a celebrity figurehead; I could not have been more wrong. Regardless of what one thinks of his politics, few Americans have ever taken their citizenship as seriously as Spock. The people who wrote to him during the Vietnam War understood this better than his biographers (we are long overdue for a study that takes Spock's second career in politics as seriously as his first as a pediatrician), and I thank them, too. In many ways, technological advances have stolen from us our most basic instruments of democratic participation; the pens, pencils, and typewriters used to write long, thoughtful letters to public figures have become historical artifacts, replaced by the e-mails and voice mails that we instinctively sense go ignored by their recipients. Americans cannot afford the resulting discouragement. I hope the letters in this volume inspire more active citizenship—in many forms—particularly during wartime.

Dr. Spock's papers are carefully tended, organized and made available to researchers at the Bird Library, Syracuse University, in New York State. There, in the Special Collections Research Center, I have made innumerable research (and photocopy) requests from both on-site and off-site Spock Collection record groups and was never met with anything but good cheer. Carolyn Davis, in particular, has been an enthusiastic and thoughtful supporter of the project. Nicolette Schneider has succeeded Carolyn ably, and helped with critical last-minute details.

Even before they became my in-laws, John and Pat Dale opened their home to me as a comfortable base for my research runs into Syracuse. They have so spoiled me with a place to stay, tasty meals, and even a parking pass for the SU campus that I almost dread the lonely research trips to distant archives that future projects will undoubtedly bring.

Their genuine interest in my work and loving support have meant the world to me.

The City University of New York and, specifically, the College of Staten Island extended invaluable institutional support. A PSC-CUNY grant provided much needed funding for travel and research, and a dean's reassigned time grant gave me time to prepare a first draft. Dean Francisco Soto has been unwavering in his support, and my colleagues in the History Department continue to inspire me with their own work and offer steady encouragement for mine. François Ngolet, in particular, has been a steady presence in the life of this project, gently prodding me along while working on his own book. Thanks, too, to Kate Crehan and the Women's Studies seminar for comments on an early sampling of letters.

The staff at the Library of Congress Prints and Photographs Division helped me find and duplicate about half of the images in this book—and at a reasonable price. My friend Katie Porter hand-delivered my photo duplication request to the Library of Congress and, thus, greatly reduced my anxiety. The rest of the images required significant deficit spending on my part, but I was fortunate to receive generous help in erasing some of that debt, thanks to Dean Soto and the CUNY Research Foundation, NYU Press, and my friend Kevin Vickery. I have known Kevin since we were undergrads, and we later worked for the same company for more years than I care to remember; although I changed careers and he moved to Seattle, this is not the first time he has bailed me out in the ensuing years.

One often toils in isolation for long stretches in this profession, so the confidence and prodding of mentors, peers, and friends always comforts me and frequently hits like an adrenaline rush. In addition to those mentioned above, Harvard Sitkoff, Michael Ferber, Sandi Cooper, James Carroll, Robert McElvaine, Harriet Alonso, Chris Appy, Ian Lekus, Thomas LeBien, and Marc Favreau were responsible, at one point or another, for such jolts of support. Many long conversations with David Lichtenstein have helped me to (more often than not) keep moving forward. And my life is so much richer for the intellectual pursuits, marches, protests, concerts, baseball games, and countless stories that John McMillian, Tim McCarthy, and Jeremy Varon have shared with me.

For reading complete drafts of the manuscript, I am especially indebted to Amy Schneidhorst, Mel Small, Phil Napoli, and Andrew Hunt—each of whom made insightful, cogent suggestions that vastly improved the final draft. Andrew, in particular, helped me to completely overhaul and rearrange the manuscript from a strictly chronological presentation to a more thematic and more accessible one. It saved the book.

At New York University Press, Eric Zinner is truly an editorial *director*. He saw the manuscript's potential in my first draft, huddled with me over how to improve it, solicited exactly the kind of advice I needed from the outside reviewers, and then left me alone to do the work. Emily Park helped facilitate seemingly everything, and was especially helpful in choosing images. Copyeditor Alice Calaprice polished the manuscript with great care, and managing editor Despina Papazoglou Gimbel artfully ushered it through all stages of production.

Kathryn Dale and Emma Foley give me more than they can ever fully understand. Whenever I, in Johnny Cash's phrase, "see a darkness," Kathy rescues me. So many of the letters in this book—particularly those from parents writing about their children—make me think of Emma. Not unlike Dr. Spock in that famous *New York Times* ad, I worry about the world she will inherit. But Emma's sunny spirit, her wicked sense of humor, and her sweet, sweet affection for seemingly everyone and everything give me hope, every day.

Finally, this book is dedicated to my parents who claim to have eschewed Dr. Spock's baby and child care advice because it made a brat of my uncle Bob—a terrible thing to say about a guy, especially when it clearly did not last. My parents may have sabotaged my one chance to see the Clash in 1982 (I've recently forgiven them), but during the Vietnam War, they largely succeeded in sheltering me from the horrors while quietly wearing POW/MIA bracelets, instead got me juiced up for every Apollo launch, and later tried to explain Watergate. Thanks to them, my interest in American history and politics began in the war years. I am grateful that they also managed to instill in me lifelong passion for good music, the arts, and the Boston Red Sox. Dr. Spock, I think, would have been pleased.

①

3-2-68

Dear Doctor Spock;

We were very disappointed to learn of your taking part in the "peace" demonstrations. As young parents of 5 children, we are well acquainted with your book on child care, and have come to (and still do) respect your authority on this subject.

As you have guessed, I do support our position on Viet Nam. You must get a lot of mail these days, but I do hope you will take the time to personally read and answer this letter, and weigh my arguments.

I have read your story in several publications. I think I understand why you feel as you do. You have a lot of courage. However, here are my arguments against your position:

① You do not have the right to break the law. By participating in "civil disobedience", you have shown a serious irresponsibility; a self-centered attitude. These laws were made of the people. There are due processes for changing them. This is still a free society. By violating our laws, you have demonstrated distain for our country, our people, and our democratic processes. Can you see that you have tried to elevate yourself above us? In all seriousness, what now distinguishes you from a common criminal? Laws are set up for our common good. They make possible an atmosphere of freedom from fear and oppression, in which we can work, live, and raise our families. What if the citizens who have not the high

Sample of a letter. (Benjamin Spock Papers, Syracuse University Library, Special Collections Research Center)

Introduction

IN THE wake of the Internet and telecommunications revolutions, one strains to remember that, not long ago, Americans wrote letters—lots of letters. Long before the advent of e-mail, cellular phones, and faxes narrowed the mailman's job to delivering mostly bills, catalogs, and junk mail, that postal employee proudly bore the title of "letter-carrier" to reflect the importance of his most precious cargo. Americans wrote letters all the time. They sat at kitchen tables, at desks, at pieces of furniture called "secretaries"—designed specifically with letter-writing in mind—and composed missives, long and short, silly and serious, to friends and loved ones. And they also wrote to public figures.

For historians, the art of letter-writing carried unintended benefits, for many people kept the letters they received. Social convention dictated that the recipient should not dispose of a well-crafted letter—or of letters, well crafted or not, from a loved one. As a result, manuscript collections in archives all over the world hold vast collections of correspondence that help historians make sense of the times in which they were written. Of course, most libraries and archives hold only the correspondence of relatively elite or famous people, but on occasion, such individuals corresponded with the nonelite and less famous in their societies. Fortunately for students of the past, they did not trash the letters.

This is the case with the letters published in this book. Although they are located within the Papers of Dr. Benjamin Spock, the famed pediatrician, they were written by "ordinary" Americans. Most important, the authors wrote these letters between 1965 and 1972, during a brutal and controversial war in Vietnam, at a time when Spock had become one of the leading figures in opposing the war at home.

In short, these letters offer one of the first clear views of the American home front during the Vietnam War. Although thirty years have passed since the fall of Saigon, and although the Vietnam War ranks behind only the Civil War and World War II as a subject of historical interest and inquiry in the United States, the home front experience of ordinary Americans during the nation's longest war remains largely unexamined. Historians have, of course, written extensively about America as a divided nation during the war, emphasizing the antiwar movement and its critics.[1] Likewise, considerable attention has been given to American society in the aftermath of the war, with emphasis on the lingering "shadow" or "scar" it left behind.[2] Hollywood, too, has provided glimpses of the home front (*The Deer Hunter, Born on the Fourth of July, Dead Presidents,* and *Forrest Gump*) amid the proliferation of films on the war itself, but as so often happens, those film portrayals reduce complex experience to sometimes simplistic generalizations.

While historians have been examining American society during the Civil War and the Second World War for decades, today we know very little about the average American's home-front experience of the Vietnam War as it unfolded and persisted. Certainly, periodic polls conducted during the war provide general clues on the public's opinion of, for example, President Johnson's handling of the war, but less clear is what kind of information shaped ordinary Americans' views of the war and, more specifically, how they actually saw the war as it expanded and contracted.

This book, which presents the first collection of wartime writings on the Vietnam War by ordinary Americans, helps to plug that gap in our understanding. It is not a comprehensive study of the home front; rather, it offers a window into the minds of people trying to understand their government's policies in Vietnam and how those policies did or did not line up with Americans' varied definitions of America itself.

Americans did not write about the Vietnam War only to Dr. Spock. They wrote to Presidents Johnson and Nixon, to their representatives in Congress, and to the editors of their local newspapers. But for a variety of reasons, it makes sense to start this historical discussion with the letters to Spock. For one thing, the letters are all in one place—a library at Syracuse University—and they are relatively well organized. In contrast, although the Lyndon B. Johnson Presidential Library in Austin, Texas, houses millions of citizen letters to the president, the letters are not organized topically; instead, they are organized alphabetically by the senders' last names; to sift through all of those letters looking only for those on the war could take years. The Nixon Presidential Materials Project, housed at the National Archives, on the other hand, does have citizen letters organized by topic, but those letters begin only in 1969—after the war's escalation peaked. No doubt there are thousands of citizen letters in the papers of war critics Senators J. William Fulbright, Wayne Morse, George McGovern, and Eugene McCarthy as well as in the papers of war supporters Congressmen Mendel Rivers and John McCormack, Senator Barry Goldwater, or any number of others. But those letters, like letters to newspapers, are limited in their geographic origin and seem less likely to convey the level of familiarity seen in many of the letters to Spock.

Thanks to his career as the world's most famous baby doctor, Spock had established a special relationship with most of the letter-writers in this book long before their attention turned to the Vietnam War. Since the publication of *The Common Sense Book of Baby and Child Care* in 1946, Spock had achieved a status beyond mere celebrity in millions of American homes; as many mothers and fathers said in their letters to him, a generation of parents regarded him as extended family—a trusted, grandfatherly figure who consistently reassured them during the inevitable crises that arise when raising children. The good doctor's opening line—"Trust yourself. You know more than you think you do"—endeared Spock to millions of parents, and his straightforward advice consistently worked. By one biographer's estimate, one in three children born in the mid-1950s were raised with Spock's book. According to one poll of more than one thousand new mothers, 64 percent had read *Baby and Child Care,* and of that group 80 percent referred to the book at least twice each month.[3] The book and all its revised editions went on to sell more than any other book in the English language, save the Bible.

Consequently, through the 1950s and 1960s (and beyond) Spock received tens of thousands of letters each year, most from parents seeking answers to specific questions. He answered every one, albeit often by form letter: letters on diapers, vomiting, potty training, a wide array of behavioral issues, breast feeding, rashes, and so on. He had become, for so many Americans, a hometown doctor—accessible, thoughtful, and reassuring.

Dr. Spock did not answer letters only about babies and children, however. Beginning in the early 1960s, Spock's concern for children began to extend itself more publicly into issues of foreign policy and national defense. In particular, Spock decried the nuclear arms race, fearing the incineration of millions of children he had helped to raise if the United States and the Soviet Union did not arrive at a safe balance of power. In 1962, he appeared in a famous advertisement in the *New York Times,* paid for by the Committee for a Sane Nuclear Policy (SANE), in which he appeared towering over a small child, an expression of concern on his face. "Dr. Spock is Worried," the ad said, and, in his own words, a letter to readers went on to detail the perils of nuclear weapons testing. The next year, with wide popular support, President John F. Kennedy signed the Nuclear Test Ban Treaty with the Soviets.

Over the next several years, as Spock neared his retirement from medicine, he worked more steadily—and more publicly—for nuclear disarmament and peace. Following Kennedy's assassination, Spock saw the 1964 presidential campaign as a clear choice between a candidate more likely to lead the nation to war (Republican Barry Goldwater) and an incumbent candidate more likely to keep the nation out of war (Democrat Lyndon Johnson). This was no mere spot judgment. Spock had written to both Kennedy and Johnson regarding growing tensions in Vietnam, Laos, and Cuba, urging them to take the path of peace since 1962, and both presidents appeared to listen. Johnson, especially, impressed Spock with his sweeping Great Society agenda which Spock thought, if enacted, would do more for the health and security of children than that of any previous administration. Consequently, Spock went to work for the Johnson campaign, consistently portraying Johnson as a man of peace and a protector of children.

By 1965, however, Spock felt duped. As described at the start of chapter 1, Johnson had won passage of the Gulf of Tonkin Resolution and seemed poised to commit the United States to a protracted war in Southeast Asia. Spock, as both the co-director of SANE and a private citizen, began to speak out more forcefully on the Vietnam War. The devastation wrought by American bombing, the use of napalm and chemical defoliants, and the deaths of civilians—including children—appalled him. Moreover, he never conceded to the arguments that communism had to be stopped in Vietnam, that to pacify aggressors—as the Allies had done with Hitler at Munich—would usher in the next world war. Indeed, Spock believed quite the opposite: that continued American intervention promised to spur the Chinese to defend North Vietnam (as they had done in Korea fourteen years earlier) and possibly set off World War III. Spock was a quick study and made use of his knowledge in both public and private discussions of the war. He criticized the Eisenhower administration's successful efforts to subvert the 1954 Geneva Accords, which would have unified Vietnam under one government, and lamented the damage that continued intervention did to America's standing in world opinion.

Spock's status as America's and the world's baby doctor clearly fueled many of the letters he received about the Vietnam War. Suddenly, this trusted figure, the man to whom so many turned at 3:00 A.M. when faced with a sick child, had become one of the foremost critics of the American war in Vietnam. It puzzled some Americans, and angered or comforted others. Thousands wrote to him to share their feelings.

But who were "they?" Who wrote these letters? The answer reveals both the limitations and promise of publishing these letters. I can make no claim that the writers whose letters appear in this book are in any way representative of the broader American public during the Vietnam War. As Robert McElvaine noted in the introduction to a similar volume of letters on the Great Depression, "unlike the answering of questions in a poll, the writing of a letter obviously requires a conscious decision. Mail comes from people who are especially interested in the subjects about which they write, while polling organizations ask 'everyone' without regard for level of concern."[4] At the same time, however, the content of these letters makes clear that the Vietnam War intruded on the authors' daily lives and their consciousness. These were not professional activists or political gadflies. They were citizens of Middle America.

Indeed, it is my contention that these letters come from what Richard Nixon termed the "silent majority." Seemingly unaware of national polls showing how unpopular the war was in October 1969, Nixon responded to antiwar demonstrations that month by suggesting that a small, vocal minority of protesters garnered a disproportionate amount of attention from the nation's media. In a November 3 speech, he accused that minority of jeopardizing national security and of humiliating America, and he concluded by calling on "the great silent majority" of Americans to drown out the voices of that minority by supporting his administration's policies in Vietnam. For Nixon, the speech resulted in only a temporary increase in his poll numbers, but it implied that somewhere out there a block of Americans—presumably white, middle-class, law-abiding citizens—had been watching the war and watching the country come apart over it.

There's no way to define exactly who the silent majority included, of course; there were no membership cards, and even if there had been, one could not prove that any of the letter-writers in this book carried them. Nevertheless, it is possible to generalize from the evidence. A reasonable estimate of the number of letters Spock received on the Vietnam War would be about 5,000 to 7,000. I have read all of those letters and selected the ones for this volume as a representative chunk (the first selection process collected more than 700 letters, and subsequent rounds of winnowing brought the number to 218). A review of all of the letters will show that although they certainly do not include a proportional number of letters of support—Spock received many, many brief letters on the war that could be categorized more as "fan mail" than anything else—the ones published here are not exceptional in their ideas or in the quality of their prose.

Very few of the letters' authors identified themselves as vocal participants in either the antiwar movement or as supporters of the war; few of them, therefore, would fit the class of people pilloried by Nixon in the "silent majority" speech. In fact, few of the writers identify themselves as Democrat or Republican. The circumstantial evidence suggests that the vast majority of these writers were at least middle class. Unlike McElvaine's Depression-era letter-writers, whose contrasting educational levels are obvious from the varied quality of the writing, most of these letters are well written. These writers were not poorly educated and few seem poor. Most of the letters were typed on typewriters and many of them came on personalized stationery. In addition, while letters from the Northeast and California seem most common, some letters came from truly remote areas. Most of these people, however, made their homes in cities and suburbs, and most of the city dwellers give no hint of being anything but middle- to upper-class citizens. The Spock connection is important, too, for he had been criticized in later years for writing a baby book for the middle class. One gets the feeling from reading these letters, many of which are quite long, that these writers not only had time to read Spock's book, but that they also had time to compose long, thoughtful letters.

Admittedly, the forgoing is largely impressionistic and, consequently, may not be wholly convincing. Therefore, I pulled an unscientific sample of 300 letters—75 each from the full populations of 1966, 1967, 1968, and 1969 letters to Spock—as a way to further gauge *who* sent the letters. One might suspect, for example, that Spock would be more likely to receive mail from women than men or from people opposed to the war than supportive of it, and, sure enough, both of those generalizations hold, but only by slim margins. Of 300 writers, 143 were women (47.7 percent), 137 were men (45.7 percent), and 5 were written by couples (1.7 percent); the balance (15 letters or 5 percent) were written by someone whose gender could not be determined. Overall, of these 300 letters, 204 (68 percent) were opposed to the war, but that result is certainly skewed by the large numbers of brief expressions of support for Spock's stand—again, more accurately termed "fan mail" than anything else. Of the 75 letters chosen from 1967, when polling showed a relative balance of public opinion between those who supported and opposed the war, 35 writers (46.7 percent) wrote to Spock in support of the war and 40 (53.3 percent) opposed it. Among those writing to defend the war and administration policy, men outnumbered women, but at least 30 percent of those backing Johnson's or Nixon's handling of the war were women (and maybe more, since nearly 15 percent of the letters were written by someone whose gender was not clear, or by a male-female couple). Similarly, women outnumbered men in writing in opposition to the war, 55.9 percent to 40.7 percent.

The sample also shows further evidence that these letters came from Middle America. For example, approximately three-fourths of the letters written by women came from writers who identified themselves as married (most commonly by using "Mrs." when signing the letter or on the return address). In addition, more than half of the letters (53.3 percent, n = 160) were typed on a typewriter or came as telegrams. Eighty-four of the letters (28 percent) were written or typed on letterhead, and 115 of the letters (38.3 percent) took up two or more pages. Finally, it is worth noting that between the sample and the letters published here, 44 of the 50 states are represented (though I am confident that in the entire population of letters, Spock received them from every state), and that in the sample of 300, letters from California and New York State together account for nearly one-third (93 letters) of the mail. All of this evidence suggests, therefore, that the overwhelming majority of these letter-writers did not come from activist ranks. Instead, they reveal themselves to be rank-and-file citizens—our neighbors and co-workers—of the so-called silent majority.

Of course, if viewed as one slice of home-front life, maybe none of these statistics and assertions about the silent majority matter. Maybe what is most important is what the letters say during a period of intense national debate. In his recent provocative book, *War Is a Force That Gives Us Meaning,* combat correspondent Chris Hedges argues that during wartime, "we define ourselves. All other definitions do not count." Self-definition, and by extension, defining what it means to be American, is implicit in many of the letters in this book, but not always in the way that Hedges means. For example, while many of these letters' authors were driven to define themselves, America, and America's enemy from the same patriotic impulse Hedges criticizes, the writers who were critical of the American war in Vietnam also define themselves and their America. On the one hand, the author of letter 36, a supporter of the war, defined himself and America as loving peace, but loving freedom more: "We are aware that running from aggression is not the way to peace," he wrote. In this way, he defined himself and America as on the side of freedom in a fight against an aggressor (read: communists, North Vietnam). On the other hand, in letter 85, a mother of four wrote proudly of raising four healthy children, but frets at the prospect of having a son drafted. "I know I'm not alone in my thinking," she concluded. "I know all over the world, Russian, Chinese, Vietnamese mothers feel the same as I. And the day is here when we will not allow 'governments' to continue using the fruit of years of care as statistics in their insane plots." Clearly, this writer's definition of herself and what her country should be centers on the welfare of children—a notion seemingly irrelevant to the first writer.

The point here is that although war gives rise to much passionate debate—usually by elite commentators and public officials—public opinion polls rarely reveal the same depth of feeling or complexity of reasoning seen in these two letters. In wartime, most Americans go through a complicated process of weighing evidence before arriving at a set of conclusions about the rightness or wrongness of a particular war. But by the time polling data are sifted through the media in stories about public attitudes regarding a war, we usually get only two numbers: X percent support the president's handling of the war, while Y percent disapprove. Nuance, subtlety, and—most important—ambivalence are lost. The letters in this book show ordinary Americans struggling fiercely with their own perceptions of the war and their home country. As some of the writers assert their patriotism by summarizing long-standing anticommunist justifications for fighting in Vietnam, others resist such interpretations and insist that their dissent is patriotic. If policy makers in the Johnson and Nixon administrations had read these letters, they might have gained a better understanding of both the public's tolerance and intolerance for their war policies. At any point in the war's history, these letters give a pretty good sounding of public sentiment.[5]

The letters in this volume, therefore, complicate our understanding of what historians define all too generally as "Cold War culture." The defining variable of Cold War culture—anticommunism and its pervasive presence in American life—clearly is present in many of the letters sent to Dr. Spock. But as many of the other letters show, during the Vietnam War the pervasiveness was not as thoroughgoing as it is so often described. One leading scholar has suggested that Cold War culture "decomposed" by the mid-1960s, "when the moral distinction between East and West lost a bit of its sharpness, when American self-righteousness could be more readily punctured." Maybe so, though the anticommunist writings in these letters suggests otherwise.[6]

More recently, historians have suggested that the Cold War's impact on American culture has been "overstated," or that the home front battles of the Cold War "were fought primarily at an elite level."[7] But here again, the letters to Dr. Spock, written deep into the Cold War—even as Cold War culture supposedly decomposed—challenge such assertions. The Vietnam War, for most of Spock's correspondents, served as a representation of the Cold War. If these Americans did not debate the loyalty oaths and red-baiting of Joe McCarthy in the early 1950s, they certainly argued about loyalty and patriotism, communism and democracy in the late 1960s.

Another issue to which these letters speak is that of postwar gender roles. For decades, historians have written about the "containment" of women in their homes—in their roles as wives and mothers—going hand-in-hand with America's drive to contain communism abroad and on the home front. Betty Friedan described the middle-class suburban home as the "comfortable concentration camp," and depicted millions of unhappy women lying awake at night all over America, asking themselves, "Is this all?" Elaine Tyler May's splendid book, *Homeward Bound: American Families in the Cold War Era,* now twenty years old, does the best job of confirming that experience. The easy explanation for so many women writing about politics to a noted public figure is that they did so after Friedan awakened so many with *The Feminine Mystique,* and by 1969, as the women's liberation movement unfolded. It is more accurate, though, to view many of the letters from women— regardless of their stand on the war—as extensions of their maternal responsibilities. Jane Sherron DeHart reminds us that women have resorted to this practice throughout the nineteenth and early twentieth centuries, and notes that "in an era when dissent was routinely equated with communism, it is hardly surprising that so many women whose actions challenged containment norms used essentialist, maternalist, and familial rhetoric to justify their behavior."[8] Thus, on the one hand, in

January 1968, Spock received a letter from a New York mother who wrote, "As I sit here and fuss over my little one, I realize almost daily that women who were in my position 18 years ago are now receiving telegrams saying that their sons are dead, for the vaguest of reasons. And, perhaps even harder to bear is the picture of the Vietnamese mothers, holding their dead or disabled children in their arms and trying to figure out how they can continue to live, now that they have been blessed with 'democracy.'" A few days later, he received a letter from a Wisconsin mother who wrote, "My son is only two years old, so he can be of no help in this conflict. I can only hope that enough mothers have instilled enough love of country in their sons to erase at least part of the dark shadow of shame you have cast upon our land. I pray that if the time ever comes when my son is called on to serve, he will go forward bravely and with heart held high to do honor to America and all that she stands for."

Such rhetoric, rooted in both writers' maternal self-definitions, and written both in opposition and support of the war, makes generalizing difficult. Both use maternalist rhetoric as a way to challenge domestic containment even though one clearly endorses the concept of containment in foreign policy. Indeed, the latter also challenges arguments in the literature on women's peace activism that mothers are naturally opposed to war.[9]

Ultimately, then, this collection of letters to Dr. Spock provokes us to think about the Cold War differently, and it demands that we explore the Vietnam War home front more thoroughly. The letters herein represent, perhaps, the first pull on a new and undoubtedly long thread of historical inquiry. Maybe most important, they show that political leaders who either make war or oppose it—and invoke the mandate of "the People"—do so at their own risk. The generalizations fed by public officials to the American people during wartime—generalizations that mask the obvious complexity of thought among such a broad populace—seem, at best, trite and, at worst, disingenuous or stupid. Yet such behavior persists. Perhaps this collection can serve a modest corrective function by showing a core sample of Americans who struggled so mightily to make sense of a past war as it unfolded. Their arguments, pleas, admonitions, and praise give us a unique view into the enigmatic American mind in time of war. As the current administration braces Americans for a new global "war without end," the work of exploring this side of home-front America takes on new urgency.

A Note on the Letters

THE CONTENT of the letters printed in this volume, selected from thousands sent by Americans to Dr. Spock during the Vietnam War, are transcribed exactly as they appeared in their original form; only passages unrelated to the war have been deleted. No changes have been made to correct grammatical or spelling errors. Underscoring, italicization, and use of upper- and lower-case type likewise appear exactly as in the original letters (except in those common cases in which a man or woman handwrote a letter entirely in upper-case script). Street addresses and full names have been deleted in the interest of privacy, though initials have been retained, along with an indication of the letter-writer's sex.

Dr. Spock leading a demonstration of marchers, New York, 1965. Spock's profile as an antiwar leader rose quickly within weeks of the war's escalation in 1965. (Bettmann/CORBIS)

1 Gunfire in the Distance, 1965

IN THE summer of 1964, Benjamin Spock campaigned for President Lyndon Johnson's reelection. Spock had been impressed by Johnson's campaign pledge, repeated over and over in the spring and summer, that he would not "send American boys to fight in an Asian war." But Johnson felt pressure from the "hawks" in Congress who felt more needed to be done to contain communism in Southeast Asia. Most notably, Barry Goldwater, the prospective Republican nominee for president, had taken to blasting Johnson for not "carrying the war to North Vietnam."

In response, Johnson ordered a number of covert operations off the coast of North Vietnam, in the Gulf of Tonkin. There, American destroyers supported South Vietnamese commando raids by listening to North Vietnamese radio traffic. On August 1, North Vietnamese torpedo boats responded with a weak attack on the U.S.S. *Maddox*. The Johnson administration ignored the attack and ordered operations resumed. On August 4, when commanders of the *Maddox* and the *C. Turner Joy* again reported being under attack, Johnson went to Congress for what turned out to be a blank check for the president to wage war in Vietnam. Although the commanders on the two ships quickly reported that the ships sustained no damage and that the August 4 "attacks" may not have happened (they seemed to be the result of freak weather patterns and nervous radar and sonar men), the president did not pass this intelligence on to the Congress. Three days later, Congress passed the Gulf of Tonkin Resolution, authorizing the president to take "all necessary measures to repel any armed attacks against the forces of the United States and to prevent further aggression."

As the collection of letters below indicates, however, Vietnam appeared on the radar screens of few Americans in the fall of 1964. Letters to Spock throughout 1964 still focused primarily on child-care issues, though, thanks to Spock's position as co-chair of the National Committee for a Sane Nuclear Policy (SANE), a significant number

"Communism is Treason." Counterprotesters heckle peace demonstrators in New York, 1965. Many Americans wrote to Spock expressing similar sentiments. (Douglas R. Gilbert, photographer, LOOK Magazine Collection, Library of Congress, Prints and Photographs Division, LC-L9-65-2566-V, frame 10)

addressed issues of nuclear disarmament. But Spock received few letters regarding Vietnam following the Tonkin Gulf "incidents," perhaps because Americans saw him still as a Johnson ally, or perhaps because Johnson did not immediately escalate the war beyond retaliatory air strikes. More likely, however, is that Johnson had not yet committed ground troops and, therefore, draft calls had not yet increased.

The number of letters increased—and the tenor of the letters intensified—beginning in February 1965, following an attack on a base at Plei Ku in which nine American servicemen died. This event prompted Johnson to announce the beginning of American air attacks on North Vietnam and, soon, the introduction of ground combat troops, and led Spock to publicly distance himself from Johnson.

Taken together, the variety of letters sent to Spock reveals several general themes of Cold War life, as well as a few more specific themes prompted by the growing reality of Vietnam. For example, most of the letters criticizing Spock highlight the threat of communism to American security or the disloyalty of those who would protest American policy. Such letters not only evoke the specter of a global struggle between communism and capitalism, totalitarianism and democracy, East and West—familiar to all Americans since the end of the Second World War—but also demonstrate a faith in American government to implement the right policies and in American power to emerge victorious.

In addition, the letters expressing reservations or criticism of Johnson administration policy express other Cold War concerns about the impact of the war on children, fears of speaking out against administration policy, and frustration at citizens' inability to affect administration policy. Even so, many of the letter-writers suggest their own proposals and strategies to achieve peace.

In some ways, these letters predict themes that will persist in American opinion over the next few years: the necessity of containing communism, the need to support the troops in Vietnam regardless of one's view of the war, and early worries about the nature of the war and where it might lead. In other ways, the letters demonstrate a starting point for views that will grow more diverse and more strident as the war itself escalates. Most important, though, is that the letters in this chapter show Middle Americans trying to make sense of this new and rapidly escalating war. By the end of 1965, American troop levels increased from fewer than 20,000 to more than 180,000, and draft calls grew from 8,000 a month to more than 20,000. These letters come from engaged citizens—ordinary Americans weighing in on what would soon become the defining issue of their day.

I. Confronting the Red Threat

CHIEF AMONG the operating assumptions of the Johnson administration was the unrelenting spread of international communism. As the following letters show, it also held sway with the majority of Americans in the 1960s. Each of these letter-writers accepted the popular notion that a failure to stop the spread of communism in Vietnam would, ultimately, lead to more nations in the region falling—like dominoes—to communism. It is also worth noting that in expressing support for the president's handling of the conflict, the letters state a common perception of the impossibility of dealing honestly with a dishonest, conniving enemy. Another's confidence in using force is bolstered by a faith in American power and, by implication, justice. And, finally, in one letter, we see the first suggestion that those who oppose using force are actually helping the enemy.

1. Don't you realize that the Communists aren't going to be satisfied with just Viet Nam?

Ft. Hood, TX

15 January 1965

Dear Dr. Spock,

I have been an avid reader of your book "Baby and Child Care" for some time and after having just seen your speech (or parts of it) on your feelings about the war in Viet Nam, during the evening newscast; I would like to say that if those are your honest feelings, then all the books you may write on child care are useless—there will—in time be no way of obtaining them (they would present a threat to the Communist's way of indoctrinating children) if indeed there were children left to need them.

Don't you realize that the Communists aren't going to be satisfied with just Viet Nam? Do you seriously think that they won't want more —and more? And how long before they get to us? Another Pearl Harbor on a much larger scale, perhaps?

My husband is in the military and on orders for Viet Nam. I know he won't like what he has to do, but he will do it—possibly die for it, as my father before him in World War II—so that our daughter and many, many like her may grow up to read your book, if they so desire, and any others that may appeal to them.

If for no other reason than for the sake of yours & your publisher's bankbooks, you should consider the effect of your words, if they should come true, in 20 or 30 years from now.

Sincerely,

Mrs. J. M.

2. Are we to stand idly by and let the Reds gobble up these countries by subversion, terrorism, etc.?

Novelty, OH

February 20, 1965

Dear Dr. Spock,

As one who has followed foreign affairs with great interest for many years, I read your letter to The Cleveland Press today with great interest. I have been aware of your views for some time, not only in regard to the Viet Nam problem, but also in regard to other subjects. Invariably, Doctor, you have been on the side of pacifism, a turn-the-other cheek philosophy so to speak. I respect your outspokeness, Doctor, and would surely defend your clear right to speak out. I am not one of those who feel because you have been a doctor all your life you have no right to say your piece on other subjects.

But, Doctor Spock, have a little respect for the same rights in other people, too. I am the father of five children, and could have much to lose, in the event of a real all-Out war. However, because I am the father of five children, I am going to do everything in my limited power to make sure my children have a chance to grow up in a democracy—not a wholly-owned subsidiary of Communist Russia or China.

You say in your letter that Americans should write or telegraph the President, asking him to seek an end to the war by negotiation—to counteract the influence of the Americans who are eagerly demanding a showdown. Dr. Spock, I doubt if very many Americans anywhere are "eagerly demanding a showdown." Think that phrase over a bit. Very few of us, regardless of our politics, want any war anywhere. But, alas, I have sadly come to the conclusion that we have gone that last mile, so to speak, in trying to come to a meeting of the minds with our adversaries. I fear you cannot negotiate at all with murderers, cutthroats, liars, and men in general who find any means—any whatsoever, justifies the end.

Let's take parts of your letter and break it down. You say that "in Korea, we were held to a costly, painful draw, even though the South Koreans were on our side." The plain truth is, Doctor, that we fought that war with about 5 or 10% of our potential effort, under severe handicaps (no bombings north of the Yalu, remember?),[1] and with a business as usual philosophy in this country during those years, 1950–51–52–53. I think even you will agree that had we really wanted and tried to win the Korean War, there very probably would be no Communist China today. In fact, had we done just that—which we had every right to at the time, Communist China would not be in the position of a chronic trouble-maker all over Asia as she is.

You go on to say that we "are not losing the civil war in S. Viet Nam because of the intervention of N. Viet Nam, as we claim in our frustration, but because the South Viet-Namese people are against us." Where do you get your information and data, Doctor?? Do you have, as a doctor and a plain citizen, access to top secret facts that the rest of us don't have? Every source that I have read about, from CIA to neutral observers on the scene, indicate that thousands upon thousands of <u>North</u>

VietNamese are indeed south of the border, forming the cadres for the poor bewildered natives of the South, whom they have hornswaggled, bought, or coerced into fighting for the Viet Cong. How do you know the South Viet-Namese people are against us?? How many have you talked to, or are you naively buying the line that the Commies hand out everywhere?

You also say that "if we continue to bomb the North Viet-Namese we challenge them to enter the war full-scale (they have an army 10 times the size of the force which is beating us now)." You have the facts badly twisted, Doctor, perhaps if we continue to bomb the North-Vietnamese, they will realize they are not up against a Paper Tiger, as our Chinese friends like to call us. They are in the war now, Doctor, or don't you still believe that?

The United States has an army (and Navy and Air Force) about 1000 times (not just 10) the size of our force in Viet Nam now, so I am not worried about North Viet's unused army. I doubt very much if Lyndon Johnson, in his wisdom, will commit U.S. ground armies anywhere in Asia. Fortunately we have firm friends who have sizable ground forces there already—the South VietNamese, Chiang Kai-Chek, South Korea, the Phillipines, Thailand, all anti-Communist people. The U.S. Air Force and Navy are the power and the might that our fanatical opponents fear and are our ace in the hole.

Doctor, let me ask you just one question. Where do you propose to stop Communist aggression and expansion in the world? Are you really naive enough to believe that these so-called liberation movements are spontaneous internal revolutions?? If you do, you are really way out. The simple fact is that China does not have enough arable land to feed 700,000,000 people with 25,000,000 more each year. Therefore, they have to have, in their eyes, the rice bowl of Southeast Asia. They have just announced their plans for the independent nation of Thailand. Would you let that go by default, too? What about Burma, Malaysia, the Phillipines, and Australia. Are we to stand idly by and let the Reds gobble up these countries by subversion, terrorism, etc.?

I'm sorry. I respect you as a fine doctor, and I believe you are very sincere, but I also believe you are nearly 100% wrong. There is an old proverb that says "God helps those that help themselves." Yes, I will write the President, as I have already written my congressmen in Washington, but I will ask him to keep up a firm stand, and let our greedy bullies in China and Russia know that America will not be pushed around and kicked in the teeth forever. I sincerely wish you were on our side, but the vast majority of honest, hard-working and realistic Americans will have to struggle along without your help. . . . I suggest you consult the latest Gallup Poll, which shows that 3 out of every 4 Americans who have an opinion feel that this country is handling affairs in South Viet-Nam as well as can be done under the circumstances.

Sincerely yours,

R. W. [male]

3. We can win in Viet-Nam, Laos, and Cambodia only by fighting, by doing our own fighting for our own necks.

Grafton, Ohio

March 5, 1965

Dear Dr. Spock,

Thank you for your book on how to raise my daughter. We all survived nicely and she is a joy to behold.

Even as you are a professional, I too am a professional engineer. Thus on the subject of foreign affairs we are, perhaps, equal.

The situation in Viet-Nam is not one that needs talk. This is especially true since the Enemy never really listens to what he says. Why should we talk more when we already have two fairly good agreements on paper which are not being followed? Do you really think another paper would change the actions of the Communists?

The situation in Viet-Nam is like gangrene in a foot. Talk does nothing. A shot of pain killer and a bandage is humanitarian and a temporary solution. This is the easy way out. But in a little while we must ask if the leg and the body are worth saving.

We were defeated in Korea (in Asian eyes) by Washington policy. We can win in Viet-Nam, Laos, and Cambodia only by fighting, by doing our own fighting for our own necks. Yes, it would be nice to have a stable government give us a trained, obedient army. But there is neither of these available to us. If we wait, there will be neither a South Viet-Nam government or army.

In domestic policy, I mostly disagree with President Johnson. In South Asia, he is doing his best to make my daughter's future worth living.

Very truly yours,

R. H. [male]

4. It is incredible to me that instead of upbraiding the communist you are, with your action, actually helping to give them moral license to continue to kill, loot and murder.

Arlington, VA
[undated, ca. November 1965]

Sir:

I have long felt that an indignant passionate cry should arise all over the world to influence the communist to stop fomenting trouble, aggression, ambush killing of villagers, looting homes terrorizing and murdering innocent women and children.

Thus I was very much disturbed to learn about your intended demonstration against the President upbrading him against his policy of protecting and defending the victims. It is incredible to me that instead of upbraiding the communist you are, with your action, actually helping to give them moral license to continue to kill, loot and murder. No matter what atrocities the communists commit, the demonstrators stay home; but when someone gives help to the victims it is a different story. Even if you are a communist the sense of fair play should make you reconsider.

To right your image you must make a public announcement against the demonstrations and officially condemn the communists for their hideous acts of violence and aggression towards their neighbors.

Sincerely
E. S. [male]

II. Supporting America's Troops in Vietnam

AS FREQUENTLY happens in America, during wartime, dissenters are often criticized for abandoning the patriotic, loyal citizen soldiers who accept the country's call to service. In the following letters, the writers point to the grim experience of combat and the sacrifices made in the name of freedom; some suggest a certain wisdom that grows out of combat or just from being on the scene and understanding Vietnam and its needs better than those at home. Most important, the letter writers agree that the news of protest against Johnson's Vietnam policies is crushing to the morale of these GIs.

5. I wish you could have the opportunity to describe your views to a man who is being shot at in Viet Nahm, and is seeing his friends killed every day.

Sept. 26, 1965
Cleveland, Ohio

Dear Sir,

I was very much amused and disgusted by your letter to the Editor of the Plain Dealer[2] today. I wish you could have the opportunity to describe your views to a man who is being shot at in Viet Nahm, and is seeing his friends killed every day. When your life is being sought by someone unseen you take all necessary steps to prevent same.

If you would ever have this situation thrown in your lap I'm sure you would thank God that you are safe + sound here writing your children's books. As a youngster in School, I had many views similar to yours. I joined the marines when I was 17 and spent a year in Korea. From Nov. 1950–Nov. 1951. Believe me Sir, I was scared to death every one of those days. I never asked was it for the good of the world that I'm here in this frozen hell near Manchuria? I was there, I saw friends from home killed and mutilated. I'm glad the marines only trained infantrymen and taught a basic fact: we were in a war! Stick together, fight, forget the do gooders at home and you have a fair chance of seeing home again.

I assume that you were never shot at, were in a war, and never slept in holes for a year with the feeling you were at the end of the world and would never get home again. Have you ever seen a dead person? Not a person in a funeral parlor, but a close friend or part of him covered with blood, filth and lice staring up at you with open dead eyes and seems to be saying, "Thank God, I'm out of it"! That is death. If people of your stature would face facts and realize that Americans are being killed every minute over there. Let the men doing the fighting determine who is the enemy and let them decide what is right or wrong. You seem to be in a glass walled world. You can see out via Newspaper + T.V., but your sense of smell, fear, and the will to live is different than the men who are there. They are not there for a weekend hike. They can't come in out of the rain or eat with clean napkins + silverware. They feel let down by the public just as I did in Korea. Write all the letters you want, but preach for them instead of against them. When in Korea I wished that we could have gotten shoes, clothes, weapons that would not jam etc. Preach for these things, pray for these men, because right or wrong they are there and need our support.

Yours Truly,

D. L. [male]

6. Most of all, though, is the deep repulsion that arises at the picture of our boys fighting so gallantly while so-called intellectuals betray them at home.

Annandale, Virginia

Oct. 31, 1965

Sir,

I think you are under the false impression that we mothers who have worn out a couple of copies of your baby care book in the process of rearing a family will hark to your every word as to the Viet Nam situation. Not so, I'm afraid.

I have turned to your advice countless times raising 3 children (I managed the 4th without cracking "the Spock book" once) and appreciate your help. But on Viet Nam, sir, you are all wet.

I probably should have guessed, because on colds and measles and physical matters you were great—but I found you wrong on many personality matters.

Once, I remember, when my eldest did the baby-talk routine I looked in your book and was advised ignore it. . . .

Then, one particularly hectic day, I turned to her and yelled, "I will not answer you one more time if you speak to me in that baby-talk!"— and I didn't.

After weeks of "ignoring" the baby-talk, it disappeared forever in a couple of hours.

Ignoring doesn't always help in many things. We can't always ignore the oppression of other people or the establishment of another enemy in our back yard to point missiles our way. We <u>must</u> turn and say No more —stop.

Most of all, though, is the deep repulsion that arises at the picture of our boys fighting so gallantly while so-called intellectuals betray them at home. <u>So</u>, you "subscribe to at least five world affairs journals." So what?

Count me in as one of many "Spock" mothers who are behind President Johnson and our boys 100%.

Sincerely,

M. F. [female]

7. Let our boys learn that we are back of them 100% through our prayers for VICTORY!

Harrisburg, Pennsylvania

Nov. 28, 1965

Dear Dr. Spock,

There is something you need to do and do quickly! We parents who have raised our children by the book (Spock), who have wholeheartedly agreed with the contents of your new book on "Problems of Parents— particularly with you statement in the middle of the 2nd paragraph page 234, are quite disturbed that not only have you sanctioned the Peace March on Washington, but led it!

In Viet Nam we have a situation very much like Korea, where our boys must often say "What are we doing down here in this God-forsaken-part of the world?!" We truly hope that part of their training was in understanding the role that our country must take in stopping Communism before it reaches our borders. But in describing the terrible letdown of our boys as they were taken prisoners, you seemed so right when you said, "The greater responsibility, to my mind, lay with the millions of civilians who, like the soldiers, were unprepared to see beyond the horizon of their private pursuits, to understand the relationship of their lives to the fateful issues confronting their country and the world."

At the very end of your book you reiterate your feelings again by saying, "We only need to rouse ourselves, with the inspiration of bold leaders, and we'll have enough crusades to absorb us for decades. Then we might simultaneously find ourselves, save the world from destruction and give our children a new sense of direction and worth." Perhaps our crusades should come in form of dedicated PEACE CORP workers, but surely YOU can understand the "let-down" that our soldiers must feel now that they are in the middle of a conflict (that could by its victory keep the Communists from gaining ground) read about a march on Washington by a minority group that could and DOES DISCOURAGE A SOLDIER BEYOND ALL REPAIR!

How much better to lead our country in a UNITED moment of prayer, every Sunday at 1PM, and through the medium of newspapers, radio and television let our boys learn that we are back of them 100% through our prayers for VICTORY!

If you can understand this Mothers concern for the feelings of our boys down there, may I suggest that you be big enough to confess to a mistake and make it known by asking for time on the TODAY show. If you want parents to read your book and respect your wonderful ideas, please do this for all of us!!!

Sincerely,

Mrs. M. H.

8. Perhaps when I say that my husband is on the short end of a tour of duty in Vietnam, you will understand what this letter is about.

Clemson, South Carolina
November 28, 1965

Dear Sir:

Please let me introduce myself. I am [name deleted], white Protestant female, 34 years old, college education. I am a nurse and have been taught to respect all doctors. I am the mother of four children and have raised them with biblical respect for Dr. Spock. I am also an Army wife. Perhaps when I say that my husband is on the short end of a tour of duty in Vietnam, you will understand what this letter is about.

I read more and more of your involvement in anti-Vietnam marches. In the beginning, I could not believe that my Dr. Spock, practically a great uncle to my children, could really be doing this to us. And now I have picked up the paper and once more read your name. I understand that your participation is out of concern for peace in the world, but don't you realize that every mother's son, every father, every husband now fighting the Communists in Vietnam wants peace as much as you do? I do wish that you would take the time, if you can take the time for demonstrations, to talk to some of these fellows as they come back from Vietnam. They are the ones who really know what it is all about. They realize, perhaps as you do not, that the fight has to take place somewhere if we are not to have the fight here on our own soil. Ask Sen. Thurmond of S.C., or others who have investigated, about the Communists who have infiltrated these so-called peace movements, especially in the colleges. They take sincere young men who are fired up with enthusiasm for a cause (and what college age young man does not want a cause to believe in?) and they insidiously transform their honest zeal into a tool for the Reds.

But back to the men in Vietnam, let me cite the example of my husband's own attitude toward this war—and most people readily admit it is a war, if not like any other war that has ever been fought. He left here last January full of the knowledge of what the Communists were doing in Vietnam. Before he left, I asked him if he, too, expected to "adopt" one of the Vietnamese children that you read so much about. His answer was that he was going to fight a war, not run an aid station, or words to that effect. He had not been there a month before he wrote to me and to his parents to ask us to send any old summerweight clothes that we could get for him to have to give to the children of the families that live in his area. I sent all that I could gather, his mother collected at school (she is a teacher) and they got from members of his father's church (he is a minister). We have sent numerous boxes at our own expense, clothing that has been donated by rich, poor, Protestant, Jew—Americans all—who wish to help their fellow man. Instead of sending Christmas presents to my husband, I sent two large boxes of toys, some bought with money that would normally have been spent on our own children, some donated by local stores, and he will play "Santa" this year to dozens of Vietnamese children instead of his own. . . . What small effort we have made has been repeated many times over by other American service families and non-service families—spontaneously! Even war brings good when it can inspire us all to share what we have. Perhaps you and your demonstrators are doing the cause a service by inspiring some of this. Certainly you have read of the millions of gifts and letters others have also sent.

And now for a more personal expression of my feelings. My husband is in danger every minute that he is in Vietnam and has been in many big battles already. It breaks my heart to think that he might not return. But I have made my peace with myself and my God and know that He who leads us all will give me the strength that I need to face it if it comes because I <u>know</u> as surely as if God himself has told me that what Ed is doing is for the good of mankind and for the good of the world. Communism with its lawless and Godless way of life must not be allowed to flourish and eventually to take over America as it is trying to take over all of Asia. When I read that Dr. Spock, the same man who is a household word in every American family, is aiding this cause, though it be with good intent for the end of war, I feel as if a member of my own family had taken up a rifle and fired a shot at my most beloved of all husbands. And so, Sir, I ask you to have second thoughts and to talk to those who have been there and who know what it is like and see if you can still aid and abet the enemy. Don't you think that with your position and ability you could serve your own cause better and the Communist cause less by using your name in other ways than this? I beg you to give it some thought in the name of all American service families who must give up loved ones to the cause that they, almost to the man, most sincerely believe in. I hope you can find the time to see the other side of the story.

One last word, I am not a professional letter writer. I have often wished that I could have the opportunity to speak to some of the people who have been so outspokenly against our policy in Vietnam, but I always end up realizing that I would probably be considered just a foolish talkative female. But my conscience keeps telling me that I, too, may be hurting Ed by not voicing our side of the story, so this one time I am making the effort. I do hope that you will give it due consideration, not for me but for a very dear man who is doing what he thinks is right and for the four children that he is fighting for. Thank you for taking the time to read this.

Sincerely,
Mrs. A. J.

9. We all detest war and its monstrous results, but some wars have to be fought and won.

Omaha, Nebraska
November 30, 1965

Dear Sir:

I realize that my action is about as effective as a fly on an elephant but perhaps if enough flies took aim it might make you realize that in all the years you have been writing books, columns, making speeches, etc, in my book the good has all been undone because of your present stand, politically.

I for one have used your advise for the last time, how can a doctor, a well known and much respected authority for so long allow himself to become associated with such questionable personalities.

I am quite certain that the President of the United States, his Cabinet, his advisors, and Congress know much more about the present complex condition of the world than the group that I have seen your name connected with this past few days.

Sir, you have a responsibility to too many people to risk forfeiting it just to protest for Pacifism. We all detest war and its monstrous results, but some wars have to be fought and won.

Yours truly,
Mrs. M. C.

III. Early Misgivings about the War

IF THE writers of the preceding letters expressed more concern for containing communism or supporting American troops in the field, the following writers saw reasons for concern in Johnson's Vietnam policies. Some expressed pacifist sentiments, urging peaceful resolutions of all conflicts, while others worried about war's effect on children and the national character. Others took great pains to research the origins of American intervention in Vietnam and, on political and strategic grounds, question the wisdom of the White House's policies. Finally, in these letters, we see the first hints of frustration that the ordinary citizen cannot get his or her voice heard on issues of importance.

10. I then had to explain to my children how we of the older generation —their parents—might deny them their life, and yet express a hopefulness for its control.

Lancaster, Penn.

March 31, 1965

Dear Dr. Spock,

I have read a report of your recent talk in Baltimore, Md. concerning the cold war effects on our youth. You refer to several recent studies of cold war anxieties and I would very much appreciate receiving more details of these reports. . . .

To substantiate your views I will relate two recent incidents among our youth.

Early in March my son, who is not yet eleven, told me that two old bearded men were predicting the end of the world on March 13. Across the dinner table from him my eight year old daughter asked how the world could end, to which he replied—the BOMB. I then had to explain to my children how we of the older generation—their parents—might deny them their life, and yet express a hopefulness for its control.

At about that time I attended an informal meeting of students at Franklin and Marshall College to discuss the Vietnam situation. During this discussion the majority of the students talked so coldly and with such inhuman considerations of power, escalation, and "drawing the line" for the Communists that I finally told them that the prospects of their controlling this country's destiny frightened me.

"My Son Died in Vain." Antiwar march, Berkeley, California, 1965. Expressions of concern for children, from birth through draft age, are common in letters to Spock. (Bettmann/CORBIS)

Upon reflection I concluded that these students had most likely expressed the same apprehensions as my children and had not been offered any means of dealing with their fears. Consequently, I expect they are controlled by a neurotic reasoning regarding warfare which I also suspect could permeate the whole of their personality.

Thus I share your concerns and am grateful for your public expression of them.

> Sincerely yours,
> C. B. [male]

11. I'll say to you dear Doctor, their are thousands upon thousands, who think and feel like you, but are afraid to come forward

> Cleveland, Ohio
> Sept 30, 1965

Dear Doctor Spock,

Thank you for the letter you wrote, in last Sundays paper. Your letter said to me Here's another human being who also see's that nothing can be gained by force and brutality—only can gains be made by love and unity. I'm not a well educated man and hesitated in writing to you. But I got to tell you of my experience, beginning the first world war, I spoke up against it, How I was abused for this. Feeling heavy hearted, walking along the street, I prayed saying Oh Lord only I am left against this war, it was then as though I was walking on air, the street looked brighter and things looked distance an an answer came to me as though some one said I have thousand upon thousands who think's and feel like you. I'll say to you dear Doctor, their are thousands upon thousands, who think and feel like you, but are afraid to come forward, yes intimidated afraid of lossing their job. Hoping that the day is not to far from us, as it is written When Love and truth shall kiss each other.

Best wishes to you Doctor.

> Yours truly,
> W. R. [male]

12. I welcomed your television announcement that you would lead a march to Washington D.C. to protest the warfare in Vietnam.

East Providence, RI
November 2, 1965

Dear Dr. Spock,

I welcomed your television announcement that you would lead a march to Washington D.C. to protest the warfare in Vietnam.

For a year I have been concerned about the situation there, and I have ben corresponding with the junior senator from Rhode Island, Hon. Claiborne Pell. He has sent me official background and current information.

Thus I have gleaned that the last international agreement binding upon Vietnam was the Geneva Conference on Indochina, May 8–July 21, 1954. Delegates were from Great Britain, U.S.S.R. (joint chairmen), France, U.S., Communist China, Cambodia, Laos, Vietnam, and the Vietminh regime (North Vietnam). The main provisions are:

1. Vietnam to be partitioned along 17th parallel (to stop the fighting)
2. regulations are imposed on foreign military bases, personnel and increased armaments (the introduction of war material, arms and munitions of all typed in the form of unassembled parts for subsequent reassembly is prohibited, except to replace worn out weapons).
3. country wide elections, leading to the reunification of North and South Vietnam, are to be held by July 20, 1956.
4. an International Control Commission (I.C.C.), composed of representatives from Canada, India, and Poland, is to be established to supervise the implementation of the agreements.

The United States and South Vietnam did not sign the agreements. The U.S. issued a unilateral declaration stating that it (1) will refrain from the threat of the use of force to disturb the Geneva agreements and (2) would view any renewal of the aggression in violation of the aforesaid agreements with grave concern and as seriously threatening international peace and security, and (3) shall continue to seek unity through free elections, supervised by the U.N. to insure that they are conducted fairly.

We certainly have not kept our commitment to the second provision of the conference, and our actions are questionable regarding some of the other points.

It is the responsibility of the I.C.C. to police Vietnam. The I.C.C. is responsible to the United Nations. If we feel that injustice is being done in Vietnam, we should report the matter to the United Nations. If the U.N. moves very slowly, or if it does not move at all, it is not the responsibility of the U.S. to punish the North Vietnamese.

"Vengeance is mine, I will repay," saith the Lord. We should trust Him, and the United Nations to try to make it work.

One can argue that we fight to protect democracy. I sympathize with President Johnson in his persistent upholding of the traditional presidential helpful gesture that President Eisenhower started in 1954, because he preferred democracy to a communist government in Vietnam. But President Kennedy knew the time of a wise withdrawal. He knew the time of a wise withdrawal from Laos. . . .

One can argue that we fight to honor our commitment to SEATO,[3] but the Geneva Conference was more recent than the SEATO agreement signed December 23, 1950.

In this age of reason, and high regard for the individual, neither of these arguments justifies the purposeful and accidental slaughter going on in Vietnam.

On October 29, Mr. Chester Huntley[4] said that the I.C.C. had found South Vietnam to be at fault, and recommended a reconvening of the Geneva Conference. Would it be impossible to get these powers together again? If Russia really wants peace in Vietnam, wouldn't she come? If the People's Republic of China really represents her people, wouldn't she want to discuss the matter before being dragged into a seemingly endless war? Are there not ways to attract France and North Vietnam?

I realize that Cleveland and East Providence are in opposite directions from Washington. Where would you suggest that I join your protest march?

Yours very truly,
L. S. [female]

13. Try to impress upon our leaders that this war will only bring death and destruction.

[point of origin unknown]
Nov. 6, 1965

Dear Dr. Spock,

We, the people of the U.S., agree with you about the outrageous and shameful war the U.S. is conducting in Viet Nam. We are thankful that there are some intelligent individuals, like yourself, who voiced your opinion towards this cruel, murderous, and unnecessary war that is being carried on very much against our wishes.

We, the poor and simple class of people, are unable to express our views because we don't know how or who to appeal to. Therefore, we are hopefully looking to sincere good people like yourself, to try to impress upon our leaders that this war will only bring death and destruction.

It is very ironical. We seek to find cures and medicines to prolong life and treat many diseases, then our Administration throws us into a war, wherein everyday human lives are destroyed.

Dear Dr. Spock please continue your efforts for mankind to bring about a halt to this uncivilized manner that our nation is conducting themselves. In this day and age people should be able to conduct and settle their grievances in a peaceful way.

We thank you with all our hearts.

[unsigned]

14. To this point in my life I have never been a demonstrator, nor do I wish to become one, and only rarely a letter-writer.

[EDITOR'S NOTE: This letter was written to President Johnson, with a copy sent to Dr. Spock.]

Madison, Wisconsin
November 24, 1965

Dear President Johnson:

I should like to ask just how the "little people" in this country are supposed to communicate to their government their numbness and horror over your totally ineffectual foreign policy, especially with reference to Viet Nam. Are we to join public demonstrations against your Viet Nam policy? Do you, or does anyone, ever read our letters?

I consider myself to be one of the very "little people" in this country: well-educated, well-informed, formerly a teacher but now the middle-aged mother of young children, and without any discernible influence in the workings of my government—present or future inasmuch as my ever holding public office is wholly improbable. To this point in my life I have never been a demonstrator, nor do I wish to become one, and only rarely a letter-writer.

I have the distinct impression that your administration does everything in its power to discredit the voices of criticism in this country for your foreign policy, voices which I think you would do well to heed. You certainly cannot claim any success for the course of action you have been following. As a matter of fact, this policy is resulting in a rapidly deteriorating world situation compared with that which you inherited. May I suggest that while your own personal experience in the Senate may qualify you as a capable leader in the area of domestic policy, you would be wise in seeking the counsel of those of your colleagues who can speak with wisdom on foreign policy, such as Senator Fulbright.

All the gumdrops and chocolate bars dispersed to Vietnamese children, all the medals awarded to American soldiers now in pine boxes, all the medical aid to wounded and burned peasant women and children, all the praise and publicity for loyal college students sending letters and Christmas presents to their GI counter-parts, all will not erase the blunders in your Asian policy. Eric Sevareid[5] has done us all a favor by finally awakening the citizenry to the fact that your administration has already ignored legitimate efforts to negotiate the peace.

Two years ago at the death of President Kennedy I vowed to become more of a participator in the workings of our democracy and did indeed volunteer my services, admittedly small and insignificant, to working for your election last year, but more particularly for the defeat of Barry Goldwater. When I now recall the old campaign slogan of "whose hand on the trigger," I am somewhat bemused, somewhat sad and, somewhat disillusioned.

Sincerely,

B. G. [female]

cc: Senators Nelson, Proxmire, Fulbright, R. Kennedy, Rep. Kastenmeier, Dr. Spock, Mr. Sevareid.

15. All anyone has to do is to see that terrain and he should know how insane our policy is.

Hampton, Conn.
November 28, 1965

Dear Ben,

Just in case you don't remember us, my wife was [name deleted] sister and you took care of our two boys in 1934 and 1935 (a fact about which we do not hesitate to boast when your book is mentioned).

We think what you are doing in trying to stop the war in Vietnam is magnificent and are enclosing a contribution [ed. note: $100] to help.

Our son Hank spent two and a half years in Laos and we had the chance to visit him there early in 1964. All anyone has to do is to see that terrain and he should know how insane our policy is. We felt so strongly, that, immediately on our return, we wrote both senators and our congressman, urging them to get us out. You know how far that got us.

We believe in what you are doing and admire you tremendously for taking the time and energy to do it. Keep it up; your efforts may, I hope, eventually meet with success.

Sincerely yours,

E. & L. H. [female & male]

P.S. Just to help put the pressure on Congress, I am again writing our congressmen. I regret that on of them is Thomas H. Dodd.

16. I fear that Americanism is becoming the same kind of demonism that German Nazism was 25 years ago.

Chicago, Illinois

December 1, 1965

Dear Dr. Spock:

I want to commend you for your leadership in the campaign for peace in our country today. I was glad to read that your peace march last weekend was so well organized and conducted. This demonstration may have a slight effect on the course of national policy.

I completely agree with your article, "Why Do We Betray Peace and Justice?" in the November issue of <u>Fellowship</u>. We are certainly acting to show our contempt of the rights of other nations. I am terrified by the end result of the escalation of the war in Vietnam. It is obvious to me that our national leaders will use the ultimate weapon if it becomes necessary to win the war. They will even act to destroy the world in order to save our face. That shows the madness of the nationalism that is gripping our nation today.

I fear that Americanism is becoming the same kind of demonism that German Nazism was 25 years ago. Obviously, the opposition cannot do much to halt the trend. It is just possible that the opposition may modify the madness and keep us from going beyond a semi-demonism. That is about the most I can hope for.

Very truly yours,

F. M. [male]

2 Into the Quagmire, 1966

IN 1966, the dividing lines over the Vietnam War sharpened. Benjamin Spock, for one, had become one of the most recognizable opponents of the war, and Americans of all stripes began filling his mail box with more and more letters that alternately praised or condemned his efforts to end the war. As the number of American troops increased to more than 360,000 by December 1966, debate and analysis of the war became one of the main topics of conversation in homes all over America. To meet troop demands, the draft now called 30,000 to 40,000 men for induction each month (a sharp increase from the peacetime calls of 8,000 or 9,000 a month), and the Selective Service System's reach suddenly became clearer in communities all over the country. In 1966, the war moved closer to home.

Even so, the 1966 letters—as compared to the letters for 1967 and 1968, for example—reveal a more measured debate among the "silent majority." Americans began to zero in on a range of issues in 1966, but several core ideas are illuminated in the following letters. This chapter begins, therefore, by organizing some of Spock's mail from 1966 into three themes: letters on strategy for peace; letters on children, war, and peace; and letters on anticommunism, which, for many of the letter-writers, constituted an alternative route to peace. A final grouping of letters includes another sampling that does not fit these central ideas. It is worth noting, too, that multiple variations of these themes can appear in a single letter, so the grouping laid out here is not based on rigid categories.

I. Peace Proposals

THE AUTHORS of the following letters clearly felt comfortable conveying to Spock their own ideas on how peace could be achieved in Vietnam and beyond. While some letters suggest protest strategies designed to end the Johnson administration's war, others lay out more ambitious plans for establishing and maintaining world peace. One letter from a GI

Induction Center, Newark, New Jersey, 1966. Following the commitment of ground troops in Vietnam, draft calls quickly jumped from peacetime levels of 8,000 to 10,000 per month (nationally) to more than 30,000 per month. (U.S. News & World Report, Library of Congress)

stationed in Vietnam urges that the American military enterprise be replaced with a humanitarian one.

18. And why cannot we take advantage of this to organize a great prayer for peace, in which those of all shades of opinion might join, in this and other countries?

3 January 1966

Dear Dr. Spock,

. . . Let me say first that the only political affiliation I have is the Democratic Party and occasional attendance at Women's Strike for Peace demonstrations in Washington, as well as the protest you led there in November. When I attended these, I do so alone, because no member of my family or friend (almost all our friends are dedicated career government men) agrees that the U.S. is wrong in Viet Nam.

Without your leadership, I might not have had the courage to make even this small protest. For I am always subject to the corrosive self-doubt that some character flaw causes me to align against authority. Not until I read the recent article about you in <u>Medical World News</u>, and later one of your papers in a psychoanalytic journal, did I realize that the warmth and insight by which I, like millions, was guided as a young mother was based on your experience in this discipline, as well as on your own great personal gifts. So I am sure you understand the self-doubt, and I want to say thank you very much, from me and all of those like me.

I am not, as my 19-year-old son frequently reminds me, a political analyst, and I do not know what the real purpose of the current Johnson-style jet diplomacy is. Is he, as one of the brilliant members of the faculty here suggested, making shameless use of the Pope? But whatever he is doing, would not this be the moment for a great public prayer that bombing in Viet Nam might not resume?

If, as Reston[1] said yesterday, traditional diplomacy "must not raise popular expectations" certainly Johnson's untraditional approach has done so. And why cannot we take advantage of this to organize a great prayer for peace, in which those of all shades of opinion might join, in this and other countries?

It seems to me that such a protest could be made through the churches of all faiths by clergymen opening their churches for prayer around the clock. Negro action was made effective by the leadership of the clergy and the local resource of the church building. The Pope's role suggests that it might be possible to enlist some of the Catholic clergy. The idea is a simple and obvious one: that all organizations in the peace group support this nationwide prayer by sending groups to churches to pray and that all others in the community have a chance to come and add their prayer that U.S. bombing not be resumed. Such a mounting protest might make it very hard for Mr. Johnson to reverse, even if he does not get the response we all hope for from North Viet Nam. Perhaps prayers could be started even there—maybe Lynd[2] could do something. I know a newspaperman in Saigon who might be willing to try to enlist the Buddhists.

Is all this fantasy? Another Berkeley professor on whom I tried this housewife's idea said—"There is no leadership of the peace group to get such a movement started. King[3] has withdrawn, having been warned by the Johnson Administration."

You, Dr. Spock, are the leader of the peace group and a man whose integrity nobody can question. Can you act to enlist the clergy in initiating this outburst of public prayer? I am sure that the movement would spread, if it could only be initiated properly with all the faiths. I feel sure you could obtain King's help.

I am not a member of any church, but because my son attended the Episcopal day school, St. Alban's, in Washington I have some acquaintance among Episcopal clergy there and could ask for their support. Will you let me know if you think there is anything in this idea?

> Sincerely,
> Mrs. L. C.
> Berkeley, [Calif.]

19. There is no named man for the future presidency who wants peace.

> Van Nuys, Calif
> 5-3-66

Dear Dr. Spock,

After reading the Article in The Saturday Evening Post, that you are half inclined to run for public office, I decided to write, urging you to do so.

You are not a professional politician and that in many minds is very highly in your favor. You also are one of the best known and liked people in the country.

These lying politicians who talk that they are going to follow Pres Kennedy's policies, and don't, and lie about most everything they do, make many of us sick.

There is no named man for the future presidency who wants peace. Goldwater, Nixon, Humphrey, Johnson, all talk war. They say whoever is elected; that signifies endoresment-in-blank of their policies, which is war. Both from the Democratic + Republican parties. Let us have a choice.

Some one should run who is for peace + the welfare of the human race. The military is getting more + more into control, + the military in the long run have never done any country any good.

You are one of the best known + liked person in this country. You sincerely stand for peace + human welfare. I urge you to run not for the Senate but the Presidency.

> Respectfully,
> D. F. [gender unknown]

20. I owe it to my children to help to prepare a world they can live in with peace but I also feel responsible for children I do not even know, in Viet Nam . . .

May 17, 1966
Redwood City, Calif.

Dear Dr. Spock,

. . . This letter is intended to propose an approach you may or may not have already considered. You speak to the entire nation in you efforts to arrouse action against the mistakes our nation is making in Viet Nam. I wonder if you have directed attention on one specific group, the group of mothers who are as yet unconvinced of these mistakes but who have found your words on child rearing a real treasure, I mean, those mothers who have listened to your words faithfully yesterday, but in this "other" area, today, have either backed our Administration's policy or have not understood enough to oppose it. Am I naive when I expect some of them to say, Well, I have agreed with his ideas on child rearing, and though I have always believed "My country right or wrong " (a misquote of course), I will henceforth accept his revolutionary approach to this other field, international politics?

I am interested in this matter from a personal standpoint, also. . . .

I feel like if my wife accepted so much from your writings as she raised the children, she might give some credence to your thoughts on the Viet Nam situation. You see, she is apprehensive of my participation in "demonstration" or things like that. She doesn't like to "rock the boat" I guess we might say. And yet I cannot give up my interest in these things for a number of reasons. I would be a traitor to the university system who gave me some of the insight into the problems of our day. I owe it to my children to help to prepare a world they can live in with peace but I also feel responsible for children I do not even know, in Viet Nam or any other country that is torn by war. Another reason is my experience during the War, in burying women and children civilians on Saipan,[4] that were killed by our own bullets. You know there are many more reasons why this war and many others are wrong. . . .

Sincerely,

J. S. [male]

21. The point is . . . that although people may not give "some baby doctor" the authority to speak in behalf of the country, one would tend to support the massed intelligence of the world's best thinkers.

Covina, California

June 6, 1966

Dear Dr. Spock,

. . . I too, am much concerned with international affairs, and specifically our problems with Communism, both Soviet and Chinese. I was recently in Russia and, of course, found the people to be "just people," as they are everywhere in the world. Obviously, the current problems are typical of foreign affairs, most <u>people</u> have common needs; it is only the politics of the situation which screws everything up!

I have been reading Nietzsche recently, and sharing his feelings of superiority. This leads me to believe that those of us who are fairly intelligent ought to attempt to band together, along with similar people in all countries, and come up with some sort of intelligencia group which could become extremely influential in international affairs. . . .

What I am proposing is a society or organization of some sort, which would be basically non-political in their nature, but relatively famous, and certainly extremely intelligent and learned. Through the objective evaluation of the situation by intelligent and well respected leaders of the scientific and intellectual fields of the major powers, certain basic paths and suggestions could be given. These would have the support of the intelligencia of the countries involved, and eventually of the general public, which would create great pressures on the governmental agencies in these countries, as well as giving advice directly, somewhat as the cabinet does. In fact, this organization could be set up as the "Cabinet of the U.N."

The point is . . . that although people may not give "some baby doctor" the authority to speak in behalf of the country, one would tend to support the massed intelligence of the world's best thinkers.

Obviously, you have never heard of me, and may never. Someone like you would have to do this. If not you, I'd like to know who, and contact them. It should not be difficult to propose acceptable standards for the conduct of foreign affairs, since all international policy of all countries throughout history has been so extremely irrational, nationalistic, and just plain stupid. Such a reasonably rational analysis would gain world support not only because it had the backing of the intelligencia of all countries, but also because it would make sense and be accept-able to all the <u>people</u> concerned (although certain leaders might not appreciate it very much). . . .

The government of the world has been left too long in the hands of "mere" politicians. Scientists, who have the capacity to see the problems clearly, and who are dispassionate enough to cross national boundaries in their thought, must step to the foreground and handle the problems which cannot be handled by national politicians. The stakes are extreme-ly high, and the job seems within possible reach. The problem cannot be solved by bowing to public opinion and acting like every other common demonstrator. People who <u>possess power</u> must <u>amass</u> it, on an interna-tional level, and <u>force</u> action through their strength. This country has had a long history of government and control by various elites, and this is even more true of dictatorships. Only by the creation of a new vocal, impressive, and powerful elite which has popular support, due to their humanitarian ends and the respect which their position and intelligence demands, can the present system of political nationalism and selfishness be overcome.

Sincerely,

L. L. [male]

P.S. Our first child . . . is 2 weeks old now, and we're making good use of your books!

22. Our government would have you believe my work here is leading us toward peace; it is not so.

11 June 1966

Dear Dr. Spock,

The book has helped my wife and me better understand our children and attend to their needs thank you.

My primary reason for writing is to wish you good fortune in your peace work. I am an Army pilot flying helicopters in Vietnam. Our gov-ernment would have you believe my work here is leading us toward peace; it is not so. The "Dr. Spock Baby Book," if used by every moth-er here in Vietnam would cut infant deaths in half. That is what we need to fight here, hunger, disease, ignorance. What I do is deliver men into battle to fight and die, a useless task. I won't burden you with my views of this war, but I am sure most of the super patriots would call me unpatriotic or worse. I have read they have called you some real humdingers. We need more people like you who have the hope of future mankind based on peace. I think of my son's and I know just praying for peace isn't enough, I must in some way work for it, in a more active role. At present I have limitations because of the service. But I would like to have you write me and tell me what I can do to help you. I see the results of war every day, and I shake my head and wonder why we human's shall never understand its futility.

Once again, good luck to you.

J. S. [male]

[EDITOR'S NOTE: Although Spock was on vacation when he received this letter, it moved him to respond immediately with a three-page, handwritten letter. In it he admitted that it was "gratifying . . . to hear from a man in Military Services in Vietnam," because many "citizens at home" and other servicemen, as reported in the press, accused peace advocates of "undermining our fighting men while they are risking their lives for us." He suggested to the letter-writer that, once he got out of the army, he could join various activities of the peace movement, as some others already had; "the views of an ex-serviceman are particularly influential," Spock concluded. Several weeks later, however, Spock's letter came back stamped "Verified Deceased. Return to Sender." Spock took to reading the letter at demonstrations, including the rally in front of the Pentagon on October 21, 1967.]

23. I would like to suggest . . . an independent group of Americans organizing an air-lift for the removal of Vietnamese children in the throe of war.

August 6, 1966

Dear Dr. Spock,

The war in Vietnam bothers many people. People who formerly believed that the action of the United States reflected the will of the majority. These same people now feel helpless.

How else besides peace demonstrations, letters, etc. can we show our concern? Since your name is so famous in connection with children, I would like to suggest the following:

An independent group of Americans organizing an air-lift for the removal of Vietnamese children in the throe of war. They would live with foster parents in the United States. (language would not be a barrier with the little ones) In essence . . . we want to assume responsibility for the apparent Irreverence for Life.

The publicity which would come from this venture should spotlight the <u>cause</u> not the individual families who take these babies. The privacy of the family should not be exploited.

Sincerely yours,
Mrs. A. K.
North Haven, Conn.

II. Of War and Children

THE FOLLOWING group of letters share a concern for the future of American and Vietnamese children. Many of the writers see Spock's anti-war work as a natural extension of his pediatrics care, particularly if they raised their own children with the guidance of his child-care books. The concerns they express are varied, but it is obvious that when they think of the war, their first thought is of their children. Others express horror and sympathy for Vietnamese children in particular, as well as for the "boys" fighting in Vietnam.

24. Freedom and justice must be granted to the people of S. E. Asia as equitably as to any other part of the world.

January 12, 1966

Dear Dr. Spock,

The conscionable position you have taken in regard to the Vietnam war and your often vocalized opposition to the horrible injustices perpetrated there in the name of freedom and democracy is in agreement with my feelings and personal convictions. My admiration for you, with special note to your position and your utter disregard for it's security, is profound.

The indignation which you displayed with regard to the killing and injuring of the children in Vietnam was well taken. I especially appreciate your efforts with the organization to aid them by seeking to bring them to the U.S. for surgery, etc. My resources are limited but I hope to give to this most worthy cause.

Not a week passes that I don't write several letters protesting the inhumanity of the war and all it's encumbrances. This shall continue to

Women Strike for Peace, the Pentagon, 1967. In contrast to stereotypical images of bearded hippies protesting against the war, thousands of American women couched their protest in maternal rhetoric, thus criticizing the war for the damage it did to both Vietnamese and American children. (Bettmann/CORBIS)

be my pattern until we can see this situation resolved to the benefit of the Vietnamese people. Freedom and justice must be granted to the people of S. E. Asia as equitably as to any other part of the world. This I do not intend to be on Mr. Rusk or Mr. Johnson's terms either.

Thanks so much for the encouraging you give.

Sincerely,
H. C. [male]
Redwood Valley Calif.

25. I can't help but wonder why our government and the majority of our citizens persist in carrying on this senseless war.

Sandusky, Ohio
March 30, 1966

Dear Dr. Spock,

I read the Plain Dealer every morning after my husband and children leave, and I start the day in a state of complete frustration. After reading about the war casualties, seeing pictures of Viet children clinging to their fathers who are bound and tied, being questioned by our soldiers; seeing a picture today of a young soldier paralyzed from the waist down, receiving the Silver Star from his wheelchair; reading of the hike in taxes to finance the war effort; the profiteering and black market evils from our supplies which are sent to Viet Nam; the shortage of medical facilities and doctors and the misery of the civilian population who were not quite so miserable until we arrived to "help" them; the unpopular military government we're trying to keep in power and so on and on—I can't help but wonder why our government and the majority of our citizens persist in carrying on this senseless war. All semblance of common sense seems to be lacking in our foreign policies.

I watched the Senate hearings for hours and was much impressed with Dean Rusk and General Maxwell Taylor. They were charming and intelligent men and their arguments were most convincing, but they are not practical for this time! Even if we won, which does not seem at all likely, what have we won? And what have those "freedom-loving people" of South Viet Nam won?

One of the reasons Johnson was elected by such a large majority was because everyone thought that Goldwater would escalate the war and LBJ would not. The polls had hardly closed before Johnson was sending more troops to Viet Nam. Where are all those anti-war voices now?

Have they become brain-washed, do they only think at election time, or are they keeping quiet so they won't be called "pinks"? Many of my friends, the women especially, feel as I do, but they don't speak out because their husbands feel differently or they're afraid of being in the minority and being identified with Cassius Clay[5] and the beatniks and the peacemarchers who get such bad publicity.

My husband is an attorney and a liberal. For twenty years he has championed the cause of the negro—even when it was an unpopular cause. I know he agrees with me on Viet Nam, but his friends and colleagues whom he respects, agree with the policies of the administration, so he is on the fence and I even have to argue with him.

Several months ago when the Pope came to plead for peace, he was accorded the greatest respect and the faithful were eager to obey anything he told them. But they completely ignore him when he says "Don't go over and kill your Asian brothers!" It is as if he never opened his mouth on the subject. The Catholics I know are right in there crying for Communist blood. I'm not referring to the man in the factory either. I'm talking about our judges, lawyers, doctors and factor owners.

We're going to Virginia over the Easter holidays to visit my husband's brother and his family. He is a Colonel in the Air Force and is stationed at the Pentagon. I have made up my mind not to argue with him about our policy in Viet Nam as we will be his guests and I don't want to spoil our visit, but isn't it a terrible state of affairs that I must not speak out against a thing which I feel to be legally and morally wrong and which is ruining several countries including our own, besides killing thousands of people, innocent and otherwise, and which is leading us into more involvement for years to come. What a heritage for our children!

The purpose of this letter, if you're still with me, is to tell you that I admire you for the stand you have taken and if your letters didn't appear in the paper once in awhile, I would think I had lost my sanity. When the children were little, I always kept a copy of BABY AND CHILD CARE handy. Your common sense and practical viewpoints also show in your political beliefs. If voices like yours continue to be heard, maybe people will wake up—if it isn't too late.

Sincerely,

E. S. [female]

26. I have never seen the logic of raising a child thru all those hours of sickness, emotional upsets and happiness, then have someone snuff them out with one bullet.

Rockaway, New Jersey
April 29, 1966

Dear Doctor Spock,

My heart compels me to write and thank you for you article in Post.

In raising our "three men," I have often dragged out the book. How wonderful it was to have a friend. Your thoughts have been so like mine that I was amazed there was another nut in the world. Our boys are not perfect, heaven forbid! We have just loved them and really enjoyed growing up together.

We do hope that you will lecture in a place where I have the courage to drive. We will listen. I have never seen the logic of raising a child thru all those hours of sickness, emotional upsets and happiness, then have someone snuff them out with one bullet. There are many times along the way when I think some parents could have done the job themselves.

My people have always been the first to exchange their plow for a sword. My grandfather was the best advertisement for America that I have ever seen. Yet, the thoughts of our boys going to fight, or their children being affected by radiation, sickens me. I honestly feel it could all be avoided.

Thank you again for your article, hoping to hear you soon.

H. B. [female]

27. In short, we love this boy so much that this horrible war in Vietnam is making casualties of us.

May 2, 1966

Dear Dr. Spock:

My husband and I were happy to read the article about you in the May 7th issue of the Sateve Post. How wonderful it is with all of the warmongering going on to read of someone like you working for peace! . . .

Our only blood son is in Vietnam as a machine gunner in the 25th infantry division. We have an adopted son now eight years of age who is a veritable delight and fills a huge gap left by our son.

I never read your books while rearing my first family and made many mistakes; but somehow they turned out fine. Our kids always knew they were loved. Our son never gave us any trouble. Attended church and even took time to talk to the elderly (something most kids nowadays don't do). Of course we're prejudiced—he's our boy. He loves the outdoors. Loves to hunt and fish. If you get him started talking about guns there's no stopping him. He knows all about every gun that was ever made. In short, we love this boy so much that this horrible war in Vietnam is making casualties of us. Although we have a strong faith in God and realize that this is a brief trying ground for all of us; and we are trying to be strong so that when our son returns (if it is God's will) things will be the same as when he left.

I did not intend, when I started this letter to tell you all these things, but somehow feel you will understand and want you to know that we support your stand and will pray for you in your decision to run for the Senate.[6] We need good men, fearless men to aid our country in her time of distress as never before.

I am writing to the editors of the magazines who rejected your articles on peace; asking them to reconsider.

May our Heavenly Father bless you in all your righteous decisions.

Sincerely,

L. S. [female]

Ceddona, Calif

28. Although I do not agree with your views on the Vietnam situation, I know beyond any doubt that the reason you hold those views is because of your concern for babies.

Easton, Pa.

May 4, 1966

Dear Dr. Spock:

The article about you in "The Saturday Evening Post" made me realize how important you were—and still are—in our family. Early in 1946, at the time your book was published for the first time, I was a new mother, a recent college graduate, with a baby a few months old and no one whose opinion I respected sufficiently to advise me about the hundreds of questions that a first baby raises. . . .

Although I do not agree with your views on the Vietnam situation, I know beyond any doubt that the reason you hold those views is because of your concern for babies. Actually, most of us have the same aim: to give our children and grandchildren a safe world to grow up in, one with enough freedom for them to develop into the best adults, individually, they are capable of becoming. The point at which we differ is how this can best be done. The reason that your efforts for peace may be occasionally met with violent opposition is that they may be interpreted, by parents or families of Americans now fighting in Vietnam, that this country should give its military personnel there only half-hearted support. I am sure that I would react the same way if our son were in Vietnam; the only speeches I would want to hear would be ones urging more and better supplies and equipment so that he would have a better chance of survival.

But as you have said before, let us trust that there are enough friendly people in the world, enough of us who are interested in the survival and health of all children, to bring an end to aggression, in time.

Thank you for all the information and understanding your book has given me and mine.

Yours truly,
Mrs. C. G.

29. I think our use of napalm is the most savage thing a supposedly civilized nation could use.

Atlanta Ga.
May 15—66.

Dear Dr. Spock:

I am glad a person of your stature has taken a stand for peace. The two Atlanta papers in their editorials and columns actually call people ignorant and unpatriotic who are against the war in Vietnam. There was one columnist who took a sane, objective look at the war but he has now left the paper.

I can't for the life of me see how by destroying crops, desolating the land killing innocent babies and children we are giving the So. Vietnamese freedom. If I were them I would want none of it.

Here is something I read recently "It is one things for Americans to say 'better dead than Red' but are we morally entitled to say to the Vietnamese 'You would be better dead than Red and our Mr. McNamara will make the necessary arrangements."

I think our use of napalm is the most savage thing a supposedly civilized nation could use. I have seen pictures of small children terribly burned and my heart just ached. A Catholic priest said at one time his little flock were all horribly burned. What kind of monsters are we?

I know it goes against the grain of most American boys to do this, as one American soldier remarked "It is one thing to fight men, the soldiers, but when it happens to children, it is terrible["] but our soldiers . . . must do as they are told to do.

A draft official in Georgia said recently men aren't anxious to go into this war, there is no gung ho spirit today and a recruiter in Louisiana who was asked about the young men's motivation in joining the Army said "Motivation there is none, we shoot them in the fanny with the glory gun, our country right or wrong."

We have been in almost continuing war the past few years. There must be something wrong with us, we can't always be right. We meddle too much in other countries affairs. When I was in Europe sometime ago in every country I visited people would say to me "just who appointed the U.S. policeman of the World."

I think the meeting in Washington today was a magnificent one. The people I saw on T.V. were good solid substantial citizens, not the kooky looking group one usually sees. I am a conservative person, not extreme, a life long Republican (yet as a young girl the first time I voted it was for Al Smith as I admired him as a sincere man. . . .)

In the last election I couldn't vote for Goldwater because he was too war like (but he was honest) and I couldn't stomach the devious, slippery, cunning LBJ, so I didn't vote.

Although I abhor the long hair and sloppy dress of most of the young anti-Vietnam demonstrators, I feel they have a gripe coming as nowadays a young man can't plan his life. The threat of being forced into the Army and sent 12,000 miles to fight in that hell hole Vietnam where it is doubtful that the majority of the people are on our side is enough to make any young man angry.

In years to come I think the historians will view this war as one of the blackest spots in our history. My family doesn't agree with me, they think this war is to save the Vietnamese. We who are against the war take a lot of abuse, but I feel a loyalty first to my conscience and My God. No country or person comes ahead of that with me.

C. M. [female]

30. It is impossible to put into words the anguish that I and other mothers feel in this situation.

Cleveland, Ohio
May 25, 1966

Dear Dr. Spock:

May I express my appreciation and admiration of what you are doing for your country and for mothers and children in taking a courageous stand opposing the war in Viet Nam.

I admit that I have a personal interest in this opposition, as my son, a freshman at W.R.U., is now in the Marines, stationed in San Diego, and probably will shortly be sent into this conflict. It is impossible to put into words the anguish that I and other mothers feel in this situation, especially since, for many of us, this is our second experience in sending a near and dear person into conflict.

May I join the many others who urge you, with your superior endowments intellectually and you education and dedication of purpose, to take a continuing stand in opposing our involvement in this war. May I beg you to enter politics if this is necessary to achieve our goals, as there are so few either as able or willing.

I thank you, along with thousands of other mothers!

Very truly yours,
Mrs. D. S.

31. Because of an incident that happened with my nine year old son, I am now revamping my opinion of the war.

June 5, 1966

Dear Dr. Spock,

I have just finished reading your article in the TV Guide Magazine, and read another article by you in the Post I believe. Being a housewife and mother, I haven't really been too interested in Politics—outside of voting every four years—so didn't give Viet Nam much thought until lately as I thought that was "man's stuff". Because of an incident that happened with my nine year old son, I am now revamping my opinion of the war and am wondering if you have heard from any other parent who have had the same problem.

My son is nine years old and in the fourth grade. He is a normal child in every respect—his room looks like the Dover dump, he can get

B's but will settle for barely passing, and has every ache and pain the world can dig up if asked to take out the trash, but within minutes feels fine if someone come around to play. Not too long ago, he came home from school and his shoulders were hunched and his feet dragging, and for three days he just hung in his room in a very deep depression. He had no interest in ANYTHING. After much talking and worrying, he confided that between classes he had heard some teachers in the hall talking about the war in Viet Nam and that it would last ten years. They were discussing this because a local boy had just been killed and so my son immediately figured they meant all the boys in his particular class or something would be killed and he just couldn't see any sense in anything. News reports say the same thing so he was just scared to death. It has taken much talk and encouraging to get his mind off of this, but I do think it is a terrible cloud for any child to have hanging over him.

I would be interested in any comments you have to make.

Sincerely,
Mrs. D. M.
Dover, Dela.

III. "Our Enemy Is Communism"

JUST AS the previous two groups of letters articulated various strategies for peace and profound concern for children in the shadow of war, the authors of the following group of letters—all of whom support the administration's handling of the war—see the commitment to defeat communism as the surest road to a lasting peace and the safety and security of the world's children. Some invoke the "Domino Theory," arguing that if communism is not contained in Southeast Asia, one country after another will fall to communism. Others focus on the treachery of communist leaders, arguing that they cannot be trusted to negotiate honorably or honestly with the United States. Finally, others focus on the "atheism" of the communists as proof that differences between America and the communist nations are irreconcilable.

32. Peace is something that will unfortunately have to be fought for in very bloody wars.

Brattleboro, VT
4/27/66

Dear Dr. Benjamin Spock:

I read with great interest the profile article on you in the May 7 edition of the Saturday Evening Post.

This article reveals you to be a man of character, great accomplishment + high idealism.

My previous opinion of you from what I had read + seen on T.V. of your comments re the war in Viet Nam was that you were some kind of left winger or Commie sympathizer or crackpot or naive dove.

I sympathize with you in your desire for peace but I think the weak spot in your armor is that you are not aware that there are two kinds of peace—the peace the U.S. wants and the peace the Communists want. The latter kind of peace means domination of the world by the Communists—it means loss of freedom to the people, ruthless domination by the bosses + tyranny.

Your ideal of peace is fine + noble but it will never be achieved by simply lying down + giving in. Peace is something that will unfortunately have to be fought for in very bloody wars.

The Communists have demonstrated repeatedly that they cannot be trusted; they make agreements only to repudiate them—they understand only one thing + that thing is superior force. This is a sad fact but a FACT.

Sincerely yours,
G. S. [gender unknown]

33. Inherent in the concept of Communism is this absolute will to destroy any capitalistic society, of which the United States of America is the prime offender.

St. Cloud, Minnesota
April 28, 1966

Dear Dr. Spock:

I was very interested in reading the feature story about you and some of your ideas in a recent issue of the Saturday Evening Post.

I was particularly heartened to note that you plan to devote a large portion of the remainder of your life time to working for peace. I heartedly agree with your contention that the kind of world we live in poses a major threat to the future of both the young and the old in our country.

I, too, realizing the importance of the times in which we live, am searching for a way to have peace.

At the present time, Dr. Spock, I must in all fairness tell you that my ideas on how to preserve peace for the future, as well as for the present, appear to be diametrically opposed to your techniques.

I happen to believe that testing nuclear devices in order to develop this force as a military weapon may very well be essential for preserving peace.

I happen to believe that our action in Vietnam is militarily sound, morally correct, and extremely wise politically.

As you can see, I am sure, these ideas calculated to preserve the peace are exactly the opposite of what you advocate.

I wonder why two fellow physicians, both wanting peace, can have the exact opposite ideas on how to achieve peace.

I would appreciate it very much, Dr. Spock, if you would show me the kindness to take some time and send me a list of references so that I may read some of the background material that you must have read in order to arrive at the conclusions you have arrived at.

If you would bear with me, I, in turn, would like to briefly outline some of the background involved in causing me to come to the conclusions I mentioned above.

We are not at peace now. This means that we have an enemy. I believe that possibly the difference in our techniques for peace may spring from a different concept of the nature of our enemy, his goals, and his techniques of operation.

I believe that our enemy is Communism. I feel that Communism is based upon dialectical materialism which teaches that every thing in the world, and indeed, in the universe, is in a state of changing flux except one thing. This one real thing is the Communist line. This means that to a dedicated Communist, for example, it is perfectly true that the United States of America dropped germ bombs during the Korean war, if the Communist party says it is true in order to help develope the Communist line. The fact that no germ bombs were dropped is not the truth in their eyes. From this basic concept also springs other concepts. For example, the idea of who are people and who are not people. In Communist thinking the people are Communists. Non-communists are unpeople.

I believe that Communism is well organized, evangelical, mystical, philosophical, atheistic and has very definite plans for the future of mankind.

Inherent in the concept of Communism is this absolute will to destroy any capitalistic society, of which the United States of America is the prime offender.

I believe this enemy intends to destroy us by psychological, military, economic, or any other method that can be used effectively against us.

With this understanding of the enemy that we face I have come to the conclusion that it is very appropriate in the preservation of peace to apply force in terms of military action when this is necessary. I sincerely believe that this is necessary now. . . .

I truly hope that mankind eventually will learn to live with ourselves in a peaceful world. We are not doing that now and I believe that the only way we can preserve any semblance of peace now and to protect ourselves in our way of life for a hopefully free life for future generations, is to be strong now, to have the will to resist now, to defend what we believe in, and, if indicated, to intelligently take the aggressive position needed in order to weaken our enemy.

I do not happen to agree with those individuals who under-estimate the nature and the desires of our enemy in so far as they feel that it is possible to negotiate and reach agreements which will guarantee the future peace of the world. I believe we must negotiate from power. I believe that we must be able to have the moral courage to face force and to defeat it when this is indicated to defend ourselves from Communist threat.

At any rate, I would appreciate very much hearing from you and particularly receiving any references that would fully develope the basis for the kind of thinking and talking and other activities that you are at present engaged in.

Sincerely,
R. K. [male], M.D.

34. "This is my Country, and right or wrong—it's still _my_ Country."

Baton Rouge, La.
24 May 1966

Dr. Spock:

It is with ever growing certainty that the good you might have accomplished is eclipsed by the wrongdoing you now are engaged in.

As a loyal American it is no longer possible for me to regard your treatise in the best interest of my country. As a Christian father I reject your efforts and relegate them to the usual scrap-heap of indoctrination employed by the Communists, their fellow travelers, and those whose actions are so thinly seperated from similar ilk, they can only be considered traitorous. Finally, I offer this regret; That I have squandered 50 [cents] toward furthering your devious and equivocal works.

Now I must be on with the business of educating my daughter to (among other things) love and respect her Country and its effort to preserve (not only her life) but her God granted heritage, and to instill in her this: "This is my Country, and right or wrong—it's still my Country."

Sincerely,

J. B. [male]

35. By all means, in this day and age, when the hand of every country is against us . . . let us teach our children to be soft.

June 1, 1966

Editor, TV Guide

Radnor, Pennsylvania

Dear Sir,

So the great Dr. Spock, having told (presumably) 19,000,000 mothers what kind of food to cram down their children's throats, now decides he is capable of prescribing the right sort of intellectual food to cram into their minds. For the sake of these poor children I can only hope he was not as hopelessly inept at feeding them physically as he has shown himself to be at prescribing mental fare. . . . [EDITOR'S NOTE: The letter then goes on to criticize Spock's analysis of the impact of television on children, as reported in TV Guide, for more than two pages.]

And now, says Dr. Spock, maddened by blood lust, off we go, brutally bombing the gentle North Vietnamese who, according to the favorite literature of the doctor, and other intellectuals—the foreign press—only want to be truly free; free to rape and murder, to intimidate and oppress, to playfully toss a few bombs into night clubs or military barracks and kill, however incidentally, a few women and children who probably shouldn't have been there, anyway. And the death of a few more brutal, murdering American soldiers is always something to be thankful for, isn't it, Dr. Spock.

By all means, in this day and age, when the hand of every country is against us, when we are surrounded by—infiltrated with—vicious and treacherous enemies (not all of them citizens of other countries) ready to move in on us at the first sign of weakness, oh, definitely, let us teach our children to be soft—to equate civilization with simple-mindedness—consideration for other people's feelings with a cowardly yielding to blackmail, physical or moral. Oh yes, indeed, let us teach our children to follow the lead of the civilized rulers of Austria, Czechoslovakia, or Hungary, who met, in a civilize manner at the conference table to settle their differences with their enemies, offering them sweet reasonableness, conciliation, and a consideration for their feelings.

Dr. Spock admits to a limited personal knowledge of television, although this does not deter him from diagnosing its ailment and prescribing for it. One wonders if he would diagnose a baby's illness and prescribe medication for it on the basis of a worried mother's report and the sound of a sick child's cry over the telephone.

In that same manner, and over a distance of thousands of miles, I, too, would prescribe for Doctor Spock: Watch something other than a daytime soap opera. Sit your swelled head in front of a television screen and watch a few of the documentaries you speak of so feelingly—you will find that most of us agree that they are anything but dull. Invite some of you philanthropist friends to watch with you, and watch them glow with satisfaction as native mobs stone American Embassies, and burn and loot libraries, and warehouses filled with American food. Gather round with some of your fellow intellectuals and cheer as American soldiers are killed trying to protect American nationals—some of our privileged rich who have travelled around the world to see at first hand how other people appreciate the benefits of American Aid.

And then go take a long walk off a short pier, Dr. Spock. Spock—Schlock—who needs you?

N. C. [female]
Poquonnoc Bridge Conn.

36. We are aware that running from aggression is not the way to peace. We are aware that to withdraw from one battlefield means only to prepare for the next.

[EDITOR'S NOTE: This letter came on the letterhead of the president of the United States Jaycees, affiliated with Junior Chamber International.]

Tulsa 2. Okla.
June 6, 1966

Dear Dr. Spock:

Yes, we are worried, too, that freedom is not valuable enough to the American people to sacrifice for. The U.S. Jaycees officially have gone on record endorsing our government's position in Vietnam. Jaycees love peace, but they love freedom more. We are aware that running from aggression is not the way to peace. We are aware that to withdraw from one battlefield means only to prepare for the next. History has chartered our course, we must do our share.

Dr. Spock, the patriots who founded our country were not controlled by the price they paid and many of them did pay dearly. Freedom must continue though the price remains dear. Compromise did not win in 1876 and did not succeed in the 1930's. Freedom must succeed today!

Sincerely,
J. S. [male]
President

[EDITOR'S NOTE: The letter-writer included a copy of the following declaration, issued the previous fall.]

The Jaycees of America have always stepped forward in defense of freedom because we believe oppression and wars against free men anywhere constitute a threat to the life and the liberty of free men everywhere. Our nation is now engaged in the defense of freedom in Vietnam where the God given rights of free men are threatened by Communist subversion and aggression. The United States Jaycees, representing 260,000 young men in more than 5,700 communities all over this country, are young men who believe:

1. That to protect our own rights we must always fight for the rights of others, especially when they ask for our help because no man can be completely free as another man is enslaved.

2. That to achieve total victory over Communist aggression it is sometimes necessary to use force as well as diplomatic resources.

3. That responsible action in Vietnam using military force, diplomacy and all other public and private resource to protect these principles is for the ultimate benefit of all freedom-loving people.

We are proud to inform the President, the Congress and other responsible governmental officials that the attitude of young men is a positive one for freedom of all peoples everywhere.

Signed and Attested to this Twenty-Ninth Day of September,
   One Thousand Nine Hundred and Sixty Five.
Signed [Name deleted], President
Attested [Name deleted], Executive Vice President

37. We do have selfish motives but our selfishness includes the welfare of millions who are not U.S. citizens, and not just for today.

Bloomfield Hills, Michigan
November 13, 1966

Dear Dr. Spock:

Recently I read your article on "Why Man Gets Into Wars."

Your points appear valid until one realizes that you are either unconscious of the nature of our present enemy or (like most other critics of our Vietnam involvement) thoughtlessly ignore it.

I agree that Mao can probably change policy because of his one man rule. He won't however, for Communist long stated policy is to bury the free world. How then, can we consider changes in their policy as anything but steps to that end, and consequently, only temporary camouflage?

I also agree that "we should look into our own wishful thinking." When we do, we find no wish to take over the world but a most generous attitude toward others and a genuine and active desire to help the under dog. In spite of this contrast, you imply the Communists are to be trusted and we aren't. We do have selfish motives but our selfishness includes the welfare of millions who are not U.S. citizens, and not just for today.

It is high time critics go beyond proposing we get out of Vietnam. Tell us what will follow our getting out. But you won't because if we relax not only southeast Asia but India, the Philippines and Australia will soon be lost to freedom and we will have only a very precarious freedom of our own.

I'm sure that doesn't appeal to you. If it doesn't, what do you suggest.?

Sincerely,

H. B. [male]

IV: Reflections on the Expanding War

THIS REMAINING sample of letters fleshes out the breadth of concerns of Spock's letter-writers in 1966. Some accuse Spock of treason and disloyalty, while others challenge the legality and moral justification of the war. Still others argue that it is futile, that the Vietnamese want communism and will get it.

38. . . . While our boys (God bless them) are suffering and dying in Viet Nam, Dr. Spock is a ringleader in the protests against these boys, our country and the action of our President.

January 8, 1966

Mr. Mike Douglas
Station KYW TV
1619 Walnut St.
Philadelphia
Dear Mr. Douglas,

I am writing you at the suggestion of WOR TV Channel 9, and Westinghouse Corp, 90 Park Ave, New York, to express my objection to the appearance on your program of Dr. Benjamin Spock.

My objection is based on the fact that while our boys (God bless them) are suffering and dying in Viet Nam, Dr. Spock is a ringleader in the protests against these boys, our country and the action of our President. I have a son in Saigon and could not in fairness to him and the thousands of boys who have had to leave homes and loved ones, listen or watch a program with that man as guest. . . .

I am sincerely sorry to have to write this letter and to discontinue watching your program. Have advised Westinghouse I will not buy any of their products.

Hope you understand my feelings in this matter.

Yours,

Mrs. A. W.

Bronx, NY

39. Backward nations ruled by immensely wealthy "royalty", ARE helped by Communism. We should recognize the fact.

Boonville, Missouri
April 28th [1966]

My dear Dr. Spock:

It would be impossible to express my delight over the article in the current Sat. Eve. Post. But as usual, I was not a <u>little</u> <u>bit</u> troubled over the letters which some gullible, dumb, politically-biased mothers wrote to you. If their babies are shot to death in a foreign war 15 or 20 years from now, I wonder if they will remember how eager they were for OTHER mother's sons to be killed in a war that's none of our business.

If Kennedy had lived, we would not be in Viet Nam as <u>killers</u> today. Being a student of psychology, I know that the majority of people are ignorant and susceptible to propaganda, but it's quite beyond me to understand why the very ones who boasted that Harry Truman "stopped Communism in Asia", are now insisting that Johnson is doing the same thing. As a man from Holland told me, Hitler didn't "take" Holland. The people secretly wanted to TRY Nazi-ism because they belived it was the thing to boost prosperity. Some brave congressman said; "What this country refuses to see is that a lot of small nations think Communism is a GOOD THING". I don't know what they did to that congressman; but if his body was found in the Potomac I didn't read about it.

They flatly refuse to admit that the starving Chinese are better off under Communism—but the fact remains. Backward nations ruled by immensely wealthy "royalty", ARE helped by Communism. We should recognize the fact. Of course, WE don't want it. But that doesn't mean that some small nations SHOULD be liberated from hard-hearted and selfish rulers.

Laura Bergquist, one of the very best journalists, spent a month in Cuba (incognito) and wrote that she found little discontent among the people; just about the average opposition of any people against ANY ruler. WHAT IS WRONG WITH THE REPUBLICANS?? <u>WHY</u> DON'T THEY STAND UP AND FIGHT?? We are a one-party nation. A dangerous and distressing condition.

Mrs. A. W.

40. Dr. Spock, we call on you in the name of humanity and reality to renounce this stand.

Denver, Colorado
May 16, 1966

Dear Dr. Spock,

In view of your past and present pronouncements in favor of abandonment of the Vietnamese people to tender mercies of the Viet Cong murderers, we feel strongly it compellingly urgent to state that we most certainly <u>do</u> <u>not</u> agree with you using and abusing your position as a Medical Doctor for this activity.

We cannot help but wonder in the light of recent history if voices such as SANE's were at work in England and France during and after the "Munich" epochs when Hitler's particular brand of National Liberation was crunching its way across a sea of bodies in Europe. We wonder at how tragically misinformed those "peace peddlers" were. Their motivations most surely were—innocent.

It becomes increasingly difficult for us of the "inferior, unthinking masses" to subordinate our "poor mental" processes to you of the "chosen class"; you who have proven your obvious "cerebral superiority" even though this SANE dogma flies in the face of incontestable historical totality.

Dr. Spock, we call on you in the name of humanity and reality to renounce this stand. Your actions and a continuance of these frightful demonstrations can only help lead the aggressor to the same conclusion gained by our last great despot—that the Democracies were entirely too soft, corrupt, and divided to halt piecemeal barbarity.

This is a very innocent assumption, Doctor, and one which very likely will lead us, with an abundance of help, to a very deadly conflict.

Very sincerely,
R. H. [male]
B. H. [female]

41. There is no question that help is needed in Vietnam but not in the form of bullets.

APO Ny, NY
20 May 66

Dear Dr. Spock,

Thank you and your associates for your fervor and dedication to preserving the American way of life. It has become a sad and alarming concept that to disagree with the present administrations foreign policy is considered by some officials treason. Our great country was built on a foundation of freedom of speech and a government of the people and by the people. The President of the United States is no longer a guide and administrator for the people but has become an overbearing dictator.

It is time for all true Americans to voice their dissatisfaction of the administrations policies both at home and abroad. Vietnam is a sad mistake for the United States but tragic for the Vietnamese people who have been shot, burned, gassed and driven from their homes. There is no question that help is needed in Vietnam but not in the form of bullets.

I have written "letters to the editor" that have been published in the European edition of the Herald Tribune and talked to my fellow Americans in a small attempt to get people to think and at least take a stand on government policy. Lethargy is as dangerous to our freedom as ignorance. . . .

Please continue your fine efforts to keep Freedom Ringing in the United States of America.

Sincerely,

Mrs. L. H.

42. I think we citizens of the United States should demand a clarification of such acts which, in my judgment, are in violation of our constitution.

Fulton, Missouri
May 24, 1966

Dear Dr. Spock,

I have read with much interest your opinions of the Viet Nam War. I am sure that millions of American citizens are in agreement. In my opinion, the undeclared war is the most ridiculous thing that our government has ever done.

I am enclosing a copy of a letter which I wrote to our two Senators from Missouri and which was also read on a program of the television station (KRCG-TV) of Jefferson City, Missouri. . . .

You will note from this letter that I requested a Supreme Court decision as to the constitutionality of both the foreign aid program and the undeclared war in Viet Nam. Neither Senator has made any reply on that point. I think we citizens of the United States should demand a clarification of such acts which, in my judgment, are in violation of our constitution.

I am sending these copies, provided by the television station, to our other congressman in Missouri and some of the leaders of both parties in other states.

If this government is to be saved from a complete degeneration and loss of democracy it seems obvious that it must be done through the efforts of the citizens of this country and not the politicians.

Very truly yours,

D. S. [gender unknown], D.O.

43. It makes me sick at heart, and physically ill too, when I read of the many fine young boys being killed in this horrible conflict.

Friday, September 9, 1966
Marion, Ohio

Dear Dr. Spock:

Your writings have guided the raising of our two sons, one of whom is now married with three children of his own, and my daughter-in-law to whom I gave your book with their first baby also respects your opinions and has been guided by them. Now in desperation I am writing to you in response to your article in August Redbook Magazine on "Protest in Adolescence" which had contained within it all the most crushing problems facing me at this particular time with our younger son, who is now twenty years of age. He reflects the same thinking of many of his contemporaries about this Vietnamese non-war. . . .

My son has had two years of college, and wishes to complete his college education, but the threat of the draft hangs over him as over all the boys in his category. The stepped up draft calls could easily change the student deferment ruling at any time.[7] It makes me sick at heart, and physically ill too, when I read of the many fine young boys being killed in this horrible conflict which seems not to be solving anything but placing our country more deeply into jeopardy and contempt by all the other nations, even our so-called allies. I have lived long enough to observe that this year's allies may well be next year's enemies. When people who are obviously good people—as for example U. Thant, and countless others including yourself, feel that we are wrong in our handling of this problem, I feel not quite so alone in my own thinking.

We are middle class people of the Lutheran faith, not super-religious, but we believe in God and in Christianity generally, try to do our little part to improve things that need improving, etc., and I confess that I cannot see that we are making any progress at all at the moment toward living as Christ advocated we should live. We are supposed to pray for our enemies as for ourselves, for we are told that God loves us all. It isn't easy to pray for ones enemies in war. I try to do it, though, and have come to see that they are in most cases victims of circumstances beyond their control as are we. Their mothers grieve for their dead sons as we do. My two brothers took part in world war 11, there were cousins in our family in World War 1, my great-grandfather fought in the Civil War on the side of the North, though it looks as thought that horrible slaughter didn't really settle things for long either, judging from the state we are in at the moment with our Negro people. I can't help but feel that it is more love and understanding among one another that we need rather than more war. Where will it all end? God pity us.

I am now 52 years old. My mother lives with us and she is 72. We have both seen too much war during our lifetimes. Tell us what we can do toward peace.

> Sincerely with hope and prayer,
> Mrs. V. W

Dr. Spock after being struck by an egg during a demonstration outside the White House, 1967. Such treatment reflected the level of anger, frustration, and betrayal that some Americans felt toward Spock. (U.S. News & World Report, Library of Congress)

3 Polarization, January–October, 1967

ALTHOUGH SOME of the 1966 letters conveyed passionate pleas—both in support of and in opposition to the Vietnam War—in 1967 letters arriving at Dr. Spock's New York office more frequently expressed anguish. Supporters and opponents of the war argued their positions more stridently and in far greater numbers. In retrospect, this makes sense as the war approached peak escalation by the end of the year—with more than 500,000 troops in Vietnam by December—and as public opinion polls showed steadily declining support for the war over the course of the year.

It is worth noting that one of the primary themes present in the 1966 letters—children, war, and peace—faded somewhat in 1967. Many more letters from opponents of the war turned to expressions of (a) frustration over the antiwar movement's apparent lack of influence on the Johnson administration; (b) criticism of the draft system (now calling as many as 35,000 to 40,000 men a month); and (c) concerns about antiwar strategies and tactics. Likewise, many more writers described their reluctance to speak out against the war for fear of being branded disloyal. Consistent with this, among the letters from supporters of the war effort, more strident anticommunist arguments are complemented with many more letters accusing Spock and his kind of treason and disloyalty.

For the American citizens who wrote the following letters, nothing less than American freedom was at stake in 1967. Whether one supported or opposed the war, letter-writing was an act of citizenship in defense of American values seen jeopardized either by the war itself, or by the prospect of withdrawal from Vietnam.

One event, in particular, drew the attention of many of Spock's letter-writers. A number of letters in each of the three groups refer to a major antiwar protest—known as the "Spring Mobilization"—held in New York and San Francisco on April 15, 1967. The planning of the event generated no small amount of controversy; indeed, SANE and

Spock split over the question of whether or not to move SANE's agenda beyond nuclear disarmament to include support of such antiwar activities. After choosing to participate in the New York demonstration, Spock gradually grew estranged from SANE and, in the fall, resigned as national co-chair.

Meanwhile, by April 1967, Martin Luther King, Jr., joined Benjamin Spock as one of the highest-profile opponents of the war. For the rest of the year, Americans grew accustomed to seeing King and Spock marching at the front of growing masses of protesters at all of the nation's largest demonstrations, including the Spring Mobilization in New York. Moreover, King and Spock became favorites of the Sunday morning television news programs such as *Meet the Press* and *Face the Nation*, as well as weekday talk shows hosted by Merv Griffin, Mike Douglas, and others. Many of the 1967 letters respond to such appearances.

I. "Let Us Survive by Being Victorious"

THE FOLLOWING letters from Americans who support government policy in Vietnam extend the earlier themes of achieving long-term peace through force because, in their view, force is the only approach that seems to work with an enemy they see as fundamentally untrustworthy. Some of these same generalizations appear here, too, but with new twists. For one, there is a common thread in several of the letters in which some of the writers try to get beyond the stereotypes of the enemy by stating their own understandings of how U.S. intervention in Vietnam began. For all of them, the Americans came in response to communist aggression, and they paint the enemy—not the United States—as the one responsible for the current state of the war. There are a number of references to the Korean War (in which communist North Korea attacked, unprovoked, noncommunist South Korea in 1950) and Hungary (where, in 1956, the Soviet Union invaded to crush a mass uprising that demanded economic and political reform, independent from Soviet influence). For the writers, these episodes were clearly analogous to the situation in Vietnam. In addition, a certain contempt for intellectuals and public figures like Spock begins to show through in these letters. At their mildest, they suggest that just because someone like Spock achieved notoriety in one field, it does not make him a foreign policy expert; at the most extreme, they accuse Spock and others like him of treason. Such was the tenor of the debate by 1967.

44. Napalm is terrible but would you have the U.S. army issued black-pajamas and sent out to fight the Viet Cong on their terms?

Edmonds, Wash.
March 27, 1967

Dear Dr. Spock:

I have noted, with interest, your decision to retire from your post at Western Reserve University to "devote more time to the peace movement" and also your march with Dr. Rev. Martin Luther King in Chicago on March 24, 1967. I wonder if you could find time to answer the below questions for a simple fellow physician who is attempting to keep an open mind on the Vietnamese question. 1) Is it not true that the Vietnamese conflict is being primarily fought in <u>South</u> Vietnamese soil and not in North Vietnam? 2) Was not the conflict initiated by a relatively small proportion of the South Vietnamese population, the militant Peoples Liberation Front, with the support of North Vietnam, China and Russia? 3) Is not the North Vietnamese army now present in South Vietnam in the form of organized units carrying on an act of military campaign against the U.S. and South Vietnamese forces and their allies? 4) Does not this leave the <u>initiative</u> in the hands of the Viet Cong and North Vietnamese and their backers? 5) Therefore, is not the <u>responsibility</u> for the result of suffering and destruction more squarely on the shoulders of the initiators of the war than on the U.S.? 6) Napalm is terrible but would you have the U.S. army issued black-pajamas and sent out to fight the Viet Cong on their terms? 6) Do you feel that total United States withdrawal should take place from South Vietnam and that the Peoples Liberation Front, i.e. Communism, should be allowed to fill the vacuum? If your answer to this is in the affirmative would you be willing to stand by and see a similar movements succeed in other Southeastern Asian countries such as Thailand, the Phillipines and Indonesia? 7) Do you feel that the United States has any obligation to support the current governments of these countries against millitant groups?

United States involvement in Vietnam to this extent is indeed repugnent and difficult for us to understand. But at present I can see that we have no option, can you suggest one? I see that Dr. King was quoted to the effect that he is obliged to campaign for peace in Vietnam because the war there is distracting attention from the civil rights movement in this country. Is this correct and if so do you subscribe to this point of view?

I would be exceedingly interested in obtaining answers to the above questions should you be able to find time to respond.

P. O. [male], M.D.

45. I sincerely believe that you have no indication of the seriousness of your position and the great dis-service you are doing to our fighting men in Viet Nam.

Chicago, Illinois
4–4–67

Dear Dr. Spock,

Your viewpoints on child care have had my respect for a number of years. In fact, I have recommended highly your book to every young married couple with whom I have come in contact. Your professional knowledge is of the highest order. Your knowledge of the Viet Nam situation, seems to me, to be of the lowest order.

Seeing your picture in one of our local newspapers parading down one of our streets with your "friends" and "acquaintances" was most shocking. A man with your professional skill equated with "draft card burners," as some of the men appear marching with you, is hard to comprehend. Are you sure that you aren't being used by these "doves"?

The fact that Mr. Johnson sent a personal letter to Mr. Ho Chi Minh in which letter Mr. Johnson expressed a sincere desire to establish communication with Hanoi is proof of Pres. Johnson doing all he can to terminate the war.

The fact that the U.S. accepts the U.N Sec. Gen. U Thant's peace proposal indicates the willingness of the U.S. Gov. to cease hostilities.

Both of the above were refused by Mr. Ho Chi Minh!! He insists upon stopping the bombing AND ALL ACTS OF WAR! A man of your intellect knows where this would leave all our fighting men. Look at some of the current issues of the "U.S. News + World Report," and see how trustworthy the people you are marching for are shown to be by their infraction of the conditions laid down for both sides during the Christmas celebrations and Tet—the Lunar New Year. In fact, if you are really interested in checking on their sincerity, honesty + integrity, have one of your office staff give you a breakdown of the number of Americans killed and wounded during the South Korea truce talks!

Getting back to your march in Chicago, I am enclosing an article written by an American soldier who recently returned from Viet Nam. The letter appeared in the "Chicago Daily News", 4-3-67. This man's logical handling of facts places him in a position far superior than the position you have assumed. In your field of pediatrics, this man's knowledge would be inferior to yours, but his intimate knowledge of Viet Nam and his logical conclusion will not get the publicity on TV, Jerry Williams' Radio Program and pictures in newspapers as you have received. Your reputation as an expert pediatrician seems to be giving you a reputation as an expert on Viet Nam.

As a veteran of an armored division fighting in Europe during WW II, I can speak intimately of the horrors of war and the tragic waste of human lives on both sides! I have some knowledge of the necessity of soldiers having proper support, and of the <u>necessity</u> of disrupting your enemies fighting potential by destroying his base of supply etc.

I sincerely believe that you have no indication of the seriousness of your position and the great dis-service you are doing to our fighting men in Viet Nam.

Your stand is comparable to a situation that existed in WWII. This is an experience that occurred to me. We were pushing the German Army out of Holland back into Germany. The retreating German Army blew-up some dikes and the water was flooding a large area. This slowed our advance. We were in mud, literally speaking, to our knees. The first town we occupied in Germany—Selsten—gave us a breather. I had an opportunity to read an issue of the "Stars + Stripes" the Army newspaper. In that issue appeared a small notice that the men back in Detroit who were testing tanks were going on strike for higher wages. You can well imagine how our tankers felt about those men.

You can well imagine how our fighting men in Viet Nam feel about you and your friends in this peace march; stop the bombing marches, and draft card burners.

Yours Truly,

Dr. R. S. [male]

46. "America does not realize what the Communists are—we are so thankful to be in America but still afraid because Americans are so apathetic."

April 9, 1967
Salem, Oregon

Dear Dr. Spock:

When I received in the mail a copy of "Views on Violence, War and Vietnam by Dr. Spock," I read with interest down to the paragraph: "Why has America been so much more fearful of Communism than European nations which have been closer to it?"

At this point I literally gasped. Since 1921 I have been doing Public Health nursing and Social Work and through my mind marched the countless numbers of Hungarian, Polish, and Estonian and Austrian Immigrant people with whom I worked and those with whom I was associated—their one fearful, reiterated, almost frantic cry was "America does not realize what the Communists are—we are so thankful to be in America but still afraid because Americans are so apathetic—they do not know what the Communists are—what they do—the only thing we fear in this wonderful land is that unaware state of mind of Americans —oh what if what has occurred in our land should again happen in America?" This cry was said in many different dialects in many ways— had you, Dr. Spock, heard this you could not make the statement you did or ask that question, if indeed you asked it as quoted—and how do you account for the people trying to escape from East Berlin and the Hungarian revolution and all the desperate attempts at trying for freedom. . . .

Sincerely yours,
E. B. [female]

47. As far as being an expert on war and government policy, you are naive and uninformed.

4/13/67

Dear Dr. Spock,

As a pediatrician and author of books on the care and raising of children you are an expert. As far as being an expert on war and government policy, you are naive and uninformed. When I read that you are to speak at a rally against the war in Vietnam and it is part of an ad that reads

"Dad: Where were you when the U.S. was killing the Vietnamese?" I ask you where were you when the bombs were being thrown into Saigon restaurants and other public NON-MILITARY establishments, killing Americans and Vietnamese women and children alike. Where were you Dr. Spock when we halted our bombing and the Communists said nothing about peace talks but rushed men and supplies in record amounts into South Vietnam? Where were you Dr. Spock when the North Vietnamese and V.C. destroyed and maimed helpless South Vietnamese villagers?

What kind of day for humanity would it be, what kind of day for the South Vietnamese would it be if the U.S. pulled out and left the field wide-open for the Vietcong and North Vietnamese to overrun South Vietnam?

Think about that Dr. Spock and go back to pediatrics where you belong.

Very truly yours,
H. R. [male]
Plainview, NY

48. In practical effect what you are doing is as great an act of direct treason against this country as that of anyone in history.

Sewickley, PA
27 Apr 67

Dear Sir:

You made some statements on the Merv Griffin Show yesterday afternoon concerning the Vietnam situation, of which I happened to hear only the last part, which you either must know were absolutely untrue and therefore were deliberately lying, for reasons which can only be surmised, or which certainly reflect no credit upon either your judgement or your intelligence.

How can you possibly state that North Vietnam has not been guilty of direct, deliberate, and vicious aggression against South Vietnam, and therefore that any action against it by this country to try to prevent or discourage such actions by them is unjustified and represents wholly unwarranted aggression against them on our part, in the face of all the clear evidence to the contrary.

You have not had the common honesty or even intelligence to go to Vietnam to try to determine the facts, as such as Senator Brooke have done, before uttering your presumably well-intentioned but muddle-headed do-good pronouncements to the American people. It is precisely such individuals as you, far out of your element, who are doing far more than anyone else to prolong the agonies of the present situation and are lending so much encouragement to Hanoi to continue their efforts to take over South Vietnam, in the belief that this country has neither the will nor principles or stamina to resist their aggression.

In practical effect what you are doing is as great an act of direct treason against this country as that of anyone in history. Nothing fills me, and I believe most Americans, with more utter contempt, resentment, and disgust than the pious mouthings by you and others that an attempt is being made to equate the right of dissent in this matter, with treason. It is not the right of dissent which is being questioned at all, but the manner in which this is being done by you and some others, which is so reprehensible and unpardonable. You are apparently willing to prostitute whatever reputation you may have in other fields to achieve publicity for yourself, at whatever expense to this country, and it is a shameful exhibition of lack of principle and loyalty on your part.

Very truly yours,

A. G. [male]

49. I agree that these elections would have united Vietnam, and if "peacefully" means the type of peace which now reigns in Red China and Cuba, then you are right.

Pittsburgh, PA.
May 9, 1967

Dear Dr. Spock,

Thank you for replying to my letter of April 24, 1967. I can see from your reply that you are a peaceful and reasonable man. No doubt your actions and public statements have stemmed from an early conclusion that the United States really started all the trouble in Vietnam by preventing an election in 1956.

There is some question as to whether or not the United States was responsible for the failure of that election, or whether it would have taken place even if the United States had taken no position on that matter. But let us assume for the sake of argument that you are right and that the United States did prevent such an election. Do you think that this would have peacefully united Vietnam? Just remember for a moment that the elections which were held in Poland and Czechoslovakia after World War II were watched closely by the communists who made sure that there was no opposition, or that any opposition was quickly silenced. What chance would a democracy-loving person have had in such an election?

I agree that these elections would have united Vietnam, and if "peacefully" means the type of peace which now reigns in Red China and Cuba, then you are right.

Sincerely,

J. M. [male]

50. But this country only became great because, when necessary, its citizens had the guts you seem to so conspicuously lack, to stand up and pay the price to try to end such horrors imposed by others.

[EDITOR'S NOTE: The author of this letter is the same as that of letter 48.]

Sewickley, PA

16 May 67

Dear Dr. Spock:

I wondered, with great interest and curiosity, how you might be able to answer such a letter as my recent one in answer to yours. To be frank, from what you have said and done so far, I did not believe you either could or would be able to do so, for you had placed yourself in such an indefensible position by any standards of responsible conduct.

It is noted that nothing further has been heard from you publicly since your incredible appearance and statements with Martin Luther King. Let it be hoped, for the sake of your own reputation in other fields, that this blessed silence on your part may continue as far as the Vietnam situation is concerned, about which you obviously know so little yet could do so much potential harm to this country.

I do not like many things about the Vietnam situation either, but I believe there are limits in such situation beyond which no loyal citizen has the right to go in dissenting or registering any protest, and that you overstepped those bounds in an irresponsible manner of which I hope, by now, you may have become thoroughly ashamed, as you should be. Having served in two wars—in the Marines in World War I and the Engineers in World War II, and nearly losing my life in the business at Attu[1]—I know at first hand the horrors of war, and am certainly no 'hawk' in this situation. But this country only became great because, when necessary, its citizens had the guts you seem to so conspicuously lack, to stand up and pay the price to try to end such horrors imposed by others.

Very truly yours,

A. G. [male]

51. In the name of our Lord what is it going to take to wake you so called intellectuals up.

Tampa, Fla.

May 18, 1967

Dear Sir,

Last night I listened to you + watched you on the Merv Griffin Show —from what you said this program was taped before the—to me infamous New York Vietnam protest.

Sir if you are not a communists you certainly give much aid + comfort to their cause + devilish system.

I am a young person by comparison to you—only in my 30s but with ideas such as yours I shall surely age rapidly. As I listen to you + men of like ideas who are old enough to know better and are schooled enough to think more logically, I lose much sleep.

As Mr. Griffin said it sounds like the era surrounding the rise of the third Reich.

When are men of your stature and mental capacities going to wake up to the reality that we are in a life + death struggle with God-less atheistic forces who are out to destroy us + any other nation that stands in their way.

You refer to us as aggressors, brutal, etc., etc., what about what these people do, to try to gain control of the people,—they have not changed just their methods—they are more subtle + devious than before, that is all.

In my short life upon this earth, I have become so weary of my nations trust of this nation + that + leaders in various fields being taken in by sly-smiling wicked men.

Don't you remember the uprising in Hungary, don't you remember the firing squads in Cuba—the terrorist activities in Algeria + the killing on purpose of village leaders + other civilians in Vietnam?

In the name of our Lord what is it going to take to wake you so called intellectuals up.

You may or may not be aware of it but the Bible predicts so many of the things that are occurring today.

I do not know if you have any religious belief or not, I do not see how one could + be as blind as you appear to be. May God open your blinded eyes to see things as they really are.

Our involvement in Vietnam is against communism this in itself makes our being there justified.

If you + others like you—(God forbid) should have your way about things you will not believe that these power mad leaders of these communist nations mean what they say until you see them walking down Main St. with fixed bayonets. You are a fearful + misguided idealist, but you cannot be idealistic with murderers.

With the representation + pictures + posters at the march you participated in I cannot but believe it was communist inspired + instigated + those participating are blind leaders of the blind—+ dupes of the communist conspiracy.

Russia should never have been given diplomatic recognition by this country, we should never have entered into any treaty agreements with that nation + if we continue on the path which we are following in continuing to deal with her it shall be to our own destruction—May God divinely intervene as He is our only hope.

They have broken hundreds of treaties with us + others—treaties to them do not mean anything—they sign these things to gain advantage + when it is to their advantage to break them they do so.

We should declare war in Vietnam—get out of the U.N., give Red China our seat—they will be at home with the crowd that is there—+ fight using every weapon at our disposal to crush this tyrannical Anti God system.

You should read the old Testament to find out how God used different nations to destroy other nations who rejected Him and who bowed down to idols, He has not changed, only man had—man is as changeable as the shifting sands—but Praise God—He stands firm as a Rock in dealing in righteousness—mercy—+ wrath upon the ungodly. . . .

My mother who was not a Christian brought us up with much discipline, she raised 15 children with out the aid of any advice, but good common sense + high standards of morality + not one of her children was ever brought into a court room or ever had any trouble or caused any trouble in school or else where. I say all of this to point out the fact that many of these young people who are demonstrating are or never have known good discipline + high standards of morality for they would not be so rebellious if they had. They think they are rebelling against society, their parents—authority etc—but they really are rebelling against God, as man has done + I suspect will continue to do until God says that's enough! May God in His Infinite mercy save our nation, + open the minds + hearts of men to His Son our Saviour the Lord Jesus Christ is my hearts desire + prayer daily.

Most Sincerely,

Mrs. P. S.

52. No nation in history has done more for others than this one, or been better-intentioned and principled.

[EDITOR'S NOTE: The author of this letter is the same as that of 48 and 50.]

Sewickley, PA

July 19, 1967

Dear Sir:

Surely one of the most pathetic figures and spectacles around today is that of Benjamin Spock, floundering around in a miasma of personal vanity and illusions about himself and his imagined importance and influence, in an area he knows nothing whatever about and is apparently incapable of understanding in any way. The very idea of such an individual, so obviously lost and misguided, being seriously 'willing' to become a candidate for the Presidency of the United States is just too absurd and ridiculous to even be comprehensible.

All of this would be sad enough if it were not for the overtones of disloyalty and outright treason involved in some of your recent befuddled pronouncements from on high. There is ample room for dissent in this country, but it is the obligation of every citizen, worthy of that citizenship, to do so in an intelligent, <u>responsible</u> manner, and <u>within the framework of loyalty to his country, which you are not doing</u>.

In my view you have made yourself quite undeserving of your citizenship. If you profess to be even reasonably honest, you should at once apply for citizenship in some other country more to your liking, such as France, or Ghana, or Russia or China, or perhaps Syria or Egypt. Yet nothing could be more certain than that you simply do not have either the guts or common honesty to do this, but are perfectly willing to hide behind the great protection of your present citizenship, however undeserved, because you know that in no other country would such actions as yours, such antics, be tolerated. Fortunately, most Americans do have a sense of humor and can appraise and snicker at your absurdities for what they are.

Yet you have gone so far with these that one can really no longer even laugh at you, but only feel sorry that a once-respected figure should so incredibly lose all perspective on himself and the facts of life, and his obligations to his country, and be willing to make such an utter jackass of himself. Such considerations as honest responsibility and loyalty do not seem to exist in your lexicon. I think most Americans, whatever their views, deeply resent your cheap and tawdry slurs against her principles, honor, and integrity. No nation in history has done more for others than this one, or been better-intentioned and principled, and the sooner you realize this, the sooner you will regain some trace of respect for yourself, which you have been throwing away so stupidly.

> Very truly,
> A. G. [male]

53. As a sensitive, intelligent man you should see the direct parallels between the appeasers of the 1930s and the "Doves" of today.

Oct. 9, 1967

Dear Dr. Spock,

People of liberal persuasion never get upset when Communists take over a country (Hungary) with ruthless brutality. Imperialism from the left—Cuba, Vietnam, Korea—is rationalized away as "agrarian reform" or "wars of liberation."

Strangely, aggression from the right—Rhodesia, Portugal, Germany, Spain—is vigorously opposed. Why this distinction in aggression?

Liberals formed no ad-hoc committees and took out no ads in the Times when Hungarians were slaughtered. Why?

As a sensitive, intelligent man you should see the direct parallels between the appeasers of the 1930s and the "Doves" of today. An attempt is being made to repeat Munich ("doves" deny but never explain why) the comparison is valid.

Why don't liberals demand free elections in <u>No. Vietnam</u>?

Why don't they demand <u>Ho-Chi-Minh</u> come to the conference table?

Why don't they condemn the <u>N.L.F.</u> for murder + kidnapping in the South?

Why does Dr. Spock condemn the U.S. for not holding elections as required under the Geneva Accord? Don't you know that elections were not to be held until people could vote without fear of assassination + torture? Don't you know that as soon as Geneva was signed, Ho-Chi-Minh sent bands of assassins South to terrorize and kill? How could free elections be held in that atmosphere? Don't you realize that Ho-Chi-Minh is looking for the Dr. Spocks to convince us to withdraw? Without the Fulbrights, Spocks, Morses, Percys, etc. encouraging him to hold on, Ho Chi Minh would probably have called it a day.

You give the impression of a kind, gentle, highly civilized humanitarian. Many of those on your side of the Viet Nam controversy have baser motivations. You should be in better company than the inmates at the "New Politics" bedlam at Palmer House.

You find it impossible to believe that self-doubt, vacillation, debaseing one's countrie's motives, etc., are looked upon with contempt and as evidence of weakness by most of the world. Power is respected and understood. It is unfortunate that the world is like this but is has been since the beginning of time. Those nations that did not understand this have vanished.

You seem to refuse to believe that there are nations in the world that are working for the day that the U.S. will be destroyed. You seem to think the Russians have mellowed since Stalin. What about missiles in Cuba, the Berlin Wall, billions in arms to despots in the Mid-East? You will not believe it but realists see Vietnam as another probe by Communism to subtract a little more real-estate from western markets + deny access to the mineral resources of S.E. Asia to the U.S. and its allies. Success in Viet Nam for Ho will launch more "liberation wars" to keep us off balance.

Because of the influence of those neurotics who worry about "world opinion" (whatever that means!) We have tried to fight a severely limited war in Viet Nam. The result has been a vast amount of unnecessary damage and casualties. The Israelis fought a war too—with maximum, brutal force—ruthlessly applied from the <u>outset</u>. The result was victory —fast and with a minimum of damage + casualties. We could have ended the war in Vietnam years ago if our govt. would have turned a deaf ear to the doubters, idealists, pacifists and their companions with baser motives—the communists.

If you want to be a humanitarian, Dr. Spock, you should join forces with those who want to apply maximum power—short of atomic weapons—to bring this war to an end. The "limited war" Johnson is pursuing could go on for years.

Your trouble is that in your humanitarian, idealistic world, kindness, forbearance, and understanding will be reciprocated. Unfortunately, only the U.S. and some countries in N.W. Europe feel this way. In the real world only weak, decadent people act this way and aggression and wars follow—started by the predatory nations looking for easy victory.

Dr. Spock, please leave the dream world to others + do something to solve problems in the <u>real</u> world.

As with the Israelis, let us survive by being victorious. You way insures continuous war and possible destruction of this country by encouraging more + more probes by communists that we must resist or be slowly cut down to a state where a nuclear war will be deemed a good risk by Moscow or Peking.

G. R. [male]
Bronx, NY

II. Voices of Moderation

A GREAT many Americans wrote to Spock neither to argue the finer points of American policy nor to criticize his behavior directly. Most of these writers seemed to be opposed to the war, but writing in more moderate tone, expressed a range of concerns over the nature of the war, antiwar movement tactics, and the larger wartime political climate in America. They appear less likely to be antiwar activists taking to the streets, participating in demonstrations, than those in the next section; yet it is clear that they are close observers of those protests. Some wrote to Spock to suggest specific strategies for the peace movement—highlighting the draft or focusing on electoral politics, for example—while others pleaded that movement leaders and participants avoid extreme speech and acts (notably flag burning). The *appearance* of the antiwar movement is on the minds of most of these writers; some specifically wrote in desperation about keeping the idea of dissent in a democratic society legitimate. To dissent, they suggested, did not mean they were communists or that they did not support American troops in Vietnam. The "you're either with us or against us" political dynamic so familiar in wartime seemed especially troubling to these writers.

54. The draft should be eliminated before it eliminates our freedom here at home . . . as well as the flower of our youth.

April 10, 1967

Dear Dr. Spock:

Aren't we all responsible for what is going on in Vietnam? In a republic, the <u>people</u> are the government. For 20 years we citizens have never questioned the right of our public servants to impress young men into a kind of American Foreign Legion.

Instead of starting off to ban the bomb, your peace group should begin to <u>abolish the draft,</u> and the terrible waste of American lives in foreign wars. The debate should be intellectual however, not unpatriotic. Radicalism in the Peace Movement promotes confusion and anarchy, not peace. Some people might be trying to do just that, and they should be stopped. The draft card burners, hecklers, rioters etc . . . should be soundly rebuked for giving an aire of <u>respectability</u> to a very un-American law. May I suggest the following:

1. Stop the appeasement line and sympathy plea for the Viet Cong. It isn't going over with the public. Mothers are too worried about their <u>own sons</u>. ALL SYMPATHY SHOULD GO TO AMERICAN SOLDIERS. WE HELPED PUT THEM THERE.

2. Americans can <u>abolish the draft</u> through political action and through the vote. It's a little harder to convince the <u>world</u> to abolish war. First things first. The Congress is now conducting hearings on the draft. I would hope that you and Luther King would make an appearance to question the constitutionality of the law. A draft is completely contrary to our tradition and a serious threat to our country as a free society. It is "involuntary servitude." A continuing draft, which is never questioned can, in time pave the way for universal conscription, not just for our sons and daughters, but for professional people, workers etc. . . . Congress may be usurping power it does not have, for in a free society, a draft should exist only if the country is under imminent threat to its safety and security. No such threat exists. If it did, congress would declare a state of emergency, war would be declared, and all trade would cease with enemy

nations. Both Johnson and Goldwater promised to abolish the draft during the 1964 presidential campaign. THIS SHOULD BE BROUGHT UP AGAIN AND AGAIN.

3. People with such diverse political philosophies as Sen. Brooke and Gov. Reagan have come out against the draft, in favor of a well paid volunteer army. They should be supported because they are leading us out of the "draft mentality". There is nothing sacred, or American, about the draft. The contrary is true. It is also outmoded, and it is ridiculous and unethical for a country to draft its men to occupy friendly and peaceful countries which can and should be protecting themselves with their own manpower. Why should a country like America (supposedly free) have a draft, to maintain 3 and one quarter million men under arms to patrol the whole world . . . and a country like India with its teeming millions, no draft, and a common border with Red China have only 800,000 men for home defense? Our Congress should be booted out of Washington. They are as expendible as they seem to think American youths are.

4. Twenty years ago when this foreign aid thing started, Harry Truman said we would help other countries reach their own self-determination with economic and technical assistance. What does the draft have to do with this? Maybe we need some "self determination" at home. Our government has spread itself so thin, it has become shallow in regard to its own American families and it treats its youth and their human rights with impunity. The draft should be eliminated before it eliminates our freedom here at home . . . as well as the flower of our youth.

> A citizen,
> Mrs. J. F.
> Shaker Hts, Ohio

55. I respect your integrity, but I am worried deeply about the direction the peace movement is taking.

April 15, 1967

Dear Dr. Spock:

I appreciate your deep concern about the Vietnam situation—It is a hellish war. I have deep distrust, though, of directions the "peace" movement is taking.

Ho has rejected a major proposal for peace—largely accepted by

President Johnson and Premier Ky.[2] Ho rejected private efforts of President Johnson to begin talks. It seems to me that a <u>genuine</u> peace movement would be exerting international pressure on <u>both</u> sides to begin negotiations. That would be a genuinely moral position. In the absence of that it appears that we are being given anti-American propaganda.

I have seen liberal movements perverted by authoritarian leftists before. It seems to me that serious attention should be given to this possibility now.

I respect your integrity, but I am worried deeply about the direction the peace movement is taking.

Sincerely,

A. W. [male]

[EDITOR'S NOTE: The next letters arrived at Spock's office in the days after he participated in the Spring Mobilization march and protests in New York. The speakers and events to whom they refer occurred on that day.]

56. I did find fault, though, with the unsupported ridicule and denunciation of L.B.J. by some of the lesser speakers and particularly by some of the folk singers.

Phila., Pa.

April 17, 1967

Dear Ben:

I was in Yale, class of 1924, and knew you slightly then. I just want to express my admiration now for your wisdom and courage in the Vietnam situation, and so am enclosing my check for $100.00 for SANE.

I took a bus to N.Y. Saturday, attached myself to the "Veterans Group", marched to the U.N. and listened to your and the others' speeches. The whole thing was amazing. I never saw so many young people. Dr. King is one of my heroes. I don't think I agree with McKissick and less with Carmichael,[3] but I did not object to their presence. I did find fault, though, with the unsupported ridicule and denunciation of L.B.J. by some of the lesser speakers and particularly by some of the folk singers. I suppose the latter are a necessary evil of such an enormous gathering, but I feel it is damaging to the cause.

With best wishes and with gratitude, I am

Sincerely,

H. H. [male].

57. <u>SEE</u> to it that every individual in this nation . . . is <u>informed</u> <u>fully</u> and thoughtfully <u>NOT</u> to <u>BURN</u> <u>ANY</u> <u>FLAGS</u>—<u>OURS</u>—or any <u>other</u>.

May 3, 1967
Bronx, N. Y.

Dear Dr. Spock,

Yesterday, August Heckscher,—New York City's Park Commissioner—gave the word that no further rallies would be held in Central Park, (N.Y.). There seems to be every reason to believe that <u>ONE</u> purpose of his move has been due to the fact that protests were made by outsiders to his office because the <u>U.S.</u> <u>Flag</u> was burned by individuals there,—and which set off a chain reaction in Congress and elsewhere, reacting against it.

Mr. Spock,—whether you do so <u>openly</u> or in confidence to the peace movements—<u>SEE</u> to it that every individual in this nation, (who carries his <u>OWN</u> <u>banner</u> for <u>sanity</u> restoration) is <u>informed</u> <u>fully</u> and thoughtfully <u>NOT</u> to <u>BURN</u> <u>ANY</u> <u>FLAGS</u>—<u>OURS</u>—or any <u>other</u>, where <u>STANDARDS</u> have meaning! <u>THIS</u> <u>IS</u> <u>JUST</u> <u>WHAT</u> <u>THE</u> <u>"DAILY</u> <u>NEWS</u>",—(with its poisonous, corrosive <u>idiotorials</u>) <u>WANTS</u>;—and gleefully, <u>THAT'S</u> <u>JUST</u> what they congratulated Heckscher for <u>DOING</u>! Our work for world peace today is no ordinary and/or temporary crusade against fear-mongers who play with napalm bombs like firecrackers;—universal peace was pioneered by noble figures in the past who gave <u>THEIR</u> lives for <u>US</u> to carry <u>ON</u>, and which we <u>TODAY</u> and fighting to preserve and extend to the <u>NEXT</u> unborn generations. And posterity will <u>YET</u> say that <u>THIS</u> is <u>OUR</u> finest hour, in the struggle we're waging against the Goldwaters, the Johnsons, the Birch Societies, etc, all of whom <u>USE</u> the flag which <u>ONCE</u> was <u>OURS</u>—and which <u>STILL</u> is ours! I certainly am no tar baby "patriot" but <u>THIS</u> much I <u>DO</u> know:—The U.S. flag which <u>ONCE</u> stood for <u>HUMANITY</u> <u>MUST</u> <u>BE</u> <u>RESTORED</u> as such. It's <u>STILL</u> the flag that gave us all the great liberals we know,—such as Franklin and Eleanor Roosevelt, —Alben Barkley,—Henry Wallace,—Fiorello LaGuardia—Al Smith,— and a legion of those who were in the vanguard of the genuine democracy we once knew as of old. It is <u>NOT</u> the flag of the drunken swine who run the "<u>Daily News</u>" and its bombastic satellites from the <u>sewers</u>—nor is it the flag of the munitions makers, the pentagonists and other circles who conspired to skyrocket us into the blood bath of Viet Namm for their <u>OWN</u> purposes. If someone occupies your house, and puts you out of it,—you <u>don't</u> <u>burn</u> <u>down</u> <u>your</u> <u>own</u> <u>home</u> <u>just</u> <u>out</u> <u>of</u> <u>spite</u>: You go

<u>BACK</u> to that home, and <u>ROOT</u> <u>OUT</u> again those within it to <u>RESTORE</u> what <u>ONCE</u> was <u>YOURS</u>!! All of us who were and are liberals are now <u>evicted</u> from the decent ideals now taken over by charlatans who play with men's lives and souls like chess on the blackened ruins of Viet Namm. None of us who fight for peace ever put American flags all over our stationery—in stickers—or even in rallies—like the super phony patriots do—that's <u>THEIR</u> way—not <u>OURS</u>,—just as facism and it's "corporative state" of Franco Spain is <u>THEIR</u> ideal of life—not <u>OURS</u>! <u>OUR</u> way is to <u>TAKE</u> the American flag with <u>SOME</u> respect,—<u>LEAVE</u> it elsewhere <u>in</u> it's place—<u>BUT</u> <u>WE</u> <u>DON'T</u> <u>BURN</u> it to give the hatemongers <u>ANOTHER</u> "red" issue to harp upon,—and maybe even a <u>LETHAL</u> one that can suddenly destroy <u>all</u> the work we've built up through these Viet Namm years to be demolished <u>OVERNIGHT</u>!! We might just as well burn down the White House because that clumsy ox, LBJ lives in it now,—instead of voting that dumbell <u>OUT</u> as he may <u>YET</u> be (easily?) voted out! You saw for yourself, Mr. Spock, how the recent "Loyalty Day Parade" fell flat on its face, without an audience behind the wooden horses on the sidewalks—while <u>OURS</u> was publicized throughout the length and breadth of this planet: Yet <u>all</u> this, <u>and</u> <u>more</u>, could be wiped away, by some <u>nut</u> with <u>mashed</u> <u>potatoes</u> in his head instead of <u>brains</u>, that <u>SMILES</u> in photos as he burns the U.S. standard. <u>DRAFT</u> <u>CARDS</u> we burn? <u>YES</u>! <u>MARCHES</u>? <u>YES</u>! <u>RALLYS</u>? <u>YES</u>!! <u>SIT-INS</u>? <u>YES</u>! <u>PROTESTS</u> <u>ON</u> <u>CAMPUS'S</u>? —<u>YES</u>!! <u>ANYWAY</u> we protest to gain our ends is fair. But why take this out on a <u>STANDARD</u> cloth, which was, in turn, taken away from <u>US</u>? The <u>next</u> step will be pouring tar on pictures of Lincoln and Roosevelt—defacing public buildings—maybe even bombs like anarchists, yelling behind barricades in the streets, "<u>KILL</u>—<u>KILL</u>—<u>KILL</u>!!" Fighters for peace don't <u>KILL</u>—they <u>PROTEST</u> and eventually get public opinion on <u>THEIR</u> <u>SIDE</u>!! <u>THAT'S</u> <u>WHAT</u> <u>WE</u> <u>WANT</u>—<u>PRINCIPLES</u> with <u>PROGRESS</u>. . . .

It's not enough to just say "Whoever destroyed the flag in Central Park, is not one of us"—that may be true. We must do <u>MORE</u>—we must tell our members,—one and all,—"<u>THIS</u> is <u>NOT</u> <u>OUR</u> <u>WAY</u>!—we're an <u>EDUCATED</u> group—not spawned from the gutter like the Brownshirts of Nuremberg, who <u>burned</u> <u>books</u>, and their own Reichstag."

THANK YOU,

M. M. [male]

<u>ANYONE</u> CAN BURN A FLAG, <u>BUT</u> <u>WE</u> <u>MUST</u> <u>NOT</u> <u>BE</u> <u>IDENTIFIED</u> WITH THEM. I <u>URGE</u> YOU TO MAKE A STATEMENT <u>DEFINITELY</u> <u>MAKING</u> <u>IT</u> <u>KNOWN</u> THAT <u>WE</u> <u>DO</u> <u>NOT</u> <u>DO</u> <u>THIS</u>!

58. I am a Democrat, but would <u>never again</u> vote for Mr. Johnson or Mr. Humphrey . . . but many of my friends and myself have almost given up.

Solana Beach, California
May 10, 1967

Dear Dr. Spock,

I have read with great interest your efforts to tell people the truth about our involvement in Vietnam. I certainly approved of everything you said on the Merv Griffin show and was glad that he gave you the time to present it on TV.

I'm sure that many people in the United States feel the same way, but other than write to our Congressmen and the President, we don't know what to do about it. I certainly know how my Congressmen feel about the war and President Johnson tells us he's for peace, when he's continually escalating the war. I am a Democrat, but would <u>never again</u> vote for Mr. Johnson or Mr. Humphrey . . . but many of my friends and myself have almost given up. What have we to vote for? Is any candidate going to come out AGAINST the war or some settlement for peace? Is there anyone who really wants peace?

I have a son, who is 17 and will soon be 18. (By the way, your little paperback is still in my cupboard, with loose pages, rather worn from use because I brought up two babies using it as my "Bible.") I don't want my son to fight in Vietnam for a cause that I don't believe in. I didn't work so hard to keep him good, bring him up to do right, keep him healthy and well . . . to have him go to the jungles of Asia in the pretense of keeping democracy there.

I admire Martin Luther King too, for disapproving of this war. How can we continue to build up our country, to work on the problems of race, air pollution, transportation, education, when we are spending all the money on a <u>war</u>? You are both so logical and so right, I just don't see how people could think otherwise.

Now, if we speak out against the administration or the war, we are being classed as Communists or against helping the boys in Vietnam. We are losing what our country was founded on and for. When you had the parade in New York City, you saw the report in the New York Times, which headlined that Mr. Johnson had the F.B.I. looking into marcher's records, etc. Even our good friend, Norman Cousins, editor of the Saturday Review of Literature, has been called to Washington in an effort to "Silence" him. What have we left?

Any help we can give you, we would sincerely like to do it. We thank you for your efforts and all that you have been doing is certainly appreciated by many.

Sincerely yours,

M. C. [female]

59. We are not Communists, beatniks nor hippies.

Santa Barbara, Calif.

May 19th 1967

Dear Dr. Spock,

Just want you to know that my family and I support your views of the war in Vietnam 100%. We are not Communists, beatniks nor hippies.

I believe the actions of our government in Vietnam are unworthy and unrepresentative of a Christian nation.

Sincerely,

C. K. [female]

P.S. Thank you for your book which assisted me greatly in caring for my baby. She is now 12.

60. What we may be doing now in Vietnam is simply to postpone the inevitable.

July 3, 1967

Dear Doctor Spock:

My father always maintained that there was a reason for everything.

I think that the reason they we are now involved in a war in Vietnam revolves around the fact that very few Americans understand the fundamental causes of the internal strife in this region of the world.

I was in the U.S. Navy during World War II, and I had the opportunity to see something of the conditions under which the people of the Southeastern part of Asia exist.

Although I don't like to see the spread of Communism, and while I do believe that the people of Vietnam will be making a mistake if they choose this type of government, I believe that they are sincerely trying to better their way of life.

If more people knew something of conditions in Asia, they would understand the struggle the Vietnamese are making to secure some of the benefits of civilization.

The Chinese people suffered as slaves under the rule of the various war lords in their country, for centuries, until they revolted. The war lords taxed the people heavily, took their crops and their land, and ruled with an iron fist until the natives finally had enough.

The American government established a policy of aiding such corrupt powers to perpetuate their rule, and our officials were greatly surprised at the downfall of the Nationalist government. All our military and economic aid to the Nationalist government was wasted in a campaign destined to failure.

What we may be doing now in Vietnam is simply to postpone the inevitable. Sooner or later the will of the people will be the determining factor, and I think we should have kept out of the mess.

I am 100% in favor of your policy for war peace, but I can not understand what can be done now in Vietnam if the V.C. will not negotiate. Would you be in favor of pulling our forces out of Vietnam now, if we are unable to mediate? Personally, I think this is the only course left open to us, unless we want to be engaged there for another ten years.

I have enclosed a small check for SANE, and if you have time, I would be glad to hear from you, concerning your thoughts on Vietnam.

Sincerely,

R. L. [male]

Pompton Plains, New Jersey

61. I found none, except one S. Vietnamese who is attached to our government forces here in Honolulu, who favored continuing the war.

Sheraton Hotels in Hawaii
[Letterhead]
On the beach at Waikiki
July 12, 1967

Dear Dr. Spock,

I have admired immensely your courage in combatting the vicious nature of the Vietnam war and in seeking to have our President stop this dangerous, futile and costly conflict.

A business trip now nearing completion has taken me to Bombay (after a short stop in Rome), Bangkok, Hong Kong and Tokyo. My associates and friends in these places number not only professional lawyers and business men but intelligent natives and residents to whom I could talk and listen on a personal basis. I found none, except one S.

Vietnamese who is attached to our government forces here in Honolulu, who favored continuing the war. The feeling against us is not because of lack of friendship for the U.S.A., but predominantly on the grounds that what we are doing is immoral, resented bitterly by most of the S. Vietnamese, interference with the desires of most of the S. Vietnamese to have us go home, and frustrating in that we are perpetuating a high-handed, despised, military clique (which knows little and cares less about democracy).

I should like to help in enlisting the support of the American public to expose the fallacy of the "don't let the Boys down" philosophy and in arousing our people to the realization that we are indeed "letting the boys down" and placing our country in serious peril, if this needless blood letting is not ended.

I shall be back in my New York office next week, and look forward to such suggestions as you may offer for constructive cooperation.

    Sincerely,
    H. S. [male]
    New York, NY

62. The essence of freedom is the right to dissent and the right to make mistakes within agreed-upon limits, and to chance the limits through conflict and dissent.

                Bala-Cynwyd, Pennsylvania
                8/13/1967

Dear Dr. Spock:

It was with interest and gratitude that I read the article about you in the NYT. I will not agree or disagree with your stand on Vietnam, because it is rather irrelevant to my feelings toward you. What I am grateful to you for is that a man of your prominence and undoubted high status, has publicly espoused unpopular dissent. How difficult dissent can be, even for a man as well-liked as you, the article made clear: it has brought home to me with new force how the legitimacy of dissent is one of the basic—nay, the basic—aspect of a free society. . . .

The legitimacy of dissent is a very fragile thing—and usually the first casualty in times of public hysteria. I learned it with sorrow in Nazi Germany. My father was a social-democrat, one of the few in our small town. In spite of his political dissent he was well liked, was elected to the town council, the school board, the water commission and so forth.

Twice a week, he was freely allowed to express his political dissent at the "Stammtisch", and then argue politics till 2AM under a lamppost. Dissent was legitimate and legal. It changed in 1933 almost overnight; what have been acceptable behavior became criminal and treason. For a while, my father was not harmed, but was completely ostracized with no one willing to be seen with him or talk to him. There were no Jewish people in our community, so that he did not even have the comfort of secretly sharing ideas and feelings. His business failed; his house was sold at auction for back taxes and bought for a song by the top Nazi. He refused to work as an engineer on the Autobahn—construction: "I am not going to build 'Kriegstrassen' for Hitler", he told my brother who had gotten him the job. He ended working as a common laborer on a theater building. In 1938, he was secretly offered the position of mayor of our town; times were good and no one wanted to give up business interest for a poorly paid public job: "We know how you feel, but pretend to go along." He refused: "I rather die like a dog than pretend to what I do not believe." Shortly after this, he was taken into "protective custody" from which he returned a broken man, to die in deep mental depression. His total social isolation was more than he, always a very sociable and friendly man, could bear. My mother's funeral in 1919 had been the biggest public spectacle ever in our town; at his funeral, one old friend came—Nazi enough that he could risk his presence. When I asked some of his former friends why they had isolated him so completely—after voicing to me their secret admiration for my father's stand, they told me: "I have a family." His public honor in 1945 came too late for him.

The lesson of all this? Courage, especially the courage it takes to be out of steps with our social group, is a very rare thing. It is for this reason that public dissent must not only be acceptable, it must be a public duty. We can be taught to dissent: I have taught it to my three sons—to dissent not in anger but as a matter of fact—as a right and a duty.

I hope I made myself clear. The essence of freedom is the right to dissent and the right to make mistakes within agreed-upon limits, and to chance the limits through conflict and dissent. The essence of public morality is not: "I think it is a sin and therefore you better not do it," but: "I think it is a sin and therefore I better not do it; and "I think it is socially harmful and therefore we better not do it; what do you think?" Beards, long hair, minis, unconventional garb of all sorts, are but non-verbal dissent by people who have not learned to express dissent otherwise. It may be rather ineffective except for one thing: if carried on long enough and by enough "nice" youngsters, it may make a contribution to our acceptance of the legitimacy of dissent on all levels. Perhaps you could add a chapter to your famous book: "How to teach children the 'legitimacy of dissent'"—the moral duty to voice dissent and to accept it from others.

> Sincerely your
> M. D. [female]

63. At this moment the "new left" is not constructive, is to a large extent childish . . . and is off in the wild blue yonder chasing will-o'-the wisps.

10–21–67

Dear Sir:

I heard something over the radio about difference of opinion at Sane regarding the extent and kind of activity it should support.

Maybe I heard mistaken and garbled information but it seems you were supposed to be going along with greater activity such as that of the "New Politics" or the "New Left."

May I say that I think it would be a great mistake and disservice for you to take that direction—even if you thought it correct to do so.

I think that sometimes other factors determine what's best at any moment.

At this moment the "new left" is not constructive, is to a large extent childish (without too much knowledge or wisdom + needs more level heads, which aren't accepted) and is off in the wild blue yonder chasing will-o'-the wisps. They have no goal—constructive or otherwise—and don't know how to reach anything. They are running around—chickens without heads.

My opinion is that your greatest contribution to peace and the world around us is to represent the American people as the only true peace candidate running for office—someone who will be accepted by the broadest segment of the population so that the "weasel" words of the "me-too-but better" Republicans will not offer false hopes to the American people.

If you go along with the "New Politics" you will isolate yourself from the Mass of America, who as yet don't know what gives and otherwise will have no way out of the situation they're in.

I think you are the ideal candidate for peace in 1968. I don't think Martin Luther King would be anywhere near, or do any real good. America is not ready for him yet.

This situation calls for maximum efforts for maximum results—not for token, symbolic action. If anything is done it should really show how America feels to that the world knows where America really stands.

Sincerely,

A. K. [gender unknown]

[point of origin unknown]

III. The Gathering Antiwar Storm

By 1967, in communities all over the United States, antiwar sentiment started to gain traction. As the war continued to escalate and intensify (by the end of the year, more than 500,000 American military personnel were stationed in South Vietnam), opposition to the war became more vocal. The letters that follow illuminate a number of themes, but the most notable is a sense of frustration and desperation that their voices were not being heard by those in power. In addition to expressing ongoing fears over the draft, most of the writers wrote to Spock not only to urge him on in his peace work, but also to suggest new strategies and tactics—boycotts, letter-writing campaigns, a march of parents on the White House, or starting a third party—as well as new antiwar messages —to focus on war profiteers or how the war is affecting Americans economically or to emphasize how Jesus would have sided with those pleading for peace, for example. Some of these writers identify themselves as protesters though they do not seem to fit the stereotype of the radical "long-hair" spewing invective at the administration. Others, meanwhile, seem to be participating in their first real antiwar act by writing a letter of solidarity to Spock and, in a couple of cases, actually make reference to their own process of summoning the nerve to speak up.

64. It would also help relieve the horrible feeling of helplessness I have in the undertakings of our government policies.

Jan 12, 1967

Dear Dr. Spock,

My husband and I have protested the war in Vietnam as you have done. But letters & telegrams seem to do little good.

The article in the N.Y. Times today about bringing injured children to the United States is something we and our friends have discussed. This is our responsibility.

Dr. Spock and the Rev. Dr. Martin Luther King, Jr., leading an antiwar march in Chicago, January 1967. King's outspoken opposition to the war in early 1967 made him a movement leader overnight. (Bettmann/CORBIS)

Our home is forty-five minutes from New York City. If there would be children coming here for treatment, we would be glad to help care for any who may need to stay here for out-patient treatment for a while. It would also help relieve the horrible feeling of helplessness I have in the undertakings of our government policies.

　　Very Sincerely
　　M. H. [female]
　　Suffern, New York

65. Rather than draft 20 + 21 yr olds as they have been doing—they would rather draft 19 yr olds—who the generals feel would be far more <u>tractable</u>.

Flushing, NY
March 8, 1967

Dear Dr. Spock:

　　First I would like to tell you that your book has been a most wonderful aid to me in bringing up my two sons Douglas 17, and William 13.

I recently read your article in Fact magazine and find myself in complete agreement with your views on the war in Viet Nam.

However a most chilling thing has been developing in recent months. Rather than draft 20 + 21 yr olds as they have been doing—they would rather draft 19 yr olds—who the generals feel would be far more tractable. After hearing nothing but how important college is they are now not going to permit boys to complete college. My son Douglas has done very well in his studies and worked very hard saving money to go to college. Once someone leaves school for any reason they frequently cannot go back.

My husband was in the Army for 3 1/2 years in World War II—+ received a silver star—and a bronze star. I served as a Cadet Nurse and was going to join the Navy Nurse Corps on graduation but the war ended when I received my R.N.

I think it is a sad day in America when a 19 year old boy—in school —who I don't think is mature enough to make the decision of what to do—is forced to serve—because the generals have decided they'd much rather have him than a 20 or 21 year old.

Yours sincerely,

Mrs. E. F.

P.S. I have written to congressmen + senators + have received a mimeographed form letter that had nothing to do with my letter in reply.

66. I think a display of the recognized symbols of American patriotism on peace marches might help reorient Americans to identify patriotism with peace rather than war.

Woodbridge, Connecticut

Dear Dr. Spock,

My husband . . . is planning to rearrange his schedule so that we may go as a family on April 15th to the U.N.

I went on the Women's Peace March to Washington a few months ago. In front of the Pentagon some women started to sing America the Beautiful. It was very moving but unfortunately they were drowned out by the shouts of those behind us who did not hear the singing. It struck me that none of us had thought to carry the American flag. It is unfair to ourselves and to the Peace Movement and to America to leave our flag and patriotism to the American Legion and the right wingers. We must not seek our own emotional gratification but rather effective means for winning the middle-of-the road followers to our side. I think a display of the recognized symbols of American patriotism on peace marches might help reorient Americans to identify patriotism with peace rather than war. Let us not leave these powerful symbols to the hawks as their unchallenged and exclusive possessions. Can you do anything to see that American flags are obtained and red, white, + blue used as our color scheme for the April 15th trip to the U.N. and that suitable patriotic songs are sung or played along the way? Would you pass this on to the right person or committee or notify me whom I should contact about it? . . .

Sincerely yours,
Mrs. L. R.

67. I've been a quiet dove too long. Tonight I realized that just shedding tears isn't enough.

[point of origin unknown]
April 11, 1967

Dear Dr. Spock,

It is 2:00 AM and I have just watched the program, Between the Lines, on which you appeared. It's too bad it was rerun at such a late hour. I didn't have the nerve to call my friends—but I certainly will be on the phone early tomorrow morning telling my friends what you said on the program.

Dr. Spock, I love you for the stand you have taken on this madness in which we have become involved. You must know that your name and your views give others the courage to speak up—the so called Doves are dove like; quiet and gentle people who hesitate to call attention to themselves by voicing what is too often an unpopular point of view. There, Dr. Spock, is where I think you are doing a tremendous amount of good work.

Please send me whatever literature, pamphlets, etc. that will help me to become actively involved in working for peace. I've been a quiet dove too long. Tonight I realized that just shedding tears isn't enough.

Sincerely,
M. R. [female]

68. My fellow citizens of the United States must demand a national referendum on the Vietnam involvement.

April 15, 1967

Dear Dr. Spock,

War is hell; it's also profitable. Upon this one planet divided by puddles of water, some suffer, some go without, others feel proud and patriotic, and a few rake-in cash benefit. We have deluded ourselves into thinking that one planet could not possibly have one humanity. We assure one another that our cause is just, that we are fighting for an idea, for democracy, and yet we are not. We attempt to justify our bombing of North Vietnam, but all of our major allies can find no such justification. The world sees that we become concerned whenever American business can no longer exploit cheap labor and reap profits ahead with military dictators. We violate the principles of the United Nations at will, and accuse others who do the same. With patriotic fervor we wave our flags, award medals, fill cemetaries, and even the very "bumper stickers" which express our beliefs are sold for a profit. In such a world, where large appropriations build deadlier missiles, volunteers walk from door to door with tin cans begging for pennies for medical research.

By what right do we commit American lives to keep a South Vietnamese dictator and his gang in power? How many more thousands of American boys must be killed or wounded? Close to a million Vietnamese children have been killed and maimed by our napalm bombs, and thousands made homeless.

At first we came to South Vietnam just to help. Now we have occupied the country and are fighting the whole war practically alone. By what right? By whose authority? Even our major allies find our destruction of a small nation distasteful. We accuse the Viet Cong and North Vietnam of military activity in their own land, while we persist to increase our forces and our bombing. Is America the only country that has the Divine authority to send troops into another land without the consent of its people? Without a declaration of war we are bombing because North Vietnam is sending military help to the Viet Cong. We have a hundred times more troops and machines in South Vietnam, and more is continuously being sent. Does this give the North Vietnamese the right to bomb the United States if they could? North Vietnamese involvement cannot anywhere compare to our military action in this war.

We are not fighting for democracy in South Vietnam. There exists only a ruthless military dictatorship that is despised by the Vietnamese and is kept in power only by American military involvement. The officials within this dictatorship, together with American and other business interests, are reaping money profits from diverted and stolen military and other goods shipped to South Vietnam and paid for by the American tax-payer. For them, this war is profitable. They have influence, and thousands of American boys are patriotically sent off to die for a "cause" which keeps them in business. The South Vietnamese people were never asked what they want, and they have no voice in the affairs of their government, a government which seems so much closer to fascism than to democracy. Any who dare to question or criticize are punished. The South Vietnamese people do not see benefit from our economic aid, for most of it finds its way into the pockets of officials and landlords. The people suffer in perpetual poverty. They did not ask us to come and "protect" them from Communism by destroying them in the process. In the same way that we supported Batista in Cuba, and thus invited a Communist over-throw, we support military dictatorships of the fascist variety in South America and elsewhere, while millions live in terror and poverty. But there we do nothing. Is it because American business interests are permitted to exploit cheap labor and reap billions in profit with appropriate payoffs to the dictators? Why is it that we suddenly become concerned about the freedom of people only when there is a take-over by a Communist dictator, or a threat of such a take-over as in the Dominican Republic, and American business is no longer permitted to exploit and reap profits. Are we talking about ideologies or cold cash? Then our young soldiers are sent to "liberate" the people whether they like it or not. The embarrassing fact which we have not faced is that most Communist nations have proven themselves more concerned with the well-being of their people, than our allies with feudal military dictatorships.

The United Nations did not authorize our military interference in Vietnam. We are violating the principles of the United Nations when it accomodates us. At the same time, we admonish other nations for similar acts of war and aggression. The nations of the world have indicated that they consider this to be somewhat hypocritical. If North Vietnam is guilty of aggression, then the only body that has a right to judge and use force is the United Nations. Ironically, by flouting the U.N., we are inadvertently supporting those who would destroy the U.N. for we make it ineffectual. We attempt to justify our killing of civilians and burning of their villages as unintentional hazards of war and by pointing to similar acts of violence by the Viet Cong. We cannot control the actions of the Viet Cong, but we can control our own actions. Must we become as cruel and as criminal as they are? Must we destroy food and medical supplies simply because it might get into the "wrong" hands? . . . We condemned the Soviet Union, and rightly so, when it used military force to prevent a group of Hungarians from overthrowing the Communist dictatorship in Hungary. Yet we are doing the same thing by using military force in an attempt to prevent a group of South Vietnamese, because they are Communist, from overthrowing a military-fascist dictatorship in South Vietnam. Neither the Russians nor we have the right to participate in this type of illegal intervention in the affairs of other nations. . . .

One of the most evil concepts, that of "Our country right or wrong", is being sold to the American public with tactics of half-truths and deception. We are led to believe that we Americans are God's "chosen people" with a mission to save inferior Asians. We never do anything wrong; we never make mistakes. Whatever we do is "whatever must be done", though we condemn others for doing the same. . . . We point our fingers at Communist countries where those who dare to exercise their rights as citizens in a Democracy to question and criticize their government which clashes with Communism to make the world safe for Democracy. Do we really know the meaning of the word "Democracy"? The fascistic attitude of "our country right or wrong" was successfully sold to the German people by Hitler, and history is witness to the outcome. Have we been led like sheep who do not question or think for themselves, at the cost of two billion dollars a month? Are we getting the truth about Vietnam, or does our government feed us only what reflects favorably on our involvement in Vietnam?

Principles of Democracy are fought for but seldom lived. No nation can claim to be truly a Democracy when forty million of its people are suffering in perpetual poverty. Such outlets for frustration as racial prejudice and discrimination, projections of the evils of our society on Communism, practice of superficial religious ceremonies, and misguided patriotic flag-waving has been a substitute for social and economic justice within our own land. Not by pointing to evils of other nations and interference in their affairs; not through costly space ventures; but only when we can point with pride to an American where no one suffers in poverty, where everyone lives with dignity, will we win the race with Communism and regain prestige and respect in this world. . . . Can we be proud of the thousands of American children who are suffering and dying from malnutrition and lack of medical care? Shall we say more prayers, sing more hymns, and manufacture more napalm bombs? . . .

Vietnam and poverty are two symptoms of one illness. My fellow citizens of the United States must demand a national referendum on the Vietnam involvement. Let the "pros" and "cons" be heard across the land, and let the people vote and decide as to whether they want to continue this senseless killing, this shameful path towards destruction.

You are urged to support a national referendum on Vietnam.

Sincerely,

A. M. [male]

Chelsea, Massachusetts

[EDITOR'S NOTE: Here again, in the following letters, the events of the April 15 Spring Mobilization demonstrations are a frequent impetus for writing to Spock. Spock stood out on that day, in large part because he led the march—arm-in-arm with Martin Luther King, Jr.—from Central Park to the United Nations, where he also gave one of the first speeches. He and King also made the rounds to the talk shows over the weekend, and that, too, prompted some letters.]

69. Without civil disobedience, who in the government will be concerned that we merely talk against the war?

Philadelphia, PA

4/16/67

Dear Dr. Spock:

We've written to you before, but couldn't let another day go by without voicing our wholehearted appreciation for your work with the Spring Mobilization Committee! Great! . . .

I congratulate you for your opening remarks that set the tone and for the absolute lack of censorship. If it had not been this kind of meeting, the Sioux Indians would never have attended, and large numbers of Afro-Americas would not have been present. I overheard one Afro-American say to a buddy, with strong mistrust on his face and in his voice, that this rally would serve as a catharsis for many present, and then they would go on about their business.

I hope that we will all remain united, and deepen our anti-war activities. I was one of the women on February 15th who banged on the doors of the Pentagon, and who admits to a feeling of extreme frustration. What shall we do if tomorrow the war is again escalated? We have all the trappings of "democratic" freedom (we are always allowed to assemble, and the police are instructed to protect us), but is this for foreign consumption? What do the trappings matter if no one in Washington listens to us?

Nick Egleson of SDS (my son's group) made an extremely important contribution, one that no one else made, as far as I can recall. And it was that it was our society—capitalism or corporate liberalism—that is breeding racism and war. Secondly, he wanted to know if we would support the students who would not go into the army or to Vietnam. Our son is 19, and a Junior at Swarthmore College, and as opposed to the war as we are. But there are many parents who oppose their son's anti-war positions! This is tragic, and the rest of us should support these boys as tho they were our own sons! I would like to see the adult groups raise funds for just this purpose! . . .

If you're ever in Philadelphia, [we] would be honored to have you to dinner.

Dr. and Mrs. J. A.

P.S. We just spoke to our son, and he had the following comments to make:

1. All the time, effort and money that went into this—what was the impact on the more than tens of thousands who never got to hear a single speaker?

2. Why was the U.N. site of such great symbolic value when no one of the U.N. was on our program? More people (our son went on to say) would have been accommodated at Sheeps Meadow[4] or at a stadium so that they could have been inspired by some of the speeches.

3. What will it accomplish? Why wasn't it held in Washington where the offices of all legislators would have been jammed, and active opposition voiced to the draft (coming up very shortly) and to the war?

4. Without civil disobedience, who in the government will be concerned that we merely talk against the war?

5. What will come out of this?

6. What groups are going on from here to oppose the draft?

70. My proposal is that we should try to get as many people as possible to pledge that they will not purchase a new model automobile . . . until such time as the U.S. stop bombing . . . in Vietnam.

Rochester, N.Y.

June 2, 1967

Dear Dr. Spock:

. . . As an individual, I have been fairly active in the peace movement, and have taken part in various protest activities, such as the Spring Mobilization in New York. For some time, I have been feeling—in common with many others!—that marches, petitions, advertisements, political campaigns, etc., were availing us naught, and I have been casting about for some new approach—some form of protest which might attract a constituency beyond the regular peace people.

I now have an idea about which I have spoken to various people literally, and in which some interest has been expressed. If this idea is at all worthwhile, however, it can only be implemented by an organization such as SANE or New Politics.

My idea involves an economic boycott. The trouble is that large groups of people often cannot engage in a boycott without themselves suffering real hardship. But there is one item upon which our economy hinges, and which people could do without at least for a significant length of time without suffering any real hardship. That item is automobiles—or, more precisely, <u>new</u> automobiles. My proposal is that we should try to get as many people as possible to pledge that they will not purchase a new model automobile (repeat, new model—I am not proposing that anyone go car-less) until such time as the U.S. stop bombing (and/or fighting?) in Vietnam.

I realise that there could be many things wrong with such a plan. First, the question of morality. When the Negroes in Montgomery, for instance, boycotted the buses, this was fair enough since the bus company was directly a culprit—but why punish General Motors, Chrysler, etc. for something for which they are not directly responsible? My answer here is that it will never actually get to that stage—that it is a pressure tactic which, hopefully, stands a good chance of achieving the desired result without ever having to be actually put into effect.

As I visualise it, there would be advertisements subscribed to by large numbers of people, stating that these people have pledged not to purchase a new model car unless and until, etc. The text will urge all readers who agree to tear out the ad, sign it, and mail it to the manufacturer of their present car. As I see it, we do not need millions of people doing this in order to cause the manufacturers such concern that they will appeal to the Administration to make greater efforts toward peace. Several hundred thousand would be sufficient. And weren't there that many at the Spring Mobilization?

Also, such a threat to the economy would hardly make the Administration feel secure about its chances in 1968.

It seems to me that this would be a way to apply pressure to the Administration to re-think their present policy in Vietnam.

I could go on at length, but won't do so. I ask only that if you think there is even the faintest germ of an idea here, you will place it before SANE or whatever other group you think might make some use of it. At this stage, I, like so many others, have become so desperate about our disastrous course in South-east Asia that I would rather risk being thought a crackpot than discard anything at all which might be of even the slightest use.

Sincerely,

Mrs. Z. S.

71. This forfeiture of the right of dissent is, in itself, perhaps the worst blow struck at freedom, in America, in my lifetime our yours.

Miami, Florida

July 13, 1967

Dear Dr. Spock:

I recently heard on the news some mention of a possible third party in which you might play a prominent role.

I would welcome such an opportunity to again participate as a voter.

I no longer can identify with the Democratic Party, which I had supported since the times of Roosevelt.

I read in the last week an excellent column by Sydney Harris, which expresses very closely my feelings that one cannot agree with the Republicans, but cannot help respecting their integrity in clinging to their various concepts of what constitutes a good Republican.

That Democrats, on the other hand, are becoming less and less democratic, to the extent that one dare not deviate from the party-line, or disagree as to the merits of The candidate (and we all know who He is).

I am quite interested in political science, and, while not an expert, have more confidence in my own judgement than the government's as regards our involvement in Viet Nam.

I respect and envy your ability to engage in public demonstrations. I am raising a son and feel this is not a luxery I can afford myself; I am positive it would stamp me publicly as an undesirable, and put me on some list or other. This forfeiture of the right of dissent is, in itself, perhaps the worst blow struck at freedom, in America, in my lifetime our yours.

I would like you to know how very great I feel the need is for a party which will serve the needs of the many Americans, young and old, who have no where to go, and yet have strong feelings of patriotism which cry for an outlet.

While obtaining my driver's tags this year, I stood in line, in Dade County, with three others, all of whom opposed the war in Viet Nam. All of us admitted that not one would give our name to come out in open opposition in the community. I, at least, have written my senators, so as to go on record, but the replies are framed within the speech-pattern of Johnson's America.

I would like to believe it is still our America, mine and yours.

Please be assured of my support if such plans were to materialize and you may add my name and address to any such movement now underway.

M. H. [female]

72. Those that are really destroying our flag are they who are literally dragging it through the blood of our innocent youth and the unfortunate Vietnamese.

July 18, 1967

Dear Dr. Spock,

I along with millions of other mothers raised my children with my child in one arm and your paper-back book in my other. When illness would strike and the doctor arrived, before he examined my child he'd ask me for my diagnosis because he knew I had already consulted "Dr. Spock." Invariable I was right and he'd always faceciously suggest I hang out my shingle. Well, the children are grown and the well worn copy of your book sits silently on the shelf. . . .

I read the article about you in this Sunday's N.Y. Times Magazine section and decided to write now. The picture of you marching in the peace demonstration is beautiful. Physically you are a tall man—morally you are ten feet tall.

I am abhored by the mail you receive from women who doted on your every word raising their children and now write you vehement letters because you want to save the bodies you helped develop. Our sense of values are most peculiar. In our local paper recently their was a letter to the editor that contained one sentence that described our values very adequately—'We would be more perturbed if the government came into our homes and took our television sets away than when they come and take our sons away.'

Like you, I am not a pacifist per se. Unfortunately there are times when a nation must defend itself. Unlike you I am more emotional about our involvement in Vietnam. You advocate stronger efforts towards negotiations. I feel our involvement in Vietnam is barbarism and completely unjustified and I advocate complete withdrawal. I realize this attitude is unrealistic because our government believes we have a commitment to the southern part of Vietnam and even if they didn't it's now a matter of 'face saving.' Also in regards to negotiations—I feel this might have been a possibility a couple of years ago—today I feel Ho Chi Minh will persist to the bitter end—and it may be a bitter end for us all.

I personally feel helpless about the whole sad situation. I write to Congressmen (the 'doves'), letters to editors, etc. I have stopped trying to persuade people who think we belong in Vietnam for a number of reasons. Americans have a paranoic mania about communism. They are also blindly patriotic ('My country, right or wrong') and saddest of all some people actually enjoy our being at war. I am especially appalled by the attitude of veterans who knew the horrors of war but have forgotten that and in retrospect look back at war as a glorious time in their otherwise mean lives and get a vicarious pleasure from this one.

In regards to those who are astonished at the flag burnings, they are only destroying a piece of cloth. Those that are really destroying our flag are they who are literally dragging it through the blood of our innocent youth and the unfortunate Vietnamese, North and South.

Forgive me for going on and on. The purpose of this letter is really to thank you for devoting your time to the pursuit of peace in the world at a time in life when you can really sit back and rest on your laurels and enjoy the sailing you so love. . . .

My fond good wishes to you in the future.

    Sincerely

    Mrs. S. L.

    West Warwick, RI

73. Perhaps politicians who can laugh off, ridicule or denounce parades and sit-ins, etc., might be more responsible to a million or two million letters.

Lakewood, Ohio
July 19th, 1967

My dear Dr. Spock:

Let me congratulate you on your courage and express admiration for your dedicated service to the cause of peace.

But the thought occurs to me that something else must be done to bring about a considerable conversion in the Washington mind and heart.

As a reader of our own history, I recall that Samuel Adams did a tremendous job for American Independence with his letter writing; and Harriet Beecher Stowe helped to put the end of slavery across with the pen.

Perhaps politicians who can laugh off, ridicule or denounce parades and sit-ins, etc., might be more responsible to a million or two million letters.

It seems to me that we who are concerned about the cessation of this miserable conflict could do something with discretion and power.

First of all, distract the opposite side by apparently confining all activity to the public protest.

Second, organize faculty-student leadership on the campus and the clerical leadership throughout the nation, which has been disposed to oppose involvement, and get them quietly to enlist one million letters to the White House and a second million to the several Congressmen and Senators.

A certain amount of secrecy will not enable the <u>Hawks</u> to send a similar amount of mail to cancel out the work done by the <u>Doves</u>.

Certainly the friends of peace by this time will know enough of the leaders, whose acquaintance with others, could produce a million or two million letter writers.

It would be necessary for those who enlist the writers to know names of Congressmen and Senators in each district and state and be able to aid inarticulate but sincere opposition to pen a suitable protest.

Individual letters, not petitions, will do the trick.

This, of course, will require funds. I am willing to make my own modest contribution, as a virtually retired clergyman.

Sincerely,

G. R. [male]

74. Marches, petitions, and debates have not had their desired effect.

Marblehead, Mass.
July 19, 1967

Dear Dr. Spock,

Congratulations on your tireless efforts for peace in Vietnam. It is unfortunate more encouraging results have not been obtained but I'm afraid until the middle class of the country feels similarly moved your work will be largely in vain.

The seventy-five to a hundred million Americans like myself who are over twenty-five and economically self sufficient seem to be satisfied with the tragic status quo. Marches, petitions, and debates have not had their desired effect.

It seems to me notable peace advocates such as yourself would be more successful if you appealed to our self interest rather than our compassion and reason. Through a national campaign an appeal could be made which would show each of us why we personally stand to lose more and more as the war goes on. We might be aroused through economics—the prospect of increased taxes, a mounting national deficit, cut backs in domestic spending, etc. Another approach might be by explaining casualties—our out numbering the South Vietnamese in loses, projected loses over the next few years, etc.

This campaign could be carried on through the mails on the public media and while costly might actuate sufficient numbers of people who would in turn put pressure on their congressmen. I realize this attempted seduction appeals to a fairly selfish array of motives but I feel the end justifies the means. Many churches do not care if their congregations assemble Sundays to venerate God or save their souls. If the truth were known the latter motive would probably account for the greater part of the attendance.

If in theory you think my idea has merit I would be happy to communicate further with you regarding its implementation.

Sincerely,
T. P. [male]

75. Would there be any possible way for "Parents" to organize and march to Washington D.C. and see President Johnson particularly those parents who have boys in Vietnam.

Lake Grove, N.Y.
[undated]

Dear DR. Spock:

Last Tuesday evening, at our Worship & Membership committee meeting, I spoke to our minister Rev. [name deleted], in regards to my concern about the war in Vietnam.

My son, who is 20 years old has been in Vietnam for the past 5 months and my concern has caused my health to go to the Doctor and be under medication. All of this which has depressed me to think my faith in "GOD" will bring my son back safe but I am only one Mother of thousands who are also concerned. Would there be any possible way for "Parents" to organize and march to Washington D.C. and see President Johnson particularly those parents who have boys in Vietnam/

I spoke to Rev. [name deleted] about this and he suggested to write to you I personally think 2000 strong or more in person, would more effect than Editorials or petitions.

Could you give advice to us on how to promote such a gathering?

Sincerely,

D. M. [female]

76. When political and military matters are discussed do we ever hear that America cannot do that because it violates the law of God under whom we are pledged.

Memphis, Tenn.
August 24, 1967

Dear Dr. Spock—

Have just heard over the radio that one Senator said "that we had as much business in So. Viet Namm observing their election as they had here in observing ours." It seems that they have as much right to come here and put down our riots as we had to go there to settle riots caused by poverty and oppression.

David Brinkley[5] quoted you as having said you would be willing to run for President with Martin Luther King as your partner.

Dr. Spock all our lives we've seen our officials place their hand on the Bible the Word of God, and take the Oath of Office. Citizens, Boy Scouts, Soldiers, all take the Oath Under God.

When political and military matters are discussed do we ever hear that America cannot do that because it violates the law of God under whom we are pledged.

Our Generals have carried out a search and destroy program as though people who differe with us are vermin.

Is it any wonder young people are turning to marijuana and L.S.D., they are tired of talk that has no depth. Our country could do more to protect them from these drugs, if trash like this dope can occupy American streets then why expect the rest of the World to look up to us.

Our American Anthem and Motto is "In God we Trust." A Political Party with its Song, "The Star Spangled Banner," and its Motto, "In God is Our Trust" could sweep this Country I believe.

We hear and read of the Young People having Love Ins, and of the Flower Children. This proves there is a yearning for Love and Truth and a "Love and Truth Party" could be elected I believe. How can a President work for Peace without Love. I believe Truth and Peace are the values the World is seeking. There has been such an abundance of wealth, arrogance and sham that people yearn for sincerity.

I hope for America and the World that we will have for our President someone like you, or Senator Fulbright, who want this mass slaughter to stop, that the beauty and glory of this Earth and the Peoples God has placed upon it may live in Beauty as an example for the heathen.

Would that every preacher in America like Bro. King were preaching that Christ came to bring peace. He taught His Disciples to fight but to fight and destroy the works of the devil and did not say to kill millions including old people and children. It is beyond my comprehension that a preacher should say that Christ did not come to bring Peace as though Christ sanctions this war. Christ explained that the sword He came to bring was the sword of the Spirit, we know he did not mean for fathers to kill sons, daughters to kill mothers, and each kill his neighbor.

If you or someone else runs under the Party of the People, by the People, for the People under God, then we believe and pray for you a glorious victory.

Thank you, Dr. Spock.

Sincerely,

Mrs. R. H.

Competing interpretations of "supporting the troops," October 21, 1967. *Top*: Antiwar protesters march from the Lincoln Memorial to the Pentagon—with some suggesting that the best way to support the troops is to "bring them home now." (U.S. News & World Report, Library of Congress) *Bottom*: Meanwhile, in New York, students concerned that antiwar protest undermined American troops and hurt morale demonstrate on the same day in support of the war and especially the soldiers fighting it. The sign at left reads, "If You Can't Be <u>With Them</u> Be <u>For Them</u>! Support Our Boys In Viet Nam!" (Bettmann/CORBIS)

4 The Antiwar Challenge and Its Discontents, October 1967–February 1968

As THE letters in the previous chapter indicate, the Vietnam War had, by the middle of 1967, eclipsed most other public issues in the minds of most Americans. Public opinion polls showed that in many ways this did not bode well for the Johnson administration's expectations of continued popular support. By the first week of October, a Louis Harris poll revealed that only 31 percent of Americans supported President Johnson's handling of the war, and that continued support for the war had dropped from 72 percent in July to just 58 percent.

Most important, by October 1967, a variety of antiwar forces coalesced into what appeared to be—to the Johnson administration and to the larger public—a formidable protest movement. With growing national attention on the inequities of a Selective Service System that, thanks to a decades-old deferment system, drafted poor, working-class, and minority men in disproportionate numbers, antiwar organizers launched Stop the Draft Week on October 16. On that day, draft card "turn-ins" took place in cities and on campuses all over the country; in what amounted to a nationwide act of civil disobedience, draft age men turned-in their draft registration and classification documents, sometimes in elaborate ceremonies. The cards were collected and brought to Washington, where, on October 20, a group of draft resisters and older advisers—including Benjamin Spock—delivered them to a representative from the Justice Department. Meanwhile, for the rest of the week, protests continued outside dozens of Selective Service offices and induction centers nationwide; in Oakland, California, police clashed with protesters nearly every day.

The week's events culminated in a long-planned demonstration at the Lincoln Memorial in Washington and a march on the Pentagon. As many as 100,000 Americans—the largest antiwar crowd to march on

Washington to date—turned out for the rally at the Lincoln Memorial. There, lead organizer David Dellinger told the crowd, "This is the beginning of a new stage in the American peace movement, in which the cutting edge becomes active resistance." Dr. Spock spoke, too, asserting in a line widely quoted in papers the next day that "the enemy, we believe in all sincerity, is Lyndon Johnson who was elected as a peace candidate in 1964 and who betrayed us within three months."

Later in the day, an estimated 35,000 marched from the Lincoln Memorial to the Pentagon. As the marchers approached the massive building, headquarters of Vietnam War planning, they could see that U.S. marshals and army regulars surrounded the building. It marked the first time since the 1932 Bonus Army march that the federal government had called out the armed forces to protect itself against its own citizens. Almost all of the protesters assembled in the north parking lot, a space for which organizers had secured a permit; but several small groups of militants charged the troops and attempted to enter the Pentagon (a few succeeded and were beaten and arrested for their efforts). After these flare-ups settled down, a "festival atmosphere" developed as musicians played for the crowd and speakers conducted what amounted to an impromptu teach-in.

At one point, Dellinger, Spock, and others led a group of marchers toward one entrance to the Pentagon. Spock, speaking through a bullhorn, told the story of the GI stationed in Vietnam who had written to him the previous year *(letter 22)*; the soldier had been critical of the war and sought information on the peace movement; but when Spock wrote back, the letter was returned, stamped "Verified Deceased." Unmoved, the troops waded into the crowd, swinging their batons; they arrested a number of the notable leaders, though they skipped over Spock despite his best efforts to get arrested. Later that evening, the soldiers launched another savage attack on the remaining few hundred demonstrators. News reports of the Pentagon march were overwhelmingly critical of the protesters, focusing especially on the attempts to enter the Pentagon and the clash with the armed servicemen.

Most of the letters in the first three sections of this chapter thus came to Spock almost exclusively in response to the events in Washington and at the Pentagon. Again, they show ordinary Americans' deepening engagement over the issue of the war, the increasing passion driving their views, and, for all of them, the high stakes at play in this national debate over the war.

I. "Don't Stop Fighting"

Spock's high-profile participation in the Pentagon demonstration led to a flood of supportive email. Most significantly, the next sample of letters shows, in particular, how the war made so many American parents —especially mothers—worry about their children dying in this and future wars. Some describe the imminent peril confronting their adult sons— some already in the military and others facing conscription—while others anxiously imagine future wars threatening their children when they grow up in a post-Vietnam America. For all of them, the implication is that protest serves as a vehicle for protecting their children. Other letters came to Spock expressing solidarity and optimism that, as one wrote, "dissent is growing" in the aftermath of the Pentagon demonstrations. Still others continue to offer suggestions for new protest strategies to Spock, the antiwar leader. And almost all of the letters assume something that others writing to Spock in the same period dismiss: dissent is patriotic.

77. My second son, 18 years of age + myself particated in the "march" or "sit in" in Oakland. I went three days. It was not a riot or a near riot.

October 21, 1967

Dear Dr. Spock:

. . . I am writing to encourage you in your brave stand against Vietnam. Please, keep this up to bring our boys home. You are heard when you speak. People won't listen to us little people. Thank God you have taken this stand.

My second son, 18 years of age + myself particated in the "march" or "sit in" in Oakland. I went three days. It was not a riot or a near riot. I know, I was there. The government wants us to look bad. The people we met were nice. I met a Catholic priest I've known for years there + he had two other priests there. They weren't there just to be there—they are against the war in Vietnam.

My eldest boy, 20 years of age, is in the Navy. He hates the war and says the Navy gears you up to it. He is due to go to Vietnam the first of the year + work in the boats going up and down the canals.

Dr. Spock, I haven't raised my two oldest boys for a unjust war. I haven't raised them for any war—but not such an immoral one. Please continue to speak out against this awful war. Don't let hate letters and talks quiet you.

May God continue to bless you. Talk against the mass murder as much as your strength will let you.

> Sincerely,
> M. D. [female]
> Oakland, Calif.

[EDITOR'S NOTE: Two days later, before sending the above letter, the same letter-writer wrote the following brief note to Spock, and included it with the first.]

October 23, 1967

Dear Dr. Spock,

Please say how many people were on your side—against the war in Vietnam. Also build up the fact that you are for the men in Vietnam but against the war. The two go hand in hand.

> Love + Peace
> M. D. [female]

78. Thank you for helping me to raise my three children . . . and thank you for trying to help me keep my two sons from a useless death.

Philadelphia, Penna.
October 22, 1967

My dear, dear Dr. Spock:

Perhaps this can balance out all the hate mail you must be receiving after your courageous stand during this week-end's Peace Demonstrations.

Even if I didn't agree with your unselfish fight for your beliefs, I would still have to admire you for risking your popularity as a public figure for what you believe as a man. There are too few people like you, but maybe those few can make more difference than the selfish and silent.

I've read that people disagreeing with you send The Book [*Baby and Child Care*] back with venomous comments. My oldest child is eleven; my youngest, eight (with a nine-year-old tucked in-between!). I too raised them "by The Book". I now have the feeling that by following your rules, I must have given them even <u>more</u> than merely the proper baby care you recommended. I'm beginning to suspect that the popularity of your book was due not only to your common sense advice, but to the integrity and humanity that readers unconsciously picked up between the lines on how to conduct toilet training.

So, thank you, <u>thank you</u>, Dr. Spock, not only for that wonderful first line, "You know more than you think you know" that got me through all these years of motherhood . . . but for your work <u>now</u> . . . your courage and strength in the face of dangerous opposition.

Thank you for helping me to raise my three children . . . and thank you for trying to help me keep my two sons from a useless death.

With deepest gratitude and love,
Mrs. L. S.

79. Approx. 150 people went from here to Washington, my own husband . . . amongst them. He got arrested on the steps of the Pentagon.

Urbana, Ill.
Oct. 22nd 1967

Dear Dr. Spock,

Probably you are too busy to even read my letter, but just in case you do, I want to be counted amongst the many many thousands in this country, + all over the world to register my congratulations—congratulations, + more congratulations—the warmest and most sincere. Always we have admired you, but never so much as over the last few years, as your stand on this hideous war has become more bold and unflinching, even in the face of unfair, and stupid criticism. All of us involved in the protest movement, value, respect, + <u>need</u> your courageous leadership. Along with Dr. King, William Coffin, Noam Shomsky, Norman Thomas,[1] and a few others, you give the rest of us the leadership + inspiration to keep up the struggle. We are so grateful for men like you, + it's comforting in this crazy world that there are some, to whom we can really look up to + admire.

Congratulations too on your adroit handling of the "inquisition" on "Face the Nation" today. You met their questions head on, and it was superbly refreshing to watch.

We have a very active bunch of "Peaceniks" on + off the U. of Ill. campus here in Urbana-Champaign. The students are busy burning their draft cards + shutting down the draft board—the faculty + the community (i.e., mostly wives) are busy bailing them out of assorted prisons—this week Dow Chemical[2] are coming to town, so we're all after them. The community committee mailed out 600 copies of your "Resist" statement—we have no idea tho how many signed it, although since that time a lot more people have become a lot more militant + ready to sign, so we had a local one of our own.

Approx. 150 people went from here to Washington, my own husband . . . amongst them. He got arrested on the steps of the Pentagon—however he was in illustrious company!

. . . Once again dear Dr. Spock, thank you for all you are doing. You did so much for people all over the world in your first career . . . yet I think if possible you are doing even more in your second. It just occurred to me, first you had to save the kids from their parents—now you have to save them from their Government!

Good luck sir, yrs respectfully + sincerely,

J. W. [female]

80. On one hand the country seems to be in a growing paranoid fit over Communism, on the other there seems to be hope that dissent is growing.

Old Lyme, Connecticut
25 Oct. 1967

Dear Dr. Spock,

Thank you for all that you are doing in regards to Vietnam.

We believe that the Johnson administration has brought shame and disgrace to and hatred for our country—as well as terrible danger to all of mankind. It is no longer a secret that the Pentagon is attempting to draw us into war with China.

We write the powers that be numerous letters and send telegrams to deaf ears. It all seems so very hopeless. We noticed that CBS TV ignored you Monday, while they attempted to give the idea that any protest comes only from kids, crackpots and beatniks.

On one hand the country seems to be in a growing paranoid fit over Communism, on the other there seems to be hope that dissent is growing. Our little local newspaper for the lower Conn. valley has recently switched from being pro war to anti.

Anyway, my husband and I just want you to know that we are grateful to you.

Please do not answer this. We would rather think of you doing something more useful.

Sincerely,
Mrs. L. D.

81. I agree that America's provincial paranoia on the big Communist bugaboo is one of the reasons the American public can be sold a bill of goods on our outrageous intervention in Vietnam.

Friday, Oct. 27, 1967
Hartsdale, N.Y.

Dear Dr. Spock,

I was glad to see that you didn't lose your temper when that nasty needler [William F.] Buckley[3] did his best to back you into a defensive corner. That man's convoluted mind alarms me.

I agree that America's provincial paranoia on the big Communist bugaboo is one of the reasons the American public can be sold a bill of goods on our outrageous intervention in Vietnam. My husband has ruefully, and rudely, observed that every Irish Mick and Italian Guinea is all for wiping out + shooting down anyone in the world on whom the tag 'Communist' can be placed. This ignorant reaction frightens me out of my pacifist wits.

Why anyone listens to the propagandists from the armed services I can't understand. To take the word of someone who has chosen the business of killing as a profession is to mark one's self as a sucker.

No wonder the younger generation would rather 'cop out' than join their elders in this Warfare State. We do need a leader who could redirect our energies, our wealth into social problems like civil rights, urban blight, education, job preparation, health and representative government. It would surely take billions but be constructive, creative, Christian, civilized instead of expensive suicide.

My three grandchildren are being brought up by Dr. Spock. Healthy sparklers, all three.

Thank you, Dr. Spock, for using your gift of life to such good purpose. I think of Norman Thomas, another tall battler for the human family, and the victories he has won for many of his ideas. You are another who can face realities and still dream.

Sincerely,
Mrs. E. C.

82. Any violence and obscenity which can be employed to stop Dow, and the Pentagon, is entirely justifiable to a decent patriotic American.

11–1–67

Dear Dr Spock

I can't for the life of me see why you conceded to newspeople that "some were" when they said "a violent group of young people (were) acting in a violent and obscene way" at the Pentagon.

There is NOTHING which can match the violence and obscenity of Johnson's Wehrmacht und Luftwaffe und CIA-SS in Vietnam. They behave like, and they ARE, common murderers and thieves over there—and the orders for their despicably unAmerican violence and obscenity originate in the Pentagon which our young people "attacked." Those young people deserve your support and encouragement, and when the Scripps-Howard news scavenger tries to trap you into agreeing to his own opinion (that they were violent and obscene) you should present a strong united front in defense of the young people's behavior and intentions—BOTH of which are unavoidable, given Johnson's behavior, and good, ditto.

J. W. [male]
Falls Church, Virginia

Nothing in the "march" matches the violence and obscenity of Dow Chemical's making money from burning Vietnamese mothers and babies to death, either! Any violence and obscenity which can be employed to stop Dow, and the Pentagon, is entirely justifiable to a decent patriotic American.

83. It is important that history record our time as one in which people were willing to make great sacrifices to oppose the immoral actions of our government.

Philadelphia, Pa.
November 6, 1967

Dear Dr. Spock:

As participants in the October 21st demonstration in Washington, we would like to make some recommendations for future actions of this kind. Basically, our suggestion is that a similar demonstration, including civil disobedience, be organized, but with an across-the-board commitment to nonviolence, not only at the rally and march, but during the confrontation and civil disobedience as well.

We were much impressed by what we heard of the "teach-in" at the Pentagon in which you and others engaged. We understand that you committed civil disobedience, but that your nonviolent bearing made it hard for at least some of the soldiers to face their task. Similar nonviolent confrontations were taking place elsewhere, but their impact was lost on the public, whose attention was drawn to the unorganized pushing and shoving episodes as marchers tried to force their way through police lines.

We do not mean to condemn those police-line episodes altogether. While it is clear they do not command much public sympathy, there are times when unpopular actions must be taken because they are right, without much concern for their public interest. We agree with Robert McAfee Brown[4] that, regardless of the practical consequences of civil disobedience, it is important that history record our time as one in which people were willing to make great sacrifices to oppose the immoral actions of our government.

On the other hand, we hope that you and other organizers of the Mobilization agree that an action would be ideal which would <u>both</u> protest that government's position in the most direct and sacrificial way, and <u>also</u> win public sympathy.

As participants in the March, we saw numerous examples of nonviolence in action, and we were impressed by the capacity of the marchers to improvise nonviolent responses to threatening situations. At the same time, we believe that some of the aimless and unthinking actions which provoked violence for no real reason could be kept under control and channelled into creative nonviolence. Instead of encouraging all kinds of "free-lance" actions at the Pentagon at the end of the March, the organizers should lay stress on group actions well planned in advance. Marchers not associated with an action group in advance could nevertheless be encouraged to join one or another group on the day of the demonstration. They should first agree to accept the group's discipline, and should be briefed on how to conduct themselves.

Specifically, we suggest the following: (1) more careful training in non-violence in advance of the March by participating groups; (2) organization of teach-ins without civil disobedience (to a splendidly "captive" audience) in addition to those involving disobedience; (3) training of groups to advance slowly and quietly on the police or military lines until they are arrested, instead of using the inconclusive "rushing" tactics which we saw that Saturday; (this kind of organized advance was used by Ghandi's followers in the 1930's); (4) seated vigil groups in areas likely to be cleared by the police or the military; (5) entrance to the Pentagon or other buildings sought for the purpose of confronting top officials in order to explain to them the purpose of the nonviolent actions being undertaken (rather than simply for the purpose of obstructing business).

We believe that actions such as these, plus others, would be much more likely to arouse public sympathy than most of what was happening at the Pentagon October 21st. Just as in Birmingham and other civil rights demonstrations, public sympathy was aroused very strongly when police attacked and/or arrested completely nonviolent people. When demonstrators are not nonviolent, it is much too easy for the public to say, "Well they deserved it anyway—the police had every right to stop such provocations and to break a few heads."

We would wholeheartedly support another Washington March on this basis, and would appreciate knowing your reactions to these ideas. Meanwhile we all owe you a debt of gratitude for setting us all an example.

> Yours sincerely,
> R. O. [male for 4 males, 2 females]

84. Think of the effect it would have on the populace if Frank Sinatra should call a press conference and denounce the Administration as being purveyors of violence and claim that we have no business in Vietnam.

November 16, 1967

Dear Dr. Spock:

I wish to thank you for the stand you have taken on Vietnam and your bravery and honesty which you exhibited on the program "Good Company." The things you said make more sense than anything I have heard concerning the war. It was especially refreshing to hear you admit that you were ashamed that you had made speeches in favor of Johnson in 1964. How much more refreshing it would be if those of us who feel as you do concerning the immorality of our involvement in the war could convince those men who are advisors to the President that the commitments which they made so long ago were wrong!

I feel that the most good is done for the cause of peace when well-known people such as you make their thoughts known. And yet it seems that there are very few well-known people who are out-spoken concerning the immorality of the war. Is there any way in which you can sound our certain celebrities to find out if their views parallel your own? If they could be convinced to join in peace marches and to make public their concern of this injustice, there is no telling how much good they could do for the cause of ending our involvement in Vietnam and bringing our boys back home. Think of the advantages to be gained if you could convince, say, Doris Day to lead a peace march and to make a statement concerning the 13,000 of our men who have died uselessly in Vietnam. Think of the effect it would have on the populace if Frank Sinatra should call a press conference and denounce the Administration as being purveyors of violence and claim that we have no business in Vietnam. What if stands were taken by people like J.D. Salinger, Michael DeBakey, Jonas Salk, Norman Mailer—the list is almost endless—and what if these people made their stands known? The effect on the masses would be stupendous. What you have already done goes beyond greatness in my book, but perhaps you could spearhead the seemingly impossible by creating an alliance of famous people who are not afraid to take a stand and be heard, even if it means that they will come into some disfavor. I think that the people in such an alliance could persuade most of the borderline cases to decide that our presence in Vietnam is a great tragedy, and could also persuade many "hawks" to re-evaluate their positions. . . .

Sincerely,

L. G. [female]

Tulsa, Oklahoma

85. I know I'm not alone in my thinking. I know all over the world, Russian, Chinese, Vietnamese mothers feel the same as I.

Dec 5th, 1967

Dear Dr. Spock,

With hard work, lots of love, + the aid of your book, I'm raising four healthy children (girls, 4+5, + twins, a boy + girl, 15 months) but I want to take time out from my own "work" to voice my support of your anti-draft/war position.

Whenever your name is brought up, it is quite the thing to remark "why doesn't he stay with his own field, diapers + formula + leave running the country to the experts."

The experts have managed to get us into Viet Nam + day by day closer to World War III.

My husband tells me there has always been war, as if that fact makes it inevitable. I say war is obsolete, old-fashioned.

Just as there always had been the plague, with knowledge + understanding, it is no more. So is the concept of war an illness of mankind that must be cured.

My children were born in an excellent hospital with the best medical care we could afford. I nursed them to give them the best possible start. They go to the pediatrician regularly. They eat healthy meals + when the time comes they'll go to school. We'll struggle through the teens, growing pains, heartache + all. And after all those years of care, I should send my son off to war because some selective service board says it's his patriotic duty to go.

I know I'm not alone in my thinking. I know all over the world, Russian, Chinese, Vietnamese mothers feel the same as I. And the day is here when we will not allow "governments" to continue using the fruit of years of care as statistics in their insane plots.

I want peace! (And as soon as I get the laundry caught up) I'll join you in the demonstrations!

Sincerely,

Mrs. J. E.

Inglewood, Calif

86. I don't know what to tell mine, to be very honest. Children do so expect the world to be fair, and it just isn't.

Boulder, Colo

December 8, 1967

Dear Dr. Spock,

I just want to let you know how very much I appreciate your willingness to speak out and act in protest of our government's policies in VietNam. I truly cannot say that I am convinced in my mind as to what the absolutely best policy would be at this time, but I do know for certain what agony I feel seeing the pictures that show so graphically the suffering there for all the people. It is so hard not to just emotionally give up in despair—there seems to be so little we as individuals can do. I feel about explaining war and everything that the concept entails the way some people seem to feel about explaining sex to their children. I don't know what to tell mine, to be very honest. Children do so expect the world to be fair, and it just isn't. How to let them know that children their ages in other countries are dying and burning, and at the best only just barely getting by? For this is ultimately what it comes down to, as we know.

Anyway, I thank you from the bottom of my heart, cliche or no, for your actions. I know you must come in for much criticism and ridicule for the stand you have taken. There are those of us, however, who do stand behind and defend you, and I want you to know that my husband and I are two of them. People like you make it easier for us to have hope.

Thank you again,

Mrs. J. A.

87. For every ten dollars the government takes in income tax, we give six dollars to some cause or organization that is improving the world instead of smashing it.

Tucson, Arizona

December 11, 1967

Dear Dr. Spock:

I want to let you know that our family agrees wholeheartedly with your stand on Vietnam.

We aren't demonstrators, and we aren't very persuasive, but we don't feel entirely helpless. For what it's worth, here is our answer to the question, "What can we do?"

Most of us have two weapons, the power of the vote and the power of the dollar. In 1965 Americans spent forty-seven billion dollars on defense. Their personal spending included 1.3 billion dollars for church and welfare activities.

For many years our family budget has been put on this basis: for every ten dollars the government takes in income tax, we give six dollars to some cause or organization that is improving the world instead of smashing it. For us, this means no new car, no telephone, no television set, until Vietnam is over.

In 1965 Americans spent forty-three billion dollars for clothing, jewelry, and accessories, fifty-seven billion on owner-operated transportation, seven and a half billion on alcoholic beverages and tobacco, and twenty-five billion for recreation. It seems to me we could trim quite a bit of fat from these items, and maybe omit soft drinks and potato chips from the food budget without suffering too much. This would make a real difference, if enough people thought peace was that important.

Sincerely,

Mrs. M. S.

88. I raised my son to hate war and where is he? In the army because I didn't have money enough to keep him in college!

Wellsville, N.Y.

January 5, 1968

Dear Dr. Spock,

Thank you and the others for trying to correct a terrible terrible wrong: the draft!

I raised my son to hate war and where is he? In the army because I didn't have money enough to keep him in college!

My second son is <u>staying</u> in college in spite of the fact that I am going in debt up to my neck to do it, and, in spite of the fact that his tuition has been doubled, and, in spite of the fact that my youngest child is in dire need of special care which I cannot give her because of the tribute I must pay to keep one son out of the draft.

In every generation there are a few with courage enough to try to help their fellow citizens at great risk to their profession and reputation. I am glad to see you have this courage.

Sincerely,

Mrs. H. B.

89. As I sit here and fuss over my little one, I realize almost daily that women who were in my position 18 years ago are now receiving telegrams saying that their sons are dead, for the vaguest of reasons.

New York, New York

January 12, 1968

Dear Dr. Spock,

I have never written a "fan" letter of any sort in my life, but I read in the New York Times that you receive many letters from mothers who condemn you for your political beliefs and therefore refuse to buy or read your book. I think it's time that a few of us who admire your book <u>and</u> what you're doing politically chimed in.

As the mother of the most marvelous two-month-old boy on earth (ahem) I have already worn the covers off my copy of "Baby And Child Care". And I deeply admire your attitude of respect for the intelligence and basic good humor of the American mother. It is a pleasure to be spoken to as a creature of some merit, and not just a pair of mammary glands with a bird-sized brain and a tendency to panic at the slightest provocation.

But more important, as I sit here and fuss over my little one, I realize almost daily that women who were in my position 18 years ago are now receiving telegrams saying that their sons are dead, for the vaguest of reasons. And, perhaps even harder to bear is the picture of the Vietnamese mothers, holding their dead or disabled children in their arms and trying to figure out how they can continue to live, now that they have been blessed with "democracy". I am sure that your thoughts were like mine when you decided to fight for an end to this immoral war, because what is the point of creating new life, worrying and caring and fussing over babies, only to have it all end so absurdly?

I suppose all I'm trying to say is, don't stop fighting. And know that there are young mothers, like me, who sit home and make formula and wash diapers and read the newspapers and conclude that Benjamin Spock is the only hero America has.

Sincerely,

B. S. [female]

II. "I Am Ashamed of People Like You"

Dr. Spock's participation in the Pentagon march and his frequent appearances on television news programs after October 21 not only raised his profile for appreciative doves; it also made him a primary target for hawks and others who, if they were not hawks, objected to antiwar behavior. In addition to familiar references to the communist threat, the following letters often make two key points: that Spock and his child-rearing philosophy are to blame for an entire generation's authority-defying behavior, and that the peace movement is giving "aid and comfort" to the enemy, prolonging the war, and effectively killing American troops. A number of letters pressing these last points also, as a kind of corollary, assert the importance of respecting the president's authority and supporting the troops. The level of anger comes across more than in earlier letters, too, as the writers reflexively refer to protesters as "hippies," "punks," "kooks," "shirkers and ingrates," and "mobs."

Protesters confront troops at the Pentagon, October 21, 1967. Spock's participation in the Pentagon demonstration, the late night clash between troops and demonstrators, and the arrest of hundreds of protesters generated a flurry of mail to Spock. (U.S. News & World Report, Library of Congress)

90. You are responsible for today's Hippies—because you preached that <u>children</u> are wiser than parents.

Danville Virginia
October 22, 1967

Dear Dr. Spock,

At <u>last</u> I can tell you what I think of you—you have brainwashed so many parents—I don't wonder your kooky ideas are now exposed.

I'm a grandmother—and when my first grandson was born in 1958 —he kicked and screamed—and wouldn't eat—+ he <u>ruled</u> his parents, because they said "Dr. Spock said it's a <u>stage</u> babies and children go thru"—so allow permissive training—children know <u>more</u> than their parents. <u>So</u>—my two grandchildren have taken over the house—defy their parents—refuse discipline—which is what you <u>preach</u>. Where is <u>training</u> of children?

You are responsible for today's Hippies—because you preached that <u>children</u> are wiser than parents. Is a two year old—or a ten year old more intelligent than his parents? According to your theories, we should allow children to protest, have <u>no</u> discipline + lack of control, because you <u>brain</u> <u>washed</u> their parents. I wonder to <u>whom</u> you are loyal—the God fearing Americans or the unlawful kids who are more Communist than <u>freedoms'</u> children. You preached defiance <u>of laws</u>.

You thought it was "a stage" when children yelled + screamed at the dining room table—so adults were <u>cringing</u> before their <u>power</u>. They still take over the home—the parents are Dr. Spock-brain-washed.

Now I know why—the hippies + kooks of today were reared by <u>your</u> <u>book</u>. What are you, anyhow, a destructive American?

God hopes that someday other intelligent people will expose you for what you are; to bring up kids a la your <u>permissive</u> training so they'll march on our government, protest—riot + be a generation of lawless people.

I wish you'd shut up—both on your child psychology books + your new found ambition of becoming President. God help us if <u>you</u> are that important.

Very truly yours,
Mrs. R. B.

P.S. I'd like to organize a movement against Dr. Benjamin Spock! It will happen, you know.

91. I believe all such activities as these indulged in by your lovely little group of darling young people should be banned from television and all news media.

El Campo, Texas

10-22-67

Dear Sir:

At present you are attempting to answer a question in re the value of actions around the Pentagon yesterday.

Sir: as a mother of three young people, a girl—18, a boy—16, and another boy—14, I speak with considerable feeling. I believe all such activities as these indulged in by your lovely little group of darling young people should be banned from television and all news media. Disgraceful to burden serious minded, plain, ordinary citizens with the sight and sound of our President being called "enemy." (But don't jump to conclusions: I have never supported LBJ and do not intend to except insofar as he <u>stands back of our</u> MEN <u>in</u> Viet Nam.) And storming the Pentagon —darling little young people—they wouldn't hurt a soul, would they? How much money changed hands between whom for this filthy mess, anyway? And the rings through the noses—very becoming bedecked with [illegible].

But, of course, what we must blame is the news media. For if these adorable, demonstratin', fine youngsters were not photographed and written up and so highly publicized, the game wouldn't be half the fun, would it?? Well, the publicity is doing something else, it is arousing the opposition—us mediocre, tuned-out, non-flower people who don't do much except earn the taxes to keep this country going.

Oh, shame on you and on Channel 11 for burdening us with you.

<u>Most</u> sincerely,

Mrs. J. L.

92. You are giving aid and comfort to our enemy—you are abeting them in continuing this war.

Monterey, California

October 22

Dr. Spock:—

I am writing to you as a Republican, as the widow of a Radiologist. You, as a medical man, are not serving the interests of our sons and grandsons in Vietnam. You are giving aid and comfort to our enemy—you are abeting them in continuing this war.

You should know as an intelligent person (supposedly?) that our Country is sincere in its motives. We wish no territories—we only wish to curb the tenacles of a horrible communism which would take away freedom (to act as you are acting).

Surely as a medical man you should know the insidious ways of a malignancy? And that is what communism is! I have, ever, been proud that my husband was a doctor—a fellow of the College of Radiology. I am not proud of you! You frighten me for my Country's sake. Yes, and mine.

> For God and Country,
> Mrs. O. B.

And I am not a John Bircher!

93. Now by your actions and speech you are helping to kill the flower of your youth.

10/22/67

Dr. Spock,

You started your career saving life. Now by your actions and speech you are helping to kill the flower of your youth. It is the consensus of the countrie's opinion that your actions have given comfort to the enemy and recovering his will to resist, hoping that you and your ilk will make us get out. Please <u>paint</u> a gray chimney on your house signifying a Tory and a Benedict Arnold. I served in the 1st world war and my son was in the 2nd world war. These efforts gave you the freedom that you have now.

> A Listener [male]
> Wash. DC

94. I didn't vote for Pres. Johnson, but as long as he was elected to run this country, let us help him not our enemies the Communists.

October 23, 1967

Dr. Spock,

I am ashamed of you and people like you. You should have gotten all your hostility and rebellion out of you in your teens.

I have a grandson in Viet-Nam and four more to go. I don't like nor want war. There is no just nor moral war. I didn't vote for Pres. Johnson, but as long as he was elected to run this country, let us help him not our enemies the Communists.

You know about what you are doing, as Pres. Johnson knows about pediatrics. Stick to your trade if you haven't forgotten it.

D. R. [female]
Bklyn NY

95. Do you take responsibility of the cracked heads and arrests when your mobs get out of control?

Luray, Virginia
October 23, 1967

Dear Sir:

I am ashamed to call you a Doctor of Medicine and colleague. Your exhortations to young people, in your self righteous anti Vietnam War demonstrations was most regrettable. A man of high training telling the young people to disobey their government, to be judge of what is best for the United States and the world.

No wonder your book on pediatrics was so good because you are still living as a child and not as a responsible adult.

Dr. Spock, do you take the responsibility for these mobs-defying the government and breaking the laws of the land? Do you take responsibility of the cracked heads and arrests when your mobs get out of control? Where is your peace movement? You have disgusted every one who saw you on television except a very small percentage of people.

I feel so sorry for you and your kind.

M. W., M.D.

96. Do you find any justice in forcing those servicemen who have paid the price for your past political frivolities to be put in the position where they have to confront the country men of their generation on the streets of our cities?

Palisade, Colorado
October 23, 1967

My dear Dr. Spock:

As one who did <u>not</u> vote for Lyndon Johnson in 1964 and as the parent of a nineteen-year-old Navy enlistee, I feel entitled to some answers and I therefore write to you in the expectation—(not a vain one, I hope) —that you will take time to give them to me.

1. Did you, prior to the 1964 election, ask the legal infants of this country how they felt about our international commitments? Or did you consider them too young to have valid opinions?

2. Were you not cognizant of the implications of the Gulf of Tonkin Resolution passed by Congress on August 7, 1964, three full months before the election? And did you support any of the Senators or Representatives who, by virtue of this resolution, abdicated their authority and their obligation to office?

3. Were you politically tutored, sir, to the fact that Lyndon Johnson was riding to the White House on the back of a dead man? Did you suffer, along with the other millions who precipitated his land-slide election, from the illusion that the ghost of John F. Kennedy would really direct the political conscience of such an out-and-out egotist as Lyndon Johnson?

4. Where now are the voters whom you worked to influence in 1964? Are they protest-marching, being clubbed, going to jail? Or do they send their kids out to do their dirty work for them?

5. How many of the youngsters whom you lead into confrontation with seasoned troops have the right to vote? If they are old enough to demonstrated and to be drafted, are they too immature to exercise the franchise? Would you dare to live with their political decisions as they have had to live—and die—with yours?

6. How much bared young emotion, how great a social stigma, how many burned draft-cards, what number of broken heads will it take to assuage your wounded personal pride, Dr. Spock? Having worked to inflict Lyndon Johnson and his war upon us and our children, how much domestic expense and international embarrassment will you exact from us before you are satisfied?

7. Do you find any justice in forcing those servicemen who have paid the price for your past political frivolities to be put in the position where they have to confront the country men of their generation on the streets of our cities? Did you not help to make them veterans, sir? By what right do you attempt to undermine their sacrifice to your mistakes?

8. What assures you that, having been so wrong three years ago, you are now right? If you do not believe in the brutalities of the war you

helped make, why are you not in Viet Nam utilizing your professional skill to alleviate the suffering occasioned by it? Do you lack the courage of your convictions?

9. Why do you, one trained in the science of mind and body, use raw emotion rather than reason as a means of correcting a bad situation? Are you ignorant of mob psychology and, if so, how come?

10. Do you not recognize the danger of what you are doing? Or is it your intent, while the sons of the non-supporters of Lyndon Johnson are fighting his and your war, to incite a revolution here at home? Are our boys to be left to the tender mercies of the enemy because they are patriots who have been taught to abide by the rule of the majority, of which you have been one? Have you asked or even considered how they or their parents feel about all this, or do you even care?

I'd like to know the answers to these things, Dr. Spock. Perhaps then I wouldn't be so horrified at your conduct.

Very truly yours,
Mrs. J. P.

97. This son is going into the Service tomorrow. Of course I dread his involvement in the war in Viet Nam—But I know there is no other way.

October 23, 1967

Dear Dr. Spock;

I have become aware of your criticism of the Viet Nam war. I have also become aware of your attempts to organize peace parties and marches against the war.

You, are of course, utilizing your right of dissent; a right all Americans enjoy, use, and sometimes take for granted.

You have used your right of dissent to hop on to Lyndon Johnson's back. It is your right to do so. But please, Dr. Spock don't expect us to sympathize with you.

I have a son who was raised on your book. This son is going into the Service tomorrow. Of course I dread his involvement in the war in Viet Nam—But I know there is no other way.

I want you to know, Dr. Spock, that no American in Viet Nam has held an infant in his arms and killed him intentionally—as your friends the Viet Congs do every day.

Your cites of hate against President Johnson will not end the war—

it will only prolong it. Ho Che Min knows the only way to win in Vietnam as with Indo China is to let the American people chicken out first. You are giving Ho Che Min his hope. an only solution to Victory, and the leaders of this country are not about to leave S. Vietnam. You prolong the killing, suffering and fighting. Maybe this makes you happy— Maybe Communism makes you happy.

I hope you see the light and stop making a fool of yourself. From a Mother who used to think of you as a good Guy.

C. G. [female]
So. Plainfield, N.J.

98. One cannot rear their children to become good citizens if one does not teach them the price and value of freedom.

Chicago, Illinois
October 25, 1967

Dear Dr. Spock:

I am a young mother (age 25) of two small children (ages 6 months and 18 months) and I am writing to you in protest of your protest. First of all, I believe you should remember your station in life. You are not a military man nor a diplomat of our State Department. You are a doctor supposedly interested in the physical and mental care and rearing of children.

Then how, in good conscience, can you support the anti-Viet Nam marches and demonstrations and how can you refer to President Johnson as "the enemy"? How can you back a minority of people who seem to have no moral values at all?

One cannot rear their children to become good citizens if one does not teach them the price and value of freedom. Granted, the "peaceniks" have the right to dissent, but this dissension now is bordering on treason. The people of South Viet Nam have the right to freedom, a freedom for which we are helping them fight.

I would die if I ever thought my son and/or daughter would grow up without a respect for the office of the presidency and the man who holds that office. It would hurt me deeply to find they had no respect and love for their country. I would consider myself a complete failure. I do not like war, but this is something to which we have dedicated ourselves and something we must continue.

A friend of mine and I had thought of burning your books in a bonfire as the hippies do their draft-cards. Then we thought better of the idea because by burning your books we would have to buy them and therefore indirectly support you. Instead we have promised not to teach our children your doctrines and will try to spread the word far and wide in retaliation to your stand.

    Sincerely,

    Mrs. L. G.

99. Is it the wish of you and your group for us to stand by and do nothing about the communist conspiracy against all of mankind throughout our world?

Whitehall, Wis

11–13–67

Dear Dr. Spock:

    . . . The issue of Vietnam boils down this: Do we want the communists to win in Vietnam, and later take over all of Asia, imposing their dictatorships on the presently and newly created democratic government of South Vietnam as well as the rest of Asia as they promise to do?

    If we are wrong in the war in Vietnam, then we were wrong in fighting the Kaiser Wilhelm in first world war; the cruel despot Hitler and Mussilini as well as the military dictators in Japan in the second world war.

    History now proves that protesters in those wars in defense of democracy were wrong at that time; history will do the same for this present war, that protesters were wrong, and our government were right.

    We stopped the communists in Berlin; in Greece; in sending nuclear weapons to Cuba; Israel stopped them from taking over in Egypt and Israel itself; Nato is holding them in check in Europe; we are defending against them in this country, as is well known.

    Now we are defending the helpless smaller nations against them in Asia.

    Is it the wish of you and your group for us to stand by and do nothing about the communist conspiracy against all of mankind throughout our world, as they have said many times they would do?

    We know, especially those who give it serious thought, that evolution is retarded in countries where dictatorships rule; where people are not free to make their own choices; to speak and write freely; not free to worship as they would like; to form their free governments and elect their own officials. In short, they are stopped in doing what is necessary for themselves in order to evolve and advance in all fields of human endeavor.

Communist and other cruel dictators operate contrary to the will and intention of the Ruling Hierarchy of our world; the real Rulers who function in our behalf and for our advancement intellectually, morally, spiritually, and in ever other way that promotes our evolutionary progress.

When a people take up arms in defense of these principles, they are doing it for a just cause; that is the main reason we as Americans have always won in the past, and will always win in the present and the future.

We wish to protect your own right to speak and write, as well as my own.

Sincerely,

A. E. [gender unknown]

100. My son is only two years old, so he can be of no help in this conflict. . . . I pray that if the time ever comes when my son is called on to serve, he will go forward bravely and with heart held high to do honor to America and all that she stands for.

January 15, 1968

An open letter to Dr. Benjamin Spock

Dear Dr. Spock:

In America, where you have been guaranteed freedom of speech, you have spoken freely—and so shall I. There comes a time when to remain silent is as vile an act toward our country as openly defaming her.

Yes, Dr. Spock, you have spoken freely because America has given you that right. You have practiced or not practiced your religion, whichever your choice, because America will have it no other way. Indeed, if you will review the Bill of Rights, you will find that each of the promised freedoms has served you well, as they have each one of us.

You have moved about freely in a free society and become a member of an honored profession. In another country your lot might have been quite different. America allows no Hitlers or Stalins to dictate what you shall do and when, to threaten your very life if you do not cater to their lust for power.

Oh yes, America has her faults. Ghettos and starvation do exist, but

America sees her shortcomings and tries to overcome them. Efforts are being made to serve the wants and needs of her people. Even though conditions exist that are less than ideal, there are many who have risen above poverty. Whether your success was a result of your own efforts or whether you were helped along the way, in America it was possible.

Your country has done much for you, if by no other means than by letting you be and allowing you to make your own way, without interference.

We have a great country. Great countries, like truly great men, have generous hearts. They want only to see those less fortunate than themselves obtain the means to happiness. When oppressed peoples desire freedom, then America desires to help them reach their goal.

No great gifts are given without sacrifice. Freedom requires the greatest sacrifices of all—the blood of sons and husbands and the tears of mothers and wives. We ourselves paid that price, not too long ago, that America might be free.

Even if we cannot agree on the war that is now raging, we must remember that this is what America, as a nation, is fighting for. We have a debt to pay to her, to support the things she believes in.

But you, sir, evidently feel that your debt to America is paid by your yearly income tax. You, who have reaped so generously of America's gifts, have the audacity to oppose her so violently as to advise others not to do their duty. You help the shirkers and ingrates to avoid their debt, to run and hide. What a pity that you cannot direct as much energy to supporting candidates for office, candidates who share your views, as you do to opposing those who already hold office. There might, then, be less to demonstrate against.

My son is only two years old, so he can be of no help in this conflict. I can only hope that enough mothers have instilled enough love of country in their sons to erase at least part of the dark shadow of shame that you have cast upon our land. I pray that if the time ever comes when my son is called on to serve, he will go forward bravely and with heart held high to do honor to America and all that she stands for.

Mrs. J. F.
Brookfield, Wisconsin

cc: Mr. Paul Harvey
The Milwaukee Journal

101. There they are fighting and many of them dying while alot of punks are protesting the war and the draft.

January 28, 1968

Dr. Spock,

My name is [name deleted], a junior in high school, and the daughter of an Air Force sgt. I watched your interview today on Meet the Press. It aroused me somewhat. My father is in Vietnam on the U.S.S. Ranger working for the Navy and our country. He has also served his time in Thailand. My boyfriend is also in Vietnam, on the U.S.S. Canberra. Certainly I don't like the draft particularly, as most Americans dislike sending their fathers, husbands, boyfriends, brothers, and friends off to war and perhaps to die. But . . . they are dying for their country and for what they love and believe in. What do the words "freedom" and "liberty" mean to you? To me I can sum them up easily "The United States." Alot of the boys that I know joined the service, but many others need to be helped to the recruiter . . . drafted in other words. These boys couldn't have a conscience. Not to let others go and fight for them, while they sit, nice and safe in the states. Is this right? I ask you as an American.

Every week I get letters from my boyfriend telling me how good it makes them all feel to be fighting for us, yes us, you and me. But he says that the moral needs lifting over there. I can certainly see why. There they are fighting and many of them dying while alot of punks are protesting the war and the draft. It makes you think, doesn't it? It makes some of them wonder if the fighting is worth it. Even with the draft law, it's hard to get guys to join the service, think what it would be like if there wasn't a draft law. I can tell you what it would be like . . . one big mess.

Yes, you are older and perhaps wiser than I, but it could be that you can't see things as clearly from your point of view as I can from mine.

Cordially yours,
L. D. [female]
Lemoore, Calif

III. Wartime Observations and Anguish

LETTERS PRAISING Spock as well as letters criticizing him appear in the next section, but they differ from the letters in previous sections in tone and emphasis. For the most part, these letters serve as personalized dispatches from the home front, carrying observations of the war's effect at

An Hoa, South Vietnam, November 1967. In the kind of image that prompted visceral reaction in the United States, villagers await evacuation by American and South Vietnamese forces following a recent battle. (Bettmann/CORBIS)

home. Writers of the critical letters wrote in more measured language, expressing deep concern about the antiwar movement's methods and the nationwide division for which some writers in part blamed protesters. In addition, a number of writers tell personal stories conveying the impact of the war on their families and communities. The effect on children, from little ones to draft age, especially, comes through clearly. To these writers, Spock remained a trusted figure, a man to whom they again could turn for advice or help.

102. You <u>must</u> be their hero, teaching them the value of laws, respect for our national leaders, even if we violently disagree with them and their policies.

October 22

Dear Dr. Spock,

For years you've been my hero, your child raising book my simple guide to a difficult job. Your wonderful concept of the parent child relationship is a service for all of us.

Please don't spoil that Dr. Spock! You know we all need heroes—especially the young generation who are in a state of flux, not knowing just what is the proper behavior is. You <u>must</u> be their hero, teaching them the value of laws, respect for our national leaders, even if we violently disagree with them and their policies.

So please Dr. Spock, re-evaluate, and take your wonderful abilities to them. As a public figure you have influence and responsibility. We all need that, especially the younger ones. Leaders of protests are a dime a dozen—but Dr. Spocks are unique.

> Respectfully,
> L. T. [female]
> [point of origin unknown]

103. It is awful what it did to our family, + here we have him home whole + safe!

Oct 27th

Dear Dr. Spock,

I dislike Time magazine but it was so unfair to you I am writing to give you more encouragement.

My son returned from Vietnam last week. He <u>was</u> a smiling boy + despite the fact I've refused to argue about the WAR we're having a miserable 2 weeks. We wanted him back so much + I wrote over 20 cards to Washington + Gen. Gavin[5] in Boston "Another Mother for Peace" cards to express my relief + desire for other families to be united. My son + his wife had never had an argument. Now they are under a terrible strain. My husband was always so calm (a prof + writer) and spent hours with our four children. We are committed optimists; we just can't believe the strain no one can penetrate. We can't reach each other anymore. [Our son and his wife] have a lousy year ahead at Fort Walters, Texas, training other chopper pilots. He doesn't understand at all that I give full time to student peace groups (he only knows a little) not because I am agst him! It is awful what it did to our family, + here we have him home whole + safe!

So, dear Dr. Spock, I was too busy to finish your book, but how I worship your courage!

> Mrs. E. P.
> [point of origin unknown]

104. I teach First Grade at Buckingham Friends School and I am very much concerned about what this war is doing to the young children today.

Southampton, Pa.

October 31, 1967

Dear Dr. Spock,

I teach First Grade at Buckingham Friends School and I am very much concerned about what this war is doing to the young children today. The children are very much concerned about what is happening. Last year one of my First Graders looked at me sadly one day and said, "Mrs. [name deleted], I don't understand, but why do we have to have war?" How can you answer a question like that from a six year old? We discussed the war in Viet Nam and what we could do about it. The children decided that they would write letters to President Johnson. Their letters were child-like in their innocence, but full of heart-felt feeling. I sent the letters to Senator Joseph Clark, who forwarded them to the President. We received a letter from one of his assistants assuring the children that every effort was being made to settle the conflict at the conference table rather than on the battle field. When I read the letter to the class, they broke out in applause. Would that I could have had their faith in the sincerity of the letter! The class also decided to make puppets to send to the children in a hospital in Viet Nam. We took these to The American Friends Service Committee, and they said they would make an effort to get them to Viet Nam, and if this proved to be impossible, they would send them to Hong Kong. This year, I have avoided discussing the war, but it has come up numerous times in class discussions. What prompted me to write you was a meeting for worship that we had at our school on Monday. This was held in the meeting house for grades Kindergarten through eighth grade. It was a quiet meeting at first and no one spoke. Then one of our First Graders stood up and spoke about being sorry for all of the children all over the world who were hungry and had no homes. From then on, for the next ten minutes, the First and Second graders stood up and voiced their concern about the ills of the world. Many of them talked about the war in Viet Nam. As they talked, I realized how deeply they felt and how frustrated. I felt badly that such small shoulders had to go around with such a heavy burden, and saddened that their hearts were so filled with grief about what was happening. I feel that it is necessary to help them become aware of the misfortunes of others, especially because so many of them come from affluent homes, many of which are apathetic about the condition of the world: but I am also worried about what an over-concern might do to them <u>at this early age</u>. Therefore I am writing to you to see if you can give me any advice as to how to handle this in a constructive and helpful way. If you have any advice, I would really appreciate it.

I heard you speak in Washington at the Peace Demonstration on October 22nd, and am in complete accord with what you said. Thank you for speaking out so strongly. I only hope and pray that more voices will be added to yours.

Thanking you for any advice you can give me,

Sincerely,

Mrs. M. A.

105. Anti-war protesters could have a much stronger appeal if they used as their <u>main</u> slogan "Support our boys in Vietnam; bring them home alive."

Ridgewood, N.J.
[undated]

Dear Dr. Spock,

I firmly support your stand against the horrendous and worthless Vietnam War, and I respect your courage in jeopardizing your professional position in order to voice your opinion. As you seem to have much influence over peace demonstrations, I would like to give you my critical comments about one aspect of the present peace movement.

I have noticed that much emphasis is placed on the killing of Vietnamese, particularly small children. While this in itself is a very important reason for ending the war, I feel that the deaths of American servicemen deserve equal attention. All injuries and killings of all human beings in a war without a direct purpose should shock a civilized nation. There is also an interesting sidelight to decrying GI deaths: the pro-war demonstrations usually have as their theme "Support our boys in Vietnam." However, anti-war protesters could have a much stronger appeal if they used as their <u>main</u> slogan "Support our boys in Vietnam; bring them home alive." This would win over to your side the parents and friends of servicemen now fighting in Vietnam because such a message hits home. With such a stand you would not be sacrificing your principles but would be showing yourself to be more patriotic than the person who wants Americans to continue suicide in fighting in Vietnam.

Sincerely,

R. N. [male]

106. If I have to defend my country I would rather fight in Asia than on American soil.

Elmira, New York
November 9, 1967

Dear Dr. Spock:

Although I did not expect a reply to my letter I was glad to hear from you. I sincerely hope that I did not seem discourteous in my first letter. I have grown alarmed over the past few years because of the outspoken number of Americans who opposed the War in Viet Nam.

What is our purpose there? Many people say it is to stop Communism, they point to the domino theory. Is it wrong to stop an ideology that threatens our very way of life? The people of South Viet Nam have known nothing but slavery and oppression for two thousand years. Now after all their years of hardship they have a spark of hope left that someday their country may be free.

Freedom does not come easy, it costs lives. Our own freedom was bought with the lives of millions of Americans who believed that they were right in protecting freedom and fighting tierany any where in the world. A lot of Americans seem to forget that not too many years ago we were a young struggling nation. Maybe the average American had more ideals then, but I don't think so.

You say the rest of the world considers us as barbarians and killers. I am enclosing a newspaper article, one of hundreds in American newspapers everyday. After you read it ask yourself who are the barbarians. [EDITOR'S NOTE: The letter-writer included a four paragraph article from AP, "Cong Blamed in Chaining, Slaying of 12."]

I am a 17 year old highschool graduate and in a short time I like thousands of other young Americans will be facing military service. If I have to defend my country I would rather fight in Asia than on American soil. I don't pretend to know all the answers and I don't think our President can honestly say he does either, but I believe that one must draw the line and take a stand for what he believes is right and honorable. I am proud to be in the generation of Americans that will show the world that the United States of America will offer freedom and protection to any nation on earth. Thank you for your kind reply. I sincerely respect your views and your right to express them.

> Sincerely yours,
> T. G. [male]

107. I have become quite bitter and even thought about suing the United States Government for my 20-year old son, whose custody I have until age 21. . . . It is so unjust that these boys are forced to kill or be killed when their conscience tells them it is wrong.

> November 15, 1967
> Calgary, Alberta
> Canada

Dear Dr. Spock:

When one is worried and has what seems to be an insoluble problem, it seems logical to turn for help to someone considered most likely to understand and to give intelligent advice. Because of your occupation, for the past twenty-five years or more, in the field of baby and child care, your deep concern for the future of the country you so wisely helped to "raise", and your participation in the peace movement, I have decided to ask for your advice.

I have two daughters, ages 21 and 16, and three sons, ages 23, 20, and 15. For the past thirteen years I have always worked full time as a secretary-stenographer-typist for various companies, and for the past six years worked two jobs, my regular day job for the Standard Oil Company of California (10 yrs.) and a night and week-end job for Commercial Mailing (National Titanium) and Peterson Construction Co. of Whittier-Bellflower. I was divorced, not widowed, and support payments were inadequate.

Five months ago I requested a job transfer so as to move my family from Whittier, California, to Canada, because of my growing aversion to U.S. involvement in Vietnam. I brought the two youngest of my family with me, daughter of 16 and son, 15. My oldest daughter has a scholarship to Chapman College in Orange, California, and stayed to complete her last two years. All of my family is in agreement that the U.S. is making a terrible mistake in Vietnam. We have read a great deal on the subject, have written letters of protest, attended peace marches, and in general have tried to get our fellow Americans to learn more about the war. But, it goes on and our voices are ignored. My 20-year old son requested conscientious objector classification, but was turned down because his request was not motivated by religious conviction. It seems that we who are not members of a certain church are expected to favor mass killing.

In order to get the transfer to Canada I had to take a $100 per month cut in salary and also give up the week-end job, which means $250 less per month for living expenses. This loss, together with heavy indebtedness, lack of sufficient housing in Calgary, no furniture, inadequate clothes, and very cold winter weather coming up, prompted asking my sons for help. They presented my request (written) for help to the draft board and were turned down. Both of them were drafted.

Is there anyone in the United States I can get legal advice from concerning my rights? I have become quite bitter and even thought about suing the United States Government for my 20-year old son, whose custody I have until age 21 (he turned 20 on Sept. 26). It is so unjust that these boys are forced to kill or be killed when their conscience tells them it is wrong. There must be some justice and recourse for these boys and the many parents who feel as we do.

I have joined the Voice of Women here in Canada (Calgary) and my daughter, son and I marched in the October 21st International Peace march here, but Dr. Spock, our boys and the Vietnamese go right on dying. My brother, for whom my 20-year old son was named, was killed in World War II (the war to end wars, as we were told). There is so little time—I read in the papers every day of the accelerated build-up of American forces in Vietnam.

It occurred to me that I would be making a mistake to contact the draft board or a "hawk" attorney. Knowing what a busy person you are, I am hoping this letter will not inconvenience you. If you could possibly send a brief reply to me before they send my sons to VN, I hope you will do so. I have no money to pay an attorney. Is there anyone you could refer me to who could advise regarding my rights as a dependent mother. Since my 20-year old son was placed in my custody until age 21 and nothing was stipulated regarding custody in event of war, would I stand a chance in a suit against the U.S. Govt.? Having raised my children to have compassion for their fellowman, I find it impossible to stand idly by while my sons are driven to kill.

Please advise me, and I will always be grateful.
Sincerely and Very Respectfully,
M. G. [female]

108. I have reason to believe that someone I love very dearly is a prisoner of war.

Morristown, N.J.

November 20, 1967

Dear Dr. Spock,

I am writing concerning the war in Viet Nam. I have reason to believe that someone I love very dearly is a prisoner of war.

On November 10th we received a telegram stating that Air Force Sgt. [name deleted], was missing in action. He was stationed in Da Nang with the 37th A.R.R.S. He had been sent to Viet Nam on October 18th to do rescue and recovery work.

On November 12, 1967, we recieved word that [he] was dead. The helicopter that he was in had rescued two personnel and, afterwards, had been shot down, burning on impact. The crash occurred at 1:00. The pilot was rescued at 5:30—four and a half hours later. Rescue work did not continue until the following day. It was at this time Sgt. [name deleted] was determined to have died of injuries suffered in the crash.

Three successive telegrams followed. Each telegram stated that [his] remains were unknown, because of hostile action in the area preventing recovery of the body.

Today, a little more than one week after recieving the first telegram, we had memorial services for [him]. His body was never sent home.

I know that the government has made several mistakes concerning deaths of servicemen in Viet Nam. I would not trust the U.S. government concerning information that [name deleted] had been killed. I believe that within the day that it took rescue workers to get in and search for [him], he may very well have been captured by the Viet Cong, assuming that the area had been surrounded by the "hostile forces," or the Viet Cong.

I am writing to you to ask your help in finding out if [he] is a prisoner of war. Maybe I have set my hopes too high, but I cannot resign my self to his death because of a telegram from his commanding officer. Please help me. I have no one to turn to. His parents believe that he is dead. Perhaps I will believe it also, but only after I am certain that he is not a prisoner of war. I will do anything to aid you. I hope that my letter contains all the necessary information. Please acknowledge my letter in some way. I know that I have asked a lot of you, but [name deleted] was or is my whole life. Please understand.

E. F. [female]

109. When college students complain of our "apathy" I often long to tell them—it's not that we "don't care"—we're just <u>too</u> <u>darn</u> <u>busy</u> and pressured with earning a living.

Attleboro, Mass.

Nov. 28, 1967

Dear Dr. Spock,

. . . I've been so distressed by the war, that recently for the second time in two years, I've engaged in a diligent letter writing campaign, protesting U.S. involvement. Being inexperienced at political activity, (beyond League of Women Voters) and in writing to celebrities, I'm rather hesitant about the amount of good it will do. Still, nothing ventured nothing gained; and wouldn't it be a gigantic accomplishment to contribute toward a powerful peace movement!? From observation of the past three years, I believe I've garnered enough "evidence" to support my conclusions. To convince others, I need more concise statistical facts and am not sure where to obtain such "evidence" most efficiently. What I really need, is a sort of monograph assembled over the past ten to fifteen years, of American capital investments in Viet Nam and Southeast Asia. This, I believe, when presented in simplified form, might eliminate some confusion in the minds of the "conservative middle class," as to the principle reasons for this war, and a consequent demonstration that they are not valid reasons. I am eager (so far) to work on this project as quickly as possible; as I have access to the "non-entities" of the middle class (being one of them). When college students complain of our "apathy" I often long to tell them—it's not that we "don't care"—we're just <u>too</u> <u>darn</u> <u>busy</u> and pressured with earning a living, feeding, clothing, and training our kids, and coping with multitudes of minutiae, that demand our <u>immediate</u> attention! (I guess it's those adolescent kids who are perceptive enough to observe our treadmill activity, who get scared and "cop out." I wish I could tell them <u>its</u> <u>not</u> <u>so</u> <u>bad</u> once you get over the hump of self-appraisal—but <u>how</u> do you do it?) (They are locked in the academic towers of theory, and I'm chained to stove, sink, and washer. How do we communicate?!)

We <u>do</u> have a common cause now,—there's no reason for a generation gap, about ending the war through a massive peace movement.

If you can direct, advise or guide me, to appropriate agencies for the accomplishment of above stated goals, I'd be most appreciative.

Enclosed is a copy of my letters to Congressional leaders. Your criticism is welcome.

Sincerely,

Mrs. M. T.

110. Even if this war is unnecessary, the people of the United States must have more faith in the leaders of this country.

Cleveland Ohio

[undated]

Dear Dr. Spock,

I am a young man who is presently in the Army Reserve. . . .

I am of the strong belief that each American is certainly entitled to voice his personal opinion. If it were not for this aspect of the American civilization, I do not think our country would be as great as it is. It is important, however, to realize our position in this country. I am certain that when you voice your opinion, it has far more influence than when I voice mine.

I respect the power of conviction you have concerning the Viet Nam situation. I do believe, however, that you are wrong. Even if this war is unnecessary, the people of the United States must have more faith in the leaders of this country. History has proven that "A house divided against itself cannot stand." With the enormous problem of racial friction in this country, we must really strive to bring the peoples of our country together. The difference of opinion concerning this war has aided even further the weakening of moral.

Dr. Spock, people respect, listen and believe you. Please do not aid the "movement" to divide our house. Even if you are right, you are only hurting the country that has given you so much. If I am sent to Viet Nam to defend this country, I certainly would die for it. I am sure you are every bit the American I am. I am equally as sure that if you look at your "crusade" objectively, you will realize that you are not accomplishing what you sincerely want to accomplish.

Sincerely yours,

B. J. [male]

111. Please consider voting socialist not as a solution but as a moral stand.

Binghamton, New York

December 21, 1967

Dear Dr. Spock:

I don't believe that this immoral war in which we're engaged in Vietnam is the result of a few blunders by a few stupid men, and I can't accept LBJ as <u>the</u> enemy either, as you indicated in Washington on October 21st. He happens to be unusually crude, and there is no question that he lacks the style and the tact of John F. Kennedy or perhaps of Stevenson.

But herein lies the real question: Do you believe that either of these men would have behaved in a manner drastically different from Johnson? If you do, and if you accept Eugene McCarthy's[6] prescription of continuing to bomb supply bases in North Vietnam while withdrawing over a five year period, then I suppose you will endorse McCarthy.

I'm writing to ask you to consider carefully the statements that you make about McCarthy, for, if my suppositions are correct, the entire peace movement is waiting for you to speak.

Your letter to the <u>N.Y.Times</u> after the Chicago New Politics convention indicated that you have moved from liberalism to radicalism, and I applauded you. I hope that the same insight you displayed in evaluating that conference will lead you to reject any peace candidate who cloaks his anti-war statements with so many provisos. He's like the politician who says that he's against capital punishment but that there are a lot of really bad guys who need to be executed before a new law makes sense.

As a radical who remains unaffiliated with any party (although I'm technically a registered Democrat) and who, after several years of inspecting the evidence, has concluded that neither of the two major parties can effect the kind of over-all change that is necessary in order for us to rectify the egregious anti-humanitarian forces at work in our society, I appeal to you to weigh your words carefully when your inevitable "judgment" is made. If I could believe that the spirit being channeled toward McCarthy's nomination had the potentiality of liberating itself further into a third party after his probably defeat, then I might go along with my liberal and de-radicalized friends who are so enthusiastic about him because he's "so much better than Johnson." But I fear that when he's defeated (is it defeatist to assume this?), all of the fervent McCarthy

supporters will rally to the cause of Johnson because he's "so much better than Nixon or Reagan" or whoever has the GOP nomination.

At this point, I will admit that I do not want a Republican president
of the hawkish variety, but I will reject categorically the "lesser of two
evils" argument.

Eugene Debs once pled for a socialist vote by saying that it's better
to vote for what you want and not get it than to vote for what you don't
want and find that you have it. The socialist parties on the ballot in this
election have platforms in which you and I believe: they vary in form but
not in essence; they all stand for a major re-structuring of society, a re-
structuring that would prevent more Vietnams. They are weak because
people who agree with them are afraid of "throwing away their vote."
Please consider voting socialist not as a solution but as a moral stand.

I remember reading a statement by a young white father who jour-
neyed by bus from Chicago to Selma; and when he was asked by a
reporter if he thought his being there was really doing any good, he
replied, "Maybe not in the short-run, but when my grandchildren ask me
what I did to help black people get their freedom, I can say that I made
my stand in Selma."

That's how I feel about voting socialist.

Sincerely,

Mrs. E. L.

112. I fear you not because of what you think or believe, but because of the anarchistic method you have chosen to put your beliefs into effect.

Palatka, Florida
January 29, 1968

Dear Doctor Spock:

This is not intended to be a rash or vindictive letter.

You have now publicly expressed your opinions regarding the draft
and the war in Viet Nam. Although I am not dogmatically opposed to
some of your apparent basic thinking, I am deeply concerned about the
method you propose in gaining your end, and the great weight your
stature in your chosen field gives any expression you make regardless of
its logic.

The newspapers quote you as stating that you despise and fear our
president. Doctor Spock I cannot despise you because I honestly feel you
are a misguided fool; but I do fear you. I have listened to you, and I have

tried to understand you. I only hope you will now listen to me, and try to understand why I consider you dangerous.

You were asked if you felt as though you or any other citizen should have the right to obey, or disobey any law that might please you or particularly suit your purpose. You answered by saying that the German citizenry was guilty of criminal conspiracy because they did not disobey the laws imposed on them by the Nazi government.

It is my opinion that if the German people are to be blamed for any lack of conscience action, it should be made for their failure to exhort their then republic form of government and its law enforcement agencies to enforce their civil laws against that group of brownshirt troopers and their leaders who by acts of violence and anarchy were usurping the political structure and social order then in existence.

In short, one of the many reasons why Naziism was able to take hold in a civilize nation was due to a flagrant disregard and disobedience to established law. The very philosophy you are now preaching.

There are many of us who do not agree with certain aspects of our foreign policy. There are some who can give logical arguments against the draft. There are many of us who did not vote for LBJ because we feared certain areas of his political philosophy. I, for one, will vigorously oppose Mr. Johnson's re-election. But sir, I will not use, nor will I propose the use of any form of civil disobedience to accomplish what I may consider any important purpose vital to our moral or political freedom.

I say this not because of my abhorrence of violence and deliberate disobedience to established law, but because I fear the totally destructive end such undisciplined action can bring to an organized system. I fear you not because of what you think or believe, but because of the anarchistic method you have chosen to put your beliefs into effect.

Yours truly,

J. K., M.D. [male]

113. Yesterday we buried a handsome and intelligent and educated young man, 25 years old, blown to bits in Saigon.

Los Angeles, California

Jan. 31, 1968

Dear Dr. Spock,

Just one more message of encouragement and hope for you and your cause. Parents and wives and sons are with you and praying for you every step of the way. You must meet success in this trial for the sake of the thousands of young people who are leaning on you for support. How we thank God for the stand you have taken.

Yesterday we buried a handsome and intelligent and educated young man, 25 years old, blown to bits in Saigon. It is such a senseless waste of human life and such depth of despair for those left behind. He didn't want to go, either. How he suffered. But it is too late for him. Now, there are thousands and thousands of others depending on you. Didn't we come from England to avoid conscription? Why should any young man kill or be killed when life is sacred? Who is our president or anyone else to decide who shall be maimed or killed or destroyed? Surely no young man should be forced into this service for a cause in which he does not believe, and for slaughter which is immoral?!

President Johnson wants to give everyone everything money can buy. Now, in his State of the Union, he is talking about "PRE NATAL CARE." And then, when we have saved and sacrificed for their futures, and educated them to make a useful contribution in the world, and when we have instilled in them the ideals of brotherhood———THEN, he wants to send them out to be shot. How unreasonable can we be? How can we expect anything but rebellion from our young people with this future ahead! Someone said if the people in Washington had to go to war, there would be no war. Let them decide for themselves, but not for others.

Please continue your good work. Let us know if you need money, or if there is any way at all that we can help. You have made such a great decision to go through with this. It is your supreme contribution. We thank you and we pray for you, and admire and respect you for the stand you are taking for all of us.

Gratefully,

C. L. [female]

114. When a picture of a boy killed in action appears in the paper it is often a boy of Mexican parentage. These boys find no way to keep out of the front lines.

Le Grand, Calif
February 2, 1968

Dear Dr. Spock:

My family and I heard you + Dr. Coffin on Meet the Press and I for one am thankful you are willing to take this stand and place yourself in this difficult position.

There is so much injustice in this war and most people are becoming desensitized to the atrocities of the war. We sit in front of the television and calmly watch the horrors of war, very comfortable in our homes, safe and 7,000 miles away from those who are suffering. We used to wonder how anyone could watch a bull fight but that is mild compared to the horrors that are daily before our eyes.

If we must fight it would be better for all of us to suffer a little instead of sending our 18 year olds out in the front lines to be killed. Even there, is so much unfairness. The boys with intelligence find some way out—In this part of the country there are many Mexican-American people—Their children usually do not seek higher education. These boys have been drafted in a much larger percentage than boys of more prosperous families. When a picture of a boy killed in action appears in the paper it is often a boy of Mexican parentage. These boys find no way to keep out of the front lines.

We hear report after report from leaders of our country who have visited Vietnam and they tell us of the indifference of the Vietnamese such as not drafting their 18 year olds—Why should our young boys have to go at that age or any age, none want to go. I think our atrocities such as the mistaken bombing are far worse than the Vietcong atrocities.

The average citizen doesn't know how to oppose all this. I imagine there were German citizens during the Hitler days who opposed the tactics of those days and didn't know what to do.

I hope you and Dr. Coffin can help the people of this country see what is happening. Thank You.

Sincerely,

Mrs. M. J.

IV. Dr. Spock's Arrest and Indictment

EARLY IN the morning of December 5, 1967, during a second "Stop the Draft Week," New York City police arrested Benjamin Spock outside the Whitehall Street Induction Center. Spock had arrived at Whitehall Street hoping to join protesters from the War Resisters League in blocking the entrance to the induction center and, if only for a brief time, shutting the place down. Arrangements between protest organizers and Mayor John

Dr. Spock minutes before his arrest for sitting-in at the Armed Forces Induction Center on Whitehall Street in Manhattan, December 5, 1967. (Bettmann/CORBIS)

Lindsay's office guaranteed that the police would exercise restraint in arresting those engaged in civil disobedience—that they would allow each person to sit briefly before being arrested. When Spock and the others arrived, however, the huge classical building was ringed with police and wooden police barricades; 2,500 demonstrators chanted "Peace now! Peace now!" Spock endured several embarrassing minutes as he tried to crawl under the barricades only to bump his head on the shins of police officers standing so close together that he could not get past them. Finally, on his third attempt he managed to find a space in the line, walked up the steps of the building and sat down. The police promptly arrested him.

In newspapers across the country, the arrest made front-page news, but often the reports portrayed Spock as a crawling baby. He spent much of the day in jail before paying a $25 fine, but as the week's demonstrations went on and police no longer responded with restraint, Spock spoke at a press conference at City Hall condemning police brutality. He also took part in another day of demonstrations at Whitehall Street, but without getting arrested.

The next group of letters are a small sampling of the kind Spock received after his arrest. This is exactly one month before his indictment for conspiracy against the United States government.

115. I hope you are able in the future to express your dissent more suitably and effectively.

Westfield, New York
December 5, 1967

Dear Dr. Spock,

It is most distressing to see a man, who for years has advocated a calm common sense approach to the sometimes problematic situations of child raising, lower himself to the pavement in a geriatric temper tantrum over a troublesome government problem.

I do not deny your right to disagree with government policy, but one expects intelligent thinkers to do so within the framework of the law of the land which provides for "the right of the people peaceably to assemble and to petition the government for a redress of grievances."

As your concern over Vietnam deepend you might have used your skill as a physician by participating in the A.M.A. program, Volunteer Physicians for Vietnam. A two month tour of duty in Vietnam would have given you a chance to be of service to the Vietnamese people, while allowing you to access the situation first hand. Your opinions after such an experience may have been the same as they are today, but you would have been contributing to, not interfering with, your governments policy.

I hope you are able in the future to express your dissent more suitably and effectively. I do not fear for the tarnished image you reflect on medicine and motherhood—these will endure. You degrade only yourself.

Very truly yours,
Mrs. J. H.

116. There is something you seem to have left out of your books though. That is teaching your sons to be men.

[point of origin unknown]
December 5,

Dear Dr. Spock,

I was appalled today when I heard on the news that you were attempting to keep men out of a draft induction center. It is hard for me to believe that I read your books on child rearing, and that I believed every word of it. There is something you seem to have left out of your books though. That is teaching your sons to be men.

When my husband teaches my sons to catch a fish or when he takes them into the woods and teaches them to identify animal tracks, or to spot a squirrel, I look on with pride and say to myself, "My sons will be men."

If when my sons reach draft age, the forces of Communism are still trying to enslave the world, put and end to men's belief in God, and end our system of free enterprise, then I will encourage them to go and fight for the freedom of their country.

Many of our American boys have fought and died that you might have the freedom to speak out as you did today. You are a coward of the most despicable sort! Go ahead and associate with your long haired, sissy, drug taking, cowardly friends. My Dr. Spock book is going in the trash.

    Mrs. A. E.

117. I sign in anonymity for fear of recrimination (should this letter be intercepted) against my own in the armed services.

                     December 5, 1967
                     Oakpark Michigan

Dear Dr. Spock—

I grieved to see the manner in which you were dealt with by the authorities, today, as viewed on Television.

Dear Dr. Spock, call on the mothers and wives of America to demonstrate by gathering each in her own community, on the streets of her home, near her home, and ring the bells for cessation of the monstrous war—perhaps to march in silence with bowed heads.

I sign in anonymity for fear of recrimination (should this letter be intercepted) against my own in the armed services. Please understand.

    A. L. [gender unknown]

ON JANUARY 5, 1968, the United States indicted Dr. Benjamin Spock, the Reverend William Sloane Coffin, Michael Ferber, Mitchell Goodman, and Marcus Raskin for conspiring to aid and abet draft resisters—

conspiring, in effect, to stop the war machine. All five men had been active in the draft resistance movement, though only one (Ferber) was a resister himself; the others were beyond draft age, but had participated in various actions of support. Spock, Coffin, and Raskin had delivered the draft cards to the Justice Department in October. Coffin, Goodman, and Raskin had been the main architects of the "Call to Resist Illegitimate Authority," a national petition calling for an end to the war and for support of draft resisters. Ferber and Coffin had appeared together at a draft card turn-in at a church in Boston on October 16, and Spock had been arrested at the induction center in New York in December. Even though they had never been in a room, all together, the government identified them as ringleaders and indicted them in what many supporters thought would be the first in a wave of prosecutions against dissidents.

The news of the indictments stunned the public, and most commentators predicted a landmark courtroom confrontation between the government and articulate dissenters. The story dominated the news for the next several weeks from indictment to the arraignment on January 29. As a result, all of the accused were in demand with the press and within the movement. A massive support event took place at New York's Town Hall theater on January 10, and many of the defendants appeared on local and national television and radio broadcasts. In effect, the indictments gave Spock and Coffin, especially, a more prominent platform from which to state their views of the war and President Johnson.

The letters collected in this section reflect the range of citizen responses to the indictments. Some writers were outraged that a respectable figure such as Spock would be assaulted in this way by the government, or that the government now found it acceptable to trample his free speech rights (and, presumably, that of others), while others rejoiced at the government's response; for them, Spock and the others were certainly guilty of disloyalty, if not treason.

It is worth noting that in the fall of 1967, the Johnson administration had launched a public relations campaign in response to the major antiwar demonstrations in Washington and elsewhere. General William Westmoreland, commander of American forces in Vietnam, returned to tell the public that American forces were making tremendous progress and that victory was assured. The resulting image of an administration in control was furthered by the indictments of Spock and the others. But as the arraignment date approached in late January, two events in Asia shook the administration's carefully crafted image. First, on January 23,

North Korea seized the U.S.S. *Pueblo*, an intelligence-gathering ship, and accused the United States of espionage; it ultimately held the ship for 11 months, releasing it only after the United States formally apologized. Second, on January 30 and 31, during Tet, the Vietnamese Lunar New Year, North Vietnamese and Viet Cong forces violated the customary holiday cease-fire by launching a coordinated attack on dozens of targets throughout South Vietnam. Americans saw images of guerrillas engaged in an extended firefight with American forces within the U.S. Embassy compound in Saigon, and they saw bodies. Although the Americans later put down the offensive, coming as it did the day after the Spock arraignment, the difference of interpretations—between the administration and its critics—could not have been more stark. The president's credibility suffered an irreparable blow.

Thus, the following letters show that as the war intensified, and the government responded to dissenters, ordinary Americans did not stand silent. Their responses, varied as they were, reflect the social and political climate of that turbulent month. Spock received letters, in roughly equal proportion, on three themes: concern about the rule of law, concern about Spock's influence on young people, and purely personal attacks against him.

118. Rather than be intimidated by the actions against you, I have enlisted in the "Army of Dissent."

1) 6) 68
[place of origin unknown]

Dear Dr. Spock,

This letter is addressed to you but is also a message of support and admiration for the other four beautiful gentle-men and for the countless others who remain anonymous. Before having read the statement attributed to you that you would welcome, aid, and abet thousands of draft-age youths, I was moved to write you of my feelings. In order to do this in a manner that would preserve and perpetuate my integrity and, at the same time, impress upon you a most profound admiration, I wrote to those concerned and accompanied the letter with my draft-card. Your statement(s) and action(s) served not only to re-inforce a position and action that I have been reluctant to pursue but made it imperative that I and others continually and relentlessly confront the "machinery" of the country. Rather than be intimidated by the actions against you, I have enlisted in the "Army of Dissent." You are, in great measure, through the charismatic aura of your essence—responsible for my decision.

Strength and Courage in the pursuance of your noble and beautiful stand!

P.S. Perhaps more meaningful than my words of support and admiration is the action I took (+ will continue to take). Enclosed is a copy of the letter sent to Hershey (along with my draft-card). Incidentally, I am 30 and have been classified a "safe" 1-Y.

J. U. [male]

119. We have long been disgusted at the arrogance and unAmerican attitude of you and your associates, and are glad to hear that, at long last, there has been a government crackdown!

New York 21, N. Y.
January 6th 1968

My dear Dr. Spock:

I am writing as the spokesman for a large group of individuals. We have varied backgrounds—some are young,—some old,—but all are Americans!

We have long been disgusted at the arrogance and unAmerican attitude of you and your associates, and are glad to hear that, at long last, there has been a government crackdown! We hope that you will receive, and serve, the maximum sentence!

We certainly believe in freedom of opinion, and speech,—but we do not, for one moment, condone the insolence and danger of taking the law into one's own hands! It is one of the great troubles of our Country! If you decide you can stop War by the method you have pursued, then, you, as anyone else, can do as he pleases about all laws! I could mention a long list which, if disregarded, would bring chaos to our Country! Perhaps a considerable period of confinement will give you the opportunity to meditate on your mistakes! We sincerely hope so!

I happen to be older than yourself—I'm 79,—and a life of much experience has shown me that no one can seek to mold either another person,—or the government, by means of his own sense of what is right or wrong! I happen to feel that we do belong in Vietnam, but that the War has been pitifully mishandled! If you are so deeply concerned about ending the war, why do you use such antics? It only shows the world and North Viet Nam that we are not [illegible], and, as I hear from many heroic, self-sacrificing Service men, it is thoroughly disgusting to them! We suggest that you stick to baby-doctoring! Though, already, many mothers tell us that they will never touch one of your books again!

    Very truly yours,

    W. S. [male]

120. I deplore civil disobedience, but if you go to prison, so will I.

7 Jan 68

Dear Dr. Spock,

    Please add my name to any pledge to counsel, aid, + abet conscientious draft resisters. My late father [name deleted] was your classmate. Mum is raising cattle in Arizona + admires your example even more than I. I left active duty last year to work for the American Independent Movement, 6th District, where I'm a registered Republican. I deplore civil disobedience, but if you go to prison, so will I.

    Sincerely,

    B. M., Capt. USMCR [male]

    [town unknown], Conn.

121. We both are concerned about our responsibilities as members of this culture as to what form the expressions of our beliefs should take.

January 8, 1968

Dear Dr. Spock,

    I am a twenty two year old wife and student. My husband is at present teaching school but hopes to return to graduate school in psychology. We have therefore, a direct and personal interest in the present draft laws. My husband's problem involves more than the inconvenience of serving in the military while he should be preparing for a vocation. The heart of the problem is that he believes that the military objectives of our country are morally wrong. The problem is compounded by the fact that he is constantly unsure whether or not he will be drafted and whether or not he will be asked to participate in the Viet Nam war. Neither of us is a member of any group pro or con, nor have either of us participated in any demonstrations against the war. We both are concerned about our responsibilities as members of this culture as to what form the expressions of our beliefs should take. We have taken much vicarious pleasure from your expression of our beliefs and from that of other men who like yourself have taken an open stand against what we feel is a gross error on the part of our country. We could not ask for a better representative than yourself, and we hope and believe that we are among many who appreciate your stance in this affair.

In addition to thanking you, we want you to know that we are following the course of your legal fate with great interest and sympathy. We are appalled at the legal action which has brought about your indictment. The principles are horrifyingly clear. Though this is not the first time our country has resorted to expedience as opposed to wisdom, we believe we are in a period national tension which presents a greater threat than ever to the integrity of the individual. We don't know what our part should be.

. . . but we are thankful for yours.

We wish you every possible comfort.

    Sincerely,
    A. M. [female]
    Memphis, Tennessee

123. Its Bastards like you that help the enemy and prolong the war.

[undated]

So you think teaching these draft dogers to escape the draft is not against the law you must be a moron I hope you get 20 years Its Bastards like you that help the enemy and prolong the war.

You are a no good bastard an S. O. B.

    [unsigned]

124. We have one son who fled to another land when his claims to being a conscientious objector were rejected. . . . He felt that his imprisonment would accomplish little since he is unknown.

San Clemente, California
January 11, 1968

Dear Dr. Spock:

It has been a real inspiration to my wife and me to follow the accounts of your courageous confrontations with those in our country who have already led us so far down the disastrous road of militarism. I believe that, in addition to those who have dared to speak out, there are other silent millions who feel as you do. Now that the government is attempting to crack down on you and others, it is my hope that there may be a backfire which may force our national leaders to turn from the insane and inhumane course they have been charting in Viet-Nam.

Keep up the good work. It must have been tempting to take advantage of your well earned chance to retire and enjoy the rest of your life in ease. But I suspect that you are enjoying this opportunity to be of genuine service far more than you would have a life of pleasure-seeking!

We have one son who fled to another land when his claims to being a conscientious objector were rejected. He is teaching in a university and his talents are lost to our country. He felt that his imprisonment would accomplish little since he is unknown. But persecution of you, a national figure, may result in much good if it helps to arouse more of our people to the dangerous and tragic course America has been taking.

Sincerely,

R. W. [male]

125. Do you mean to say that a person's "conscience", no matter what it tells a person to do, is excuse enough for any action?

Groton, Conn.

January 28, 1968

Dear Dr. Spock:

Your answers and those of Mr. Coffin were so full of errors, when given on the Meet the Press program, that it is almost hopeless to try to cope with them. First, in comparing the Korean War, which you did not condemn, you claimed that the North Koreans invaded the south, while the North Vietnams did not invade South Vietnam. I don't know where you have been, to make such a statement, as it is incorrect. Also, you spoke of those fleeing south now as victims of our bombings. Have you forgotten, or did you never hear, of Dr. Dooley[7] and his hospital, and his reason for having that hospital? It was because of the horrible brutality of Communist North Vietnam, that Dr. Dooley tried to aleviate the suffering. But most vulnerable of all, is your argument about "conscience." Do you mean to say that a person's "conscience", no matter what it tells a person to do, is excuse enough for any action? I have read of someone killing another person, because his "conscience" told him to rid the world of an evil person. Also, a Christian Scientist mother, who allowed her child to die without medical attention which might have saved her life, was found guilty in the courts. Yet she was sincere in using her "conscience" as an excuse for what she did. Chaplain Coffin has been giving definite aid and especially comfort, to an enemy which is killing our boys, and that is an act of treason, according to the Constitution. Also, one of you said that the Constitution guaranteed the right to one's "conscience". It does not. It merely says that freedom of speech is guaranteed, an entirely diff. thing. You had freedom of speech on that program, didn't you? No one interferred with it. But when your "conscience" told you to break our laws, even when you are ready and willing to take the consequences, it does not give you the "right" to do so. Who is to decide when your conscience is right, and the other person's is wrong? Dr. Luther King brought forth the same awful argument, when he said he had a moral right to break a law that he thought was wrong. I might think a law forbidding me to enter my neighbor's house against his will is wrong, but would that entitle me to break down the door? Such a silly argument you gave.

I know only too well that you, in your early books, advocated permissiveness, and we have been reaping the evils of that teaching for a generation. Those youngsters who are breaking the law now could well be the children who would never obey their parents, who recognized no rules or laws in the home, and were never made to do so. The students who lied down in halls and in front of troop trains could well be the tantrum, kicking and screaming children who got what they wanted by yelling for it, a la Spock. . . .

Yours truly,

Mrs. B. W.

All my ancestors were Quakers, and my grandfather refused to fight in the Civil War. He was wrong, so very wrong, just as you are, I firmly believe. How much study have you ever given to history? How much study have you ever given to Communism + its aims?

126. There have always been wars, a grisly manifestation of the fact that the human race is in its infancy and will not live to grow up.

1/29/68

"Gentlemen":

As an exercise in futility this letter probably is an all-time star.

There are only 2 possible conclusions: 1. You are in the pay of the communists. 2. You don't know what you are doing.

If (1), you know very well what you are doing, and you are succeeding admirably, and your sponsors must be no end pleased with you.

If (2), the facts of the situation are available to you from reputable people who are in a position to know, and you are not even going to read, much less heed, the remarks of an anonymous housewife.

So for my own benefit I write down the obvious and marvel anew that you can ignore all this and call yourselves "Patriots".

For one thing, the only young men you are going to rally to your cause are those who already the weak sisters: the Hippies, the Rapp Brown-Stokely Carmichael[8] city-burners, the communist fellow-travelers, the cowards. Young men like my four sons and their friends, working their way through college as teachers, potential writers, musicians, nuclear physicists, mathematicians, are enlisting as soon as they have their degrees. They study the war and read about it and discuss it among themselves. They are a bit sad about Ed, who "used to be a good baseball player," but who now walks with a slouch, has been turned down by the Peace Corps, flunked a couple of courses, drinks too much, uses pot, and is shacked up with first one girl and then another. He is carrying placards of protest, and appears here and there in full beard handing out propaganda. Even he is not going to try to evade the draft, because when it comes right down to lining up on the side of Castro and the Kremlin against the United States he won't be able to go through with it.

There have always been wars, a grisly manifestation of the fact that the human race is in its infancy and will not live to grow up. Wars solve nothing, are so incredibly senseless that the rational mind cannot dwell upon them, and each one surely sets the stage for the next. This one is no more nor less stupid than the last.

If you have studied the anthropology of religion or related subjects you will know that it is natural for violence and non-violence to exist in the same cultural unit, non-violence as a way of life within the group, violence as a normal reaction when the group is attacked. So how do we know we have been attacked? Nobody comes to our door and shoots at us, we read in the newspaper that the Japanese have bombed Pearl Harbor, or the Kremlin announces it is going to create little Viet-Nams all over the globe for the purpose of involving, discrediting, and eventually destroying the United States and its system of <u>earned</u> individual privileges.

So we have been attacked, our leaders who know about these things tell us. And we have no personal sure knowledge that it is so, but all except the lunatic fringe which is always with us, have never had any doubts about what has to be done. There is no choice. Nobody knows what it is all about, nobody wants to go, but you go, or you are a traitor.

If, instead of trying to work through these poor disoriented slobs who follow such unwholesome types as Norman Mailer et al., destroying property, defiling the Pentagon, so infiltrated with joyous communists taking advantage of their confusion that they no longer know where they stand, you would bend your efforts to outlaw war forever as a means of settling differences, you could make a real contribution to all of humanity.

One of the most horrible things that your ugly little groups are doing is making a miserable situation for the men who have obeyed the law of the land and gone to fight their country's battle, as they have been led to believe is right. Instead of being treated as heroes who have done their duty, these men and their families are subjected to harassment by your good buddies.

Anyone you attract with your "sanctuary"[9] would have been a traitor anyhow, and of no use to the war effort. Except for the misery you manage to inflict on loyal Americans and their families, and the contribution you make to the delinquency of the already delinquent, I doubt that you will do much harm to the United States or its President, or whoever your target may be.

It would clear the air nicely if you could all go to Russia or Egypt or North Viet Nam or Red China where your heart lies, and let the rest of the country be on about its business, but of course they would never consent to that because you are of use to them only if you are here furthering their cause.

Very truly yours,
Mrs. D. G.
Kalamazoo, Mich

5 Shock Waves: The Aftermath of Tet and the Ordeal at Home, February–May 1968

IN THE first six months of 1968, America seemed to be coming apart at the seams. Following the Spock indictments and the Tet Offensive, the Johnson administration again found itself on the defensive. More and more reporters used the term "credibility gap" to describe official predictions of success versus the glaring reality of an enemy who seemed energized. In a matter of weeks, the president nearly suffered defeat at the hands of peace candidate Senator Eugene McCarthy in New Hampshire's Democratic primary, and then saw another Democratic rival, Senator Robert Kennedy, declare his candidacy for president. On March 31, Johnson beat his first retreat, announced a bombing curb (to bring the North Vietnamese to the negotiating table), and perhaps more important, that he would not accept the Democratic nomination for reelection as president.

Four days later, an assassin murdered Martin Luther King, Jr., who, by the time of his death, had become identified for his criticism of the Vietnam War almost as much as for his campaigns for racial justice. As April progressed, students at Columbia University shut down their campus in protest of the school's defense research connections and plans to dislocate minorities living around the school in order to build a gymnasium; when New York police brutalized many students in an attempted crackdown, most of the student body joined the strikers. By the end of May, student strikes shocked governments around the world, leading many American young people to believe in a worldwide youth revolution. In France, student protests expanded into a general strike that nearly toppled the republic.

As a result, in the United States, as the May trial of Dr. Spock approached, many Americans felt the country had come off its hinges,

A young woman in Pittsburgh, Pennsylvania, speaks for many of her generation in supporting Dr. Spock following his arraignment on conspiracy charges in Boston, January 1968. (Bettmann/CORBIS)

the world off its axis. The letters in this chapter, written from February to May 1968, reflect this near-apocalyptic atmosphere.

I. "Now It Is All Destroyed by the War"

MANY OF the following letters, even in expressing solidarity with Spock and the peace movement, reveal a new level of desperation. Although public support for the war dropped to new lows following the Tet Offensive, little optimism comes out in these letters. Instead, most writers express frustration over their inability to stop the war. They feel dismissed, ignored, and write to Spock, it seems, as a way to make themselves feel better or to seek advice from a man who seemed always to radiate optimism as he challenged the government. To one who felt impotent, Spock, soon to be tried for conspiracy, stood out as an inspiration, someone at least effective enough to merit prosecution by the same government running the war. For his part, Spock continued to publicly relish the prospect of being tried in court as an opportunity to turn the tables and put the war and the Johnson administration on trial.

127. With your help, my husband and I raised 3 beautiful sons—one of whom is now fighting in Viet Nam—and like you, I am wondering if I tried to give them a good body and a good mind only to be sent off to senseless brutal war.

Feb. 5, 1968

Dear Dr. Spock,

Please let me take a moment of your time to tell you how very much I am with you. With your help, my husband and I raised 3 beautiful sons —one of whom is now fighting in Viet Nam—and like you, I am wondering if I tried to give them a good body and a good mind only to be sent off to senseless brutal war. Be assured of our great admiration for you, believe me—you speak for me as I could never speak for myself. . . .

Sincerely,
Mrs. A. B.
Leavenworth, Kansas

P.S. I now have 3 little grandchildren and the old dog-eared book is still holding up!

128. People say I am "asinine" for not agreeing when they say we must stop communism at all costs. Some call me "insane" for saying that the war in Viet Nam is immoral and useless.

South Bend, Ind.

February 9, 1968

Dear Dr. Spock,

I am a sixteen year old girl and because of my age few "important" people feel they have to listen to me and other members of my generation who share my feelings. They will, though—Someday.

I am accused of being "naive" because I don't think we are just in risking holocaust by being in Viet Nam. I am called "foolish" because I don't believe that American democracy is perfect and communism is completely immoral and wrong. People say I am "asinine" for not agreeing when they say we must stop communism at all costs. Some call me "insane" for saying that the war in Viet Nam is immoral and useless. I don't praise napalm and because of this I am called "idiotic" not to recognize its necessity. Being an objector to the war makes me "too idealistic."

. . . It is hard to be in the minority. I felt I had to write to you to thank you for speaking out for what you believe. Sometimes I feel that everything I do is useless. All the marches and demonstrations, all the letters to Congressmen and Senators are futile. But I believe in what I'm doing. I cannot give up. I <u>am</u> idealistic. I believe in humanity.

I am not as eloquent as I wish but I hope you understand. I want you to know how grateful I am because you are an inspiration to me and to so many others. I am in a sense "a Dr. Spock baby" (that's a quote from my parents!) and I am proud to say that I sincerely think you are one of God's most beautiful people.

Best wishes,

L. L. [female]

129. We of Alpha Company want to help your organizations work for a SANE foreign policy.

Saturday February 17, 1968

Dear Dr. Spock:

We of Alpha Company want to help your organizations work for a

SANE foreign policy and a just and durable peace in Vietnam + through-out the world. Our contribution of $10.00 is enclosed.

> [Signed by 14 members of Alpha company;
> Battalion, Infantry and Brigade identifiers deleted;
> stationed in Vietnam]

130. My husband + I were at a dinner party last evening. As usual we talked of the war and our inability to do something. As my husband said —"we are all good Germans."

Feb. 19, 1968

Dear Dr. Spock,

We are concerned. We are afraid for the future of our children and for the future of our country. We feel so helpless. We see influential men ignored. We don't like being ashamed of our country. We deplore this horrible waste of lives. Our son is eight. He worries about the war and said he would go to Canada. I would help him.

We dread the elections because our vote will not elect anyone to help us get out of this war. We don't trust our leaders. We don't trust our President.

Must we stubbornly keep on killing Vietnam civilians, soldiers and our own young men?

My husband + I were at a dinner party last evening. As usual we talked of the war and our inability to do something. As my husband said —"we are all good Germans."

Please advise us, what can we do?

> Sincerely,
> Mrs. J. C.
> Lawrence, Kansas

131. I experience tremendous guilt for the many Vietnamese and U.S. soldiers who have died in my name.

Skokie, Illinois
March 31, 1968

My dear Dr. Spock:

Allow me first to congratulate you on your forthright and noble stand against our government's policy in Viet Nam. It is a pleasure to see someone who thinks enough about a cause to speak out for his position, regardless of the consequences to his personal life.

I, like many concerned Americans, am frustrated and enraged that I cannot stand up and be counted against the war and that even if this were so, my voice would be insignificant. I, like many Americans, feel disillusioned that there seems nothing I can do, and horrored that every day the war drags on I am responsible for innumerable inhumanities. I experience tremendous guilt for the many Vietnamese and U.S. soldiers who have died in my name. And the many civilians and North Vietnamese killed in the name of my protection!

I greatly admire and appreciate the work you have done in this cause but I have a further suggestion: cannot myself and other citizens pool their resources and produce a documentary television show which will present to the American public the true story of what has been going on in Viet Nam and that which is occurring today? I firmly believe that if most people were confronted with a basic history of that nation, they would change their views on the war. The nature of the French Colonial Regime, Ho Chi Minh's role as a nationalist, the Geneva Accords, the U.S. support and installation of Ngo Dinh Diem, the many suppressive military dictatorships, and the attitude of the U.S. soldier in Viet Nam are a few of the topics I would present to viewers. Presented with these, perhaps more people would commit themselves to protest now, and choose a peace candidate for president, hopefully Eugene McCarthy.

If there is anything I can do to become actively involved in the peace movement, please notify me. Since I am a medical student, my time is limited—but my desire and sincere concern is not. Remaining your admirer, I am

Sincerely yours,

H. F. [male]

132. Last night when the President announced he would not seek another term, I thought about the people like you.

Fowler Ohio
Apr 1 - 1968

Dear Dr. Spock

Congratulations!

Last night when the President announced he would not seek another term, I thought about the people like you, who have had the courage to stand up for the right, in spite of threats and intimidation.

I'm sure it was such pressure that influenced the President to take the action. So you deserve a lot of credit for it.

Again, congratulations.

M. L. [male]

133. You are also right about women caring most about the effects of war.

Quincy, Ill.
May 16, 1968

Dear Dr. Spock:

You could not hear my applause the other afternoon when you were on TV—and the audience seemed to be on the other side.

I clapped for you. I used your books for my children—now 11, 12, 14, all boys. Wore one out completely.

I now support your brave stand. It takes such courage.

Thank you for speaking out against the myths of Vietnam.

You are also right about women caring most about the effects of war.

I've spent years teaching my boys to consider animals their fellow creatures on earth—and to treat them accordingly. And now about ecology and how to protect earth and its functions which keep us all. Now it is all destroyed by the war. I do not know yet what I will do when they are draft age. Keep your stand.

Sincerely,
Mrs. M. R.

II. "The Wrath of the Communistic Whip"

THE FOLLOWING group of letters shows that the desperation on the part of those opposed to the war was matched in the spring of 1968 by those in support of it. As public support for the war slipped, it seems that these writers grew more incensed that their fellow citizens might be losing sight of the "savage" nature of communism. There is a driving "don't you realize" tone to the letters, as one after another predicts (sometimes in graphic language) the "slaughter" to come if the United States were to withdraw from Vietnam—an option more openly discussed than ever before. By extension, the implication is that the barbaric communists would eventually visit their slaughter on the United States. Given such stakes, at least one letter extends the familiar charge of Spock's responsibility for raising a generation of spoiled children and effectively crediting him with doing more damage to the republic than Soviet spies could do. And in spite of coming at the end of a decade that saw tremendous progress in civil rights thanks largely to massive civil disobedience, one letter also questions its legitimacy—a point of view that would have found considerable support among many Americans weary of constant conflict between citizens and their government.

134. If we "leave Vietnam to the Vietnamese" in order that they may "settle their own problems" these press reports leave no doubt as to how they will settle them.

5 February 1968

Dear Dr. Spock:

I am enclosing these recent press clippings for your reading pleasure, in case you have been too busy peacenicking or floundering in jail to read the newspapers.

I regret that I have mislaid another clipping I had intended to send. It depicted a grief-stricken South Vietnamese officer carrying his dead child, one of six butchered in an act of reprisal by the Viet Cong. Not a very pleasant picture, I am sure, to a man who has devoted most of his life to preventing the deaths of little children.

I just thought you would like to be kept up to date on what your friends are doing.

You have established yourself as the No. 1 protester in America. Why then, do you never protest atrocities like these? We can rest assured there will be no hippie parades to protest the murder of the little girl in my lost picture.

If we "leave Vietnam to the Vietnamese" in order that they may "settle their own problems" these press reports leave no doubt as to how they will settle them. For us to thus abandon innocent Vietnamese peasants to the Viet Cong savages would be not only cowardly and immoral, it would be lousy preventive pediatrics.

You seem to advocate that we "turn the other cheek" in Vietnam. What you really advocate is that we turn the cheeks of innocent peasants to these barbarians, in order that Spock's cheek will remain safe.

We have recently been blessed with our first child, a son now aged four months. I intend to do the best I can to instill in him the qualities of honor, courage, and love of country as he grows up. To this end, I have burned our copy of your paperback book on child rearing.

Giving aid and comfort to the enemies of the United States is the definition of treason. This makes you a traitor of the first rank. Patriotic Americans, and that includes most physicians, are thoroughly disgusted by your recent antics.

I sincerely hope that your coming jail term will be a long one.

Disgustedly yours,
J. W., Jr., MD [male]
Oakland, California

135. You and your "book" have set this country up to be full of lawless young people that are so easily led by the communists.

[undated]

Dear Mr. Spock,

I want to congratulate you on the outstanding job you have been doing.

You started it back in the late 30's or early 40's and it is really bearing fruit.

When you wrote your baby book on not telling a child no or not to correct them but to let them have their way, you started the ball rolling to really set things up for today.

You may consider yourself a "Patriot" but not of the U.S.A. for you have proven yourself one of the greatest enemies this country has ever had the misfortune of having.

You and your "book" have set this country up to be full of lawless young people that are so easily led by the communists.

Not being punished when young—not being told—No—and all has given these young people a feeling of no respect for their parents or anything or anyone that is connected with the law.

If a child is not punished when it is needed and told no sometimes, they feel that they are not loved nor wanted.

You have done more in this country to hurt this great nation than all the spies that Russia, Japan or any other country could possibly send in.

In God's word—we are told to punish our children if they do wrong—we are also told to obey the laws of our country.

You are undoubtedly not a Christian and I truly feel sorry for you.

God is a God of Love, and teaches that there must be love, trust, respect, and obedience, and you have broken this all down over a period of 25 to 30 years.

Look back if you have any doubts,—But I cannot help but believe now that you know what would happen when you wrote the book, and that you did it with a different plan in mind.

I am not by myself in the way I believe. There are many, many more that are looking back and seeing when it all started.

The thing is also this—that you are heading for Hell and taking lots of others with you with your ideas, and also seem to be striving for a complete down-fall of our country in the process.

May God have mercy on you. Praying for you.

Mrs. O. S.

Ventura, Calif.

136. If we don't begin today and this very minute, the whole world will one day feel that wrath of the Communistic whip.

Stow, Ohio

February 13, 1968

Doctor Spock:

In abated breath, you advocate Anarchy; and yet you feel that what you are doing is correct? Do you really believe, if AMERICA should pull their forces out of Viet Nam or any where in the world, that this war would end? While you Doctor Spock and others like you SLEEP—the Communists have and are still making conquests all over the world. As of today there are at least forty-four nations under the hammer and sickle.

The courts have ruled that we cannot so much as say Amen in schools yet some one such as yourself invite retaliation from the young people. To me this is nothing short of Anarchy. It is about time that the world took inventory into how the Communist system works. It is also about time we block what the Communist countries are attempting. If we don't begin today and this very minute, the whole world will one day feel that wrath of the Communistic whip.

If you are so disenchanted with our way of life, at least do the honest thing and disengage yourself from the publics eye.

Russia reaches out to you, go there or even Hanoii. Do what you are doing here in front of this government. Try it. Since you have made demands back here, go there and ask these countries to stop infiltrating into Viet Nam also. Isn't North Viet Nam fighting and killing and performing atrocities?

Why do you persist in pointing your ugly finger, just at America. AWAKE from your deep dream of sleep. If you would read more of the Communistic system you would have less time sowing seeds of hatred and discontent. PLEASE READ THE BOOK, "ROAD TO REVOLUTION".

Yours Truly,
Mrs. G. D.

[EDITOR'S NOTE: Spock replied: "I don't believe that communist nations are harmless or that we can let down our guard. But in S. Vietnam it is the U.S. not N. Vietnam or China which is the aggressor. Our aggression is no better than Communist aggression."]

137. Have you read the late Dr. Tom Dooley's "Deliver Us From Evil" or "The Road to Revolution" or An Evil Tree, or even J. Edgar Hoover's various articles on Communism?

Clinton, Ohio

Dr. B. J. Spock:

For months now your criticisms of our Vietnam policy has rankled me to no end. I have refrained from expressing personal opposition being ever hopeful you would learn the error of your opinion and desist but your recent speeches to the College youth advocating draft-dodging is more than I can bear.

You remind me of someone who on coming upon a 12 year-old bullying a 5 year-old, lambasts the 5 year-old and lectures him on why he should not be fighting, to the exclusion of the true bully.

Communism is bullying people everywhere—Vietnam one place in point.

How a man of your education and supposed concern for people can be so naive as to think that by withdrawal of our boys in Vietnam and by military stoppage we will have peace is beyond me. There is an insidious threatening menace unleashed in the world today.

Have you read the late Dr. Tom Dooley's "Deliver Us From Evil" or "The Road to Revolution" or An Evil Tree, or even J. Edgar Hoover's various articles on Communism?

Yes, perhaps this is the reason for your stand. You have been totally misinformed or kept completely ignorant as to who is actually perpetrating wrongs. Or is it that in your years of working with infants you have become so mentally infantile that you are having difficulty discerning the truth? . . .

Read what has happened and is happening to the many churches in communist controlled countries—to missionaries, to teachers + children —ones who would be the least of all to want to use arms to fight.

They've been subjected to atrocities, been mutilated, murdered by the very ones ravaging the South-East—the Viet Cong who are overrunning South Vietnam. They've already ravaged the North—I'm not speaking of the true Vietnamese, but of the infiltrators, trained in causing revolutions and tactical guerrilla warfare. If you are as intelligent as you profess by trying to project this image to the American youth, then take my suggestion and get yourself re-educated.

Hopefully,
Mrs. A. S.

138. Here are my arguments against your position: 1) <u>You do not have the right to break the law</u>. . . . . 2) <u>We are at war with communism</u>, whether we like it or not.

3-2-68

Dear Doctor Spock:

We were very disappointed to learn of your taking part in the "peace" demonstrations. As young parents of 5 children, we are well acquainted with your book on child care, and have come to (and still do) respect your authority on this subject.

As you have guessed, I do support our position on Viet Nam. You must get a lot of mail these days, but I do hope you will take the time to personally read and answer this letter, and weigh my arguments.

I have read your story in several publications. I think I understand why you feel as you do. You have a lot of courage. However, here are my arguments against your position:

1) <u>You do not have the right to break the law</u>. By participating in "civil disobedience," you have shown a serious irresponsibility; a self-centered attitude. These laws were made of the people. There are due processes for changing them. This is still a free society. By violating our laws, you have demonstrated distain for our country, our people, and our democratic processes. Can you see that you have tried to elevate

yourself above us? In all seriousness, what now distinguishes you from a common criminal? Laws are set up for our common good. They make possible an atmosphere of freedom from fear and oppression, in which we can work, live, and raise our families. What if the citizens who have not the high standards of conscience that you have now all decide to break the laws which they don't agree? What if they begin to interpret each law for themselves? The result would be anarchy, a system by which the strong does what it will, and the weak submit or suffer the consequences. The law is not perfect. It never was and it isn't supposed to be, but it reflects the best that our society can do. Now here you are, trying to break it down. No, Doctor. You are not above the law. You have the right to disagree, to try to change it by due process, but not the right to trample on it. What else but the law stands between us and savagery? You don't happen to be a supreme authority. You do not happen to have the right to impose your interpretation of the law—on your own will and conscience—upon us, the American people.

2) We are at war with communism, whether we like it or not. We have no choice. They declared war; a world war; on us years ago. To this day they have not changed their ideas or their intent in regard to this. They are not content to coexist, according to their own doctrine. They intend to impose their form of government on all peoples sooner or later, and therefore we must defend ourselves or submit to them. We should have started defending ourselves sooner, and now at last we are taking a stand in Viet Nam. It is far from being the best place to take a stand, thanks to the shortsightedness of our administrations added to their being outsmarted and outmaneuvered. But it is better than taking no stand at all. Where would you rather try to hold off a determined enemy —in the Tonkin Gulf or in Puget Sound? I happen to live near Puget Sound, and I guess you know my answer.

Do you disagree with my contention that the communists are out to destroy us? Believe me, I didn't decide this of myself. I simply read the writings of the communists themselves, wherein they outline their ideology, their aims, goals, and methods of operation. It astounded me to learn the meticulousness with which they plan, even down to anticipating our moves and how to counter them. More astounding was the exactness with which they follow up their plan with action. Their plans worked almost perfectly in country after country which have fallen to them. Our stand in Viet Nam is one of the few things on which they had not counted on to happen. That is why they are so distressed by our presence there. One more thought; the plan they have does not call for communists to do the work—only the planning. As Lenin put it, "communism must be built with non-communist hands." They are doing exactly that now, Doctor.

We have only two choices; resist or submit. When we face an advancing enemy such as this, our choice is limited. Yes, we are at war, whether we realize it or not. For my part, I would choose to resist. I value my free agency and that of my children. You probably are wondering how serious I am. Well, let me tell you that if I am called again, I would go willingly to fight them in Viet Nam or anywhere else. And although I cherish and love my four sons more than I can say, if the time came, I would send them to war. This I would do even knowing I may never get them back alive. It just happens that some things are more important than life. Freedom, for one. Nathan Hale said it better than I ever could.

> T. S. [male]
> Seattle, Wash

[EDITOR's NOTE: Spock had spent much of his life's leisure time on sailboats, and even at the height of his political activism, he usually took a month each summer to sail in the Virgin Islands. In late winter 1968, Spock had arranged to have a new boat shipped from Brooklyn, New York, by freighter to the islands. But when the Brooklyn longshoremen discovered that the boat belonged to Spock, they refused to load it on the ship. Spock eventually had to truck it to South Carolina and then hire a crew to sail it to the Caribbean. This event in part inspired the next letter.]

139. We have thousands of our boys over there trying to do a job. Why not give them the backing they need to finish up the job and come home.

March 10, 1968

To Dr. Spock—

Hooray for the dock workers!! There really had not been much good news lately, but that refusal to load your ketch was a marvelous item, and I hope it gave you an inkling of what some folks think.

Naturally you have a right to your own opinion, but in my book you are a traitor to your country, and are publicly disgracing yourself when you lead a mob of long-haired, immature kids to defy their country's laws and burn draft cards. A man of your age is old enough to have more sense. I heard you on the radio a while back and you sounded as if you'd gone into your second childhood.

It's folks like you and also the legislators who bicker in Washington who are aiding and abetting the enemy and prolonging this miserable war. Hanoi is never going to agree to negotiate so long as misguided souls like you are encouraging them by keeping things stirred up here. We have thousands of our boys over there trying to do a job. Why not give them the backing they need to finish up the job and come home. If we pulled out of Vietnam now there would be a most unmerciful slaughter of innocent people and the Communists would take over Cambodia, Thialand, etc. But I gathered from your radio answers that you think Communism is OK.

You and your ilk rave about freedom, but don't you realize that if the folks you are helping came into power you would have no freedom whatever. Those are the folks who are summarily executing anyone who disagrees with the established order, and who build walls and barbed wire entanglements to keep folks in, and shoot those who try to escape.

There are entirely too many young men in this day who have never had to shoulder any responsibility because Mother went out to work to give them every advantage. They've never had to be responsible for anything and they are not about to start now. They blame their parents for getting the world into such a state and they're weak-minded enough to think all they should have to do is grow long hair, strum a guitar and carry a sign in just about any kind of a protest parade. People like you, instead of encouraging that, should be turning them to do something constructive.

Never before have I written a letter I didn't sign, but I'm not signing this because I don't trust a Communist across the country or across the world. I'm not a Bircher, but there could be some Commies around here.

Signed,

Just an Old Square.

III. "What Can We Do?" Some Questions and Answers

DESPERATION OVER the state of the war is again a key impetus for the next group of letters, but instead of writing of their frustration at the antiwar movement's ineffectiveness or pleading in support of the war

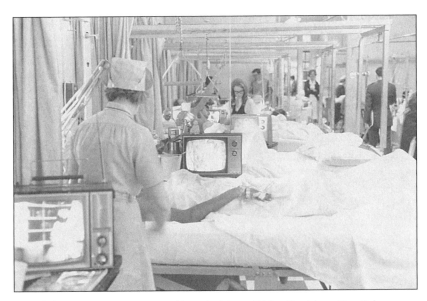

Wounded American servicemen watching television at Walter Reed Army Hospital, Bethesda, Maryland. From the start of the war, images like this one (taken in 1970) stirred public debate over the war. (U.S. News & World Report, Library of Congress)

effort, these writers contacted Spock either with suggestions for the peace movement (or the country as a whole), or seeking advice or assistance. Most interesting is that Spock received one letter from parents hoping to keep their children out of Vietnam, another from a war resister who wanted to go to Vietnam for humanitarian purposes, and yet another from an Army deserter and two from active duty servicemen. GI letters were much less common only a year before, but in the wake of Tet and the growing uncertainty over the future course of the war, it makes sense that rank-and-file soldiers—in this case, draftees—would be interested in speaking to Spock.

140. Anti-war efforts have not reached the mass public and have done little to help people accept the <u>idea</u> of withdrawal.

Durham, New Hampshire
5 February 1968

Dear Dr. Spock:
  Would you be willing to sponsor a new conference of leaders to plan

the means by which the American public can be prepared for our withdrawal from Vietnam?

New plans are needed because the old ones have not worked. Anti-war efforts have not reached the mass public and have done little to help people accept the idea of withdrawal. Perhaps our limited effectiveness has been the result of poorly conceived strategy. Do you think a group of persons opposed to the war and skilled in the arts of persuasion might come up with some new ideas?

The kind of group I have in mind would be composed of leaders of the anti-war movement, business leaders (especially persons in advertising), labor leaders, church officials, and leaders in the professions (especially psychiatrists and psychologists). Drawing upon their special insights the members of this group would attempt to:

1. Formulate the ideas that would have to become generally held to make withdrawal rationally and emotionally acceptable.
2. Plan a many-sided campaign to bring these ideas to the public.
3. Conceive a way to raise a large sum of money to finance such a campaign.

If you think this idea has merit, would you please promote it?

Sincerely yours,

H. P. [male]

141. The real enemy is subtle and can not be discovered by street fights with city authorities.

Staten Island, N.Y.
February 6, 1968

Dear Doctor Spock:

The years have flown by since my last letters to you, but my thoughts have been as much with you lately as they were when my main concerns were travel with a two-year old, and invented games to keep a recuperating child quiet in bed. I have thought again about those long years of travel and the nights alone with a sick child when your book was all that stood between me and sheer panic. I have thought of the thousands of other mothers reading and re-reading your chapters, being comforted by your quieting tone, taking intelligent action because of your advice. And so I think how it is not at all strange, really, that you should be in your present position of trying to stop this useless, hideous war. It seemed strange at first, since you are a great doctor and neither a politician nor political organizer. You are, actually, a father to this generation of children. You have to a larger degree than any other individual, helped raise them up to healthy adulthood, and it is as it should be that you now work to allow them to live and to express that life and that health. Of what use—of what possible use, to have had both children and parents weather the storms of mumps, measles, ear infections, strep throats and nightmares if they are to be maimed physically and psychologically beyond repair by the constancy of war?

I look at my boy and his generation. They are tall, healthy, and their strong bodies and good teeth indicate early Vitamin drops, vaccinations, intelligent diet. Physically they are stronger than their parents, and they are brighter too. They seem to have had greater emotional problems, the roots of which lie in World War II, and the fathers who were never the same after their face to face experience with the unfathomable horror of war; mothers whose anxiety and fear never quite left them. But these children have done well with their emotional problems. They've had the Doctor Spocks who wrote about them and let in the light of understanding. They have lived in a generation which had the courage to look at its problems in daylight.

But here we are again. War, which all men know has never really solved anything. Young men's bodies and minds to be sacrificed again in living horror; young girls and young mothers reacting to speeded up emotions, anxiety and gnawing, everlasting fear. Thank you, then, for speaking up. Thank you for again being the protector of these children-turned-young-adults.

There are things which disturb me in their behavior, though. The enemy is not the New York policemen nor the Longshoremen. They just aren't the enemy. Nor are the people of big cities who patiently get to work on transportation systems where they are treated like animals, and patiently pay taxes and taxes. The boys, in their anger, must not turn on the wrong enemy, for do to so excites violence and violence always leads to some form of war. "Hatred ceases not with hatred," said the Buddha. To end war will take intelligence and quietness, and discovering the real enemy. Is it a nation which dares not leave a war economy? Is it power lust? Has it become true that if any country anywhere threatens to have a communist form of government we must declare war? Is it possible that our churches are still teaching that Buddhists are some sort of non-thinking, non-feeling heathens?

The real enemy is subtle and can not be discovered by street fights with city authorities. While I so deeply understand the overheated emotions of the boys and the justice of their stand, I also sense that they excite wrong emotions in their parents, their supporters, or their onlookers. It troubles me. The policemen, the longshoremen are also parents. The boys must remember that these men fought a war, and won it, and the price they paid was fantastic. Had the Germans or the Japs won a direct victory, there would have been no vitamin drops, no warm clothing, no fine schools, no mothers who could be concerned with reading Dr. Spock or who could have had time to create homes physically and psychologically intact: there would have been no orthodonture, no fine guitars, no prosperity, no diets of steak and lamb chops, no democratic form of government.

It is not, of course, that the fathers of this generation believe war to be the only answer, or that they regard their sons as weak. They, more than any other group, appreciate the uselessness and the disillusion of war. It's just that there is a fantastic difference between these young men standing tall and standing in dignity to declare themselves against war, or seeming to spit on the ideals, sacrifices and the personally gained good wich has resulted from their father's war.

As these young men stand, Doctor Spock, I pray they will succeed, but I also pray they will have the depth of awareness and gratitude to salute their fathers as they stand.

I remember that I ended my first letter to you, some sixteen years ago, with gratitude that you were there. Thank you again for being there. But more—for your courage, your belief that good triumphs, your belief translated into action, thank you, Doctor Spock, for being part of my world.

Sincerely,
H. I. [female]

142. I feel that many Americans support you as I do, but many remain silent because they fear government action may be taken against them.

21 Feb 1968

Sir,

I want you to know that I support you in your stand on Viet Nam. Please do not become discouraged. I feel that many Americans support you as I do, but many remain silent because they fear government action may be taken against them.

I would like to take a more active part in the peace movement. I would like to join an organization which will inform me of demonstrations planned for this summer.

I feel that decent is the constitutional right of every American. Please continue the struggle for freedom and world peace.

> Sincerely yours,
> B. K. [male]
> Anniston, Alabama

143. This war will not be won unless America turns to God—He is our only hope.

> March 1968
> Tampa, Florida

Dear Sir,

Thank you so much for your much belated reply to my letter concerning your veiws on Viet Nam on the Merv Griffin Show.

I might also say that I with many millions of others believe that it is right to fight against atheistic—Anti God—Anti Christ Communism.

You might have also mentioned among your prominent citizens and newspapers—the Daily Worker + other prominent "leaders" in our country who are of the communist ideology.

One of the reasons this war came about was that the communist government in the north prevented the huge flood of refugees to continue from the north into S. Viet Nam. They desired to get away from the "workers paradise". There were many other reasons such as active aggression against the south etc. but to me this is reason enough for our presence there.

As in all wars the civilian casualties are occuring, if the north had taken over, these would not be victims of the war but of torture, the firing squad etc.

Some how the fear of Red China + Red Russia does not shake me as I have faith in God, that he will deliver—but America must turn to Him in repentance. . . .

This war will not be won unless America turns to God—He is our only hope.

This war will be decided not on the battle field but by those of us who spend time on our knees before God in prayer, travail + supplication.

If you do not know Him in a personal + dynamic way then your thoughts, veiws + opinions could very easily be wrong + thru the influence that God has allowed you to have, you are leading others astray.

May God help you to know Him—to love Him that you might be the influence that He intended you to be.

Yours Sincerely In the Lord,
Mrs. P. S.

PS Concerning the opinion of the world + especially Europe, I have found that if you stand up for the right against sin, against immorality against that is to say against the forces of evil—communism, modernism, etc., you will stand alone.

Europe has not done so well for its self—+ Asia for its much longer existence than us, has done even worse, so why should we take advice + worry about what they think of us—they—these continents have been war like + some of them would not exist to-day if it had not been for the blessings that God has bestowed upon us + that we in turn shared with them.

144. I have no one else to turn to and I don't know anything about the Draft laws or the deferments—I'm only interested in saving my son.

March 4, 1968

Dear Dr. Spock,

You helped me raise my son from birth to twelve years and I never thought I'd turn to you again as he nears nineteen. I've raised my son alone, as I have no family, and I've raised him close to our church, so he is a good boy and I'm so proud of him. I've always felt that hard years and the times we had barely enough food, were well worth it as he is a fine boy. He's interested in the outdoors and wants to go into that field when he's out of school. His interest is in saving life and not taking it. The thought of killing makes him sick and the thought that he may be forced to do it is on his mind constantly.

He has had asthma and Hay Fever since he was fourteen and is on Copyronil, Teldrin, and amesec. He can't run but is fairly strong otherwise so my life has become a nightmare worrying that he might be forced into a war in which he might not be able to take care of himself in an emergency. I understand the Draft Boards are not considering asthma as a deferment anymore unless hospitalization is necessary, and it hasn't been in my son's case.

I hold down two jobs in order to keep him in U. S. F. and I pray to God that this terrible war will end.

I understand that you are opposed to this senseless killing of young boys and men so I ask you for any advice you can offer that may help me save my son's life.

Dr. Spock, I have no one else to turn to and I don't know anything about the Draft laws or the deferments—I'm only interested in saving my son. If he wanted to go then, of course, I'd accept his decision no matter how I felt, but when he tells me he doesn't think he could kill a human being to save himself, I don't know what to do. I wake up during the nights praying for help.

Please sir, help me save my son. Any advice you can offer will be gratefully accepted.

If this letter is a rambling one, please know that I'm trying to give you facts without taking too much of your time.

Very truly yours,

Mrs. D. S.

San Francisco, Calif

145. The purpose of this letter, then, is to ask you to send me information about possible avenues of entrance to Viet Nam.

Kansas City, Missouri

March 5, 1968

Dear Dr. Spock,

I understand why you have chosen the position you are in. I respect it. I, too, am of the conviction that America's war in Viet Nam is wrong and that war in general is nothing but futile. I also agree with Thoreau that every citizen is morally responsible for his country's wars.

I could absolve my share of the collective responsibility by protesting and by going to jail as you have done. But I am only one twenty-year-old college junior and my confinement, unlike yours, would be but a fruitless, anonymous gesture. I want my committment to be of some positive good. I feel that the effects of my standing up in this way would be only negative and extend only to myself and to my family.

After much prayer and much effort to escape my growing awareness of what people are and what we are doing to each other in Viet Nam, I am convinced that I, by virtue of my American advantages, have a personal responsibility to the people of that country to go there with peace and healing. I am fully aware of the seriousness of this decision.

The purpose of this letter, then, is to ask you to send me information about possible avenues of entrance to Viet Nam. I know there are peaceful American volunteers there now. I also know what the Red Cross is doing. This is all I know. Any information at all would be gratefully received.

> Sincerely yours,
> J. B. [female]

146. Recently, due to a series of unfortunate incidents, I, like many other young Americans, was forced into the ranks of 'Uncle Sam's chosen.'

3/28/68

Dear Dr. Spock,

Bearing in mind the fact that you seem to be at the head of a great deal of the peace movements in this country, I write to you for compassionate assistance.

Recently, due to a series of unfortunate incidents, I, like many other young Americans, was forced into the ranks of 'Uncle Sam's chosen.' However, because of my strong convictions of opposition on the subjects of: burning civilians, torture, and all the other niceties of war, I left Fort Gordon, Ga. four weeks ago for a hunted life of hiding, stealth and extremely poor dietary conditions. It is mainly due to the latter that I am writing you.

Due to the fact that I am not at liberty to snap up the first job that comes my way, I am forced to live in not only seclusion but starvation. Usually a problem of this sort would not bother me, but, unable to contact any friends, leaves me facing the hungry wolf on $10 a week donated by my fiancé.

To come to the point, I was wondering if you could offer some help in finding me a new identity or direct me to some alternate course (turning myself in is, of course, out, as is leaving the country at this moment). The only alternative I could come up with is blowing my brains out in the interests of martyrdom, however, this plan doesn't appeal to me much.

I would appreciate it if you could hurry a reply of some sort. Time is of the essence to me now as I believe my life is hanging over precarious waters.

Enclosed find my fiancé's address. Please write me care of her.
Appreciatively,
D. S. [male]
c/o J. S. [female], Ypsilanti, Mich.

147. I am here because I failed to oppose the draft, and the position I find myself in now is a very agonizing and sickening one.

Ft. Lewis, Wash
[undated, ca. May 1968]

Dear Sirs:

I am a basic trainee in the army at Ft. Lewis, Wash. I am here because I failed to oppose the draft, and the position I find myself in now is a very agonizing and sickening one. I feel that the war is morally wrong, and can see now that the training we are receiving here is a major reason why we are causing so much deprivation and destruction in Vietnam. The seed of that terrible brutality is rooted right here in this training center.

For this reason I feel it is imperative to begin to make a protest against what is happening to me and the men with me. Therefore I would like to know if you can help me in either of two ways. First, I would like a list of organizations to which I can write for pamphlets, leaflets, and fact-sheets, and second, if you can provide information in any manner. I am aware of what is happening to me, and must do something to prevent it. A few of us here believe that what we are involved in is morally wrong, but are extremely confused as to what to do about it.

Pvt. P. G. [male]

148. As you must be aware, it is unfortunately true in our society that much of the radical opposition to the war is dismissed because of the appurtenances of radicalism.

6 May 1968

Dear Dr. Spock:

I have watched your anti-war efforts with great admiration. As you must be aware, it is unfortunately true in our society that much of the radical opposition to the war is dismissed because of the appurtenances of radicalism; the efforts of the "straight," such as yourself, are much more effective.

Thank you for how you have helped change the mood of the country: we can only hope that the Resistance will not slacken until this mood turns into peace.

My wife, my two beautiful "Spock-raised" children and I wish you the best of luck in the trial.

Sincerely,
Capt. D. N. [male]
Cannon AFB, N.M.

Mitchell Goodman, Dr. Benjamin Spock, Michael Ferber, and the Reverend William Sloane Coffin, Jr., following their convictions for conspiring to aid and abet draft resisters, June 1968. (Bettmann/CORBIS)

6 The War on Trial, May–September 1968

THE FIRST major political trial of the Vietnam War era began in Boston on May 19, 1968, and added to the growing sense of alienation and chaos felt by so many Americans that spring. The trial of Dr. Spock and his four co-defendants had been billed as a showdown between the antiwar movement and the Johnson administration, an opportunity to put the war on trial. Before the trial even began, however, Judge Francis Ford made it clear that he would not allow the defense to call witnesses to testify on the alleged illegality or immorality of the war, nor would he allow the defendants to invoke the Nuremberg principles; instead, he would limit the trial to proving or disproving the charge of conspiracy to aid and abet draft resistance. Such pretrial wrangling no doubt eluded the attention of most Americans, even those who attempted to monitor the trial through the newspapers over its three-week life. For the defendants, once the judge prohibited their primary strategy of attacking the war and the draft, the trial became a dull, technical affair, resting mostly on a free-speech defense—that they had said things in support of draft resistance but had not encouraged anyone to break draft laws.

When the jury convicted four of the five defendants on June 14—nine days after Robert Kennedy's assassination—the news shook a nation already shaken by recent events and by a never-ending war. Dr. Spock received the letters in this chapter during and after the trial; they are a very small sampling of a much larger number of letters sent to Spock at this time. Most of the trial letters were supportive, so the group that follows is fairly representative of the larger population. In some ways, this represents a high watermark in the Spock correspondence; after his conviction, the letters kept coming, but in smaller numbers, and the intense debates over the war that appeared in the first few years' letters give way to far more personal concerns.

I. "I Often Get So Discouraged": Expressing Futility

MANY OF the letters that came to Spock during and after his trial express admiration for him and the stand he took against the war, but also allude to a pervasive sense of impotence and futility in trying to stop the war. Given the way the trial went, perhaps they expected him to feel powerless and frustrated, too. Some of the following letters not only assert that Spock's trial and sentence came as part of a government effort to silence dissenters, but others argue also that the nation has its priorities mixed up. Instead of waging war in Vietnam—a war that, as one writer pointed out, had already taken 22,000 American lives—a number of writers seem exasperated that the nation does not do more to cultivate and protect its children. Here, they use "best young men" and "cream of America" to describe the children they fear are being raised only to be killed as adults in foreign wars. Similarly, another writer expresses concern for the budget cuts to antipoverty, health care, and other social programs while the expense of the war continues to soar. At least two people invoke the Bible in arguing for the peace movement as "doing Christ's work" even as they lament the movement's seeming inability to stop the war.

149. I have two sons, one of which has already gone to Vietnam and through the things that an army Draftee has to go through. Thank God my son came home without too much ill effects!

> Timberlake, N.C.
> May 19, 1968

Dear Dr. Spock:

I have just read another piece in the newspaper concerning you and the draft. I would like to commend Melvin Wulf, legal head of the American Civil Liberties Union, when he "accused the government through its prosecution of Spock of seeking to silence the most distinguished and active critic of its policy in Vietnam." How I agree with this! I have two sons, one of which has already gone to Vietnam and through the things that an army Draftee has to go through. Thank God my son came home without too much ill effects! However, as all of us honest thinkers know so many do not come back and even worse some are so maimed, they will never have "the abundant life Jesus Christ promised" and meant for us to have (especially the "cream of the crop"—our Youth). Oh, God I wish Dr.

Spock, that this nation had more Dr. Spocks! So I want to wish you an acquital. It's a shame that a person in this so-called Christian nation has to go to jail, and for doing Christ's will! It makes me sick at heart! I have another son, 15. If things stay as they are now, he also will have to be drafted against his will. It's akin to slavery! . . .
     <u>God Bless You</u>!
     Mrs. A. H.

150. There seems to be pitifully little one can do about it, except protest in every possible way, and it seems to me that you and the others have done this in a very clever, constructive manner.

                         May 28, 1968
                         Athens, Ga.

Dear Dr. Spock:
     May I just tell you how greatly I admire and support the stand you and Rev. Coffin and the other two men are taking with regard to the war in Vietnam.
     There seems to be pitifully little one can do about it, except protest in every possible way, and it seems to me that you and the others have done this in a very clever, constructive manner, and set a fine example for others.
     I sincerely hope that the present court proceedings do not tax you too severely—I am able to find very little coverage of this trial in newspapers, which is of course not very surprising.
     If there is any way to be of service to you (other than writing to my congressman, etc. which I have already done) please let me know.
     Sincerely,
     Mrs. J. G.

151. I often get so discouraged when I think that all the time I spend with little boys is actually helping them to get a 1-A rating 10 years from now in whatever "war of the week" we're fighting then.

                       [undated, ca. early June,
                       1968]

Dear Dr. Spock,
     Thank you for your stand on this war.
     I have five sons. I'm a little league baseball coach, and serving my

fourth year sentence as a Den Mother. I often get so discouraged when I think that all the time I spend with little boys is actually helping them to get a 1-A rating 10 years from now in whatever "war of the week" we're fighting then.

Most people I talk to are against you. They think this glorious fiasco is worth the lives of our boys. I don't. I hate to think I'm raising boys to become jungle, mountain, or desert fertilizer before they have a chance to live.

Thank you from the bottom of my heart, and through men like you I hope someday this country will realize that it's no crime to put the lives of our best young men ahead of other interests!

    Mrs. S. J.
    Spokane, Wash.

152. 22000 American boys lie on the fields of Vietnam, Why? It is a crime to destroy countries and people that we have never seen in our lives.

June 8, 1968

Dear Dr. Benjamin Spock,

    I am not a lawyer, but how would I like to go to court with you, and take off my chest the following:

    Yes it is a crime to burn a draft card! It is a crime to destroy government property! But it is also a crime to send our boys to the other side of the world to kill! It is a crime to leave 22000 mothers without sons. The Vietnam mothers also have sons. 22000 American boys lie on the fields of Vietnam, Why? It is a crime to destroy countries and people that we have never seen in our lives. What happened to the Bible which told us "You shalt not kill." What is crime?

    R. J. [male]
    Dorchester, Mass.

153. I permanently hate this war, my husband came home the first time alive, who knows if he'll come home to me alive the second time.

June 17, 1968

Dear Dr. Spock,

    First of all I want you to know that I am very much in favor of what you are doing. I am not a nut or someone trying to pull tricks, I am a military wife, my husband is serving his second term in Vietnam, and I applaud you for standing up for something that you think is right, this war has put me and many other wives under a heavy strain and yet the government will do nothing for the wives who have husbands in Vietnam. I permanently hate this war, my husband came home the first time alive, who knows if he'll come home to me alive the second time, I feel the government has no right to play around with a man's life the second time, and you can count on one military wife that believes in you and thinks you are right.

> Sincerely yours,
> Mrs. C. K.
> San Clemente, Calif.

[EDITOR'S NOTE: On July 10, 1968, Judge Ford sentenced Spock and his co-defendants to two years in prison and fines of $1,000 to $5,000 each. In a press conference following the sentencing, Spock and the others pledged to continue their work against the war while the case was under appeal. The next few letters came in response to the sentencing.]

154. Now, more than ever, both sides of the argument should be given room to speak and ACT intelligently on the issue of the war.

> New York, N.Y.
> [undated]

U.S. District Court
Judge Francis J. W. Ford, Jr.
District of Massachusetts
Boston, Massachusetts 02109
My Dear Judge:

With regard to you sentencing of Dr. Benjamin Spock, I am personally not entirely clear about our right to be in Viet Nam, but I am clear about one thing and as I have heard your opinion about Dr. Spock's actions, may I respectfully ask that you listen to mine.

Your words, as quoted in a New York paper, ". . . where law and order stop, obviously anarchy begins."—bring to mind the law and order of Nazi Germany. Law which was obeyed and caused the slaughter of millions. Law which, if not obeyed, would have caused the dissenter to be called an anarchist.

I am sure you spent a great deal of time consulting your conscience. I, too, have consulted mine. I have a brother in the Green Beret in Viet Nam, and perhaps it is right for him to be there. That is not my issue— my issue is that I fear for his country and mine when an intelligent, compassionate man is treated by America in such a manner as to discredit him and silence his voice of dissent. Now, more than ever, both sides of the argument should be given room to speak and ACT intelligently on the issue of the war. Why are we muzzling half of America—or more? Should even I fear to write you openly about my views—or am I safe from censure because I choose the relatively ineffectual form of a letter? When you sentenced Dr. Spock, did you sentence conscientious, involved America?

    J. K. [female]

cc: Dr. Benjamin Spock
    President Lyndon B. Johnson
    Senator Jacob Javits
    Congressman Theodore R. Kupferman
    Mayor John Vliet Lindsay
    Senator Eugene McCarthy
    Vice President Hubert Humphrey

155. The words of a father of a son murdered in Vietnam.

Mercer Island, Wash.
July 11, 1968

Dear Dr. Spock:

Your sentence today was very injust all the way.

My son was drafted out of the U. of Wash. sick with mono and sentenced to Vietnam—and never came back. "3/6/68"

As in your case there are too many inequities in our courts and draft boards.

We do not even have an act of war so why should more men, "cream of America," be sentenced to "Johnson's" Vietnam, to keep his inflation soaring.

The words of a father of a son murdered in Vietnam.

    L. W. [male]

156. I find it intolerable to see TV programs on starving babies in our own nation of supposed wealth, while at the same time I read of the billions we spend fighting a war no one but the military officers in Saigon can profit from.

[undated]

Dear Dr. Spock—

My husband and I have 2 young children and live in Wash. D.C. I saw you on TV's "Contact" while visiting my family here.

We support you 100%—we've read all we could get our hands on about Vietnam + believe we should never have been there in the first place. I'm all for losing a little "face" + follow the French withdrawal in Algeria + Vietnam.

My main concern is with our poor people here—problems of integration + health, education + more job opportunities—problems, which, if we don't solve soon will destroy us. I find it intolerable to see TV programs on starving babies in our own nation of supposed wealth, while at the same time I read of the billions we spend fighting a war no one but the military officers in Saigon can profit from.

I envy the draft dissenters for their great courage. Anyone who says they are cowards are blind. We who sit comfortably in our homes + build careers can't perceive the sacrifices they are willing to make for principles.

I cringe when Congress cuts the poverty programs + attacks it small efforts. I'm tired of inadequately provided for children, poor educations for some of our citizens, slum housing + lack of jobs + job-training.

Many of us are so discouraged by the war, Kennedy + King's assassinations, Congressional reaction to the needs of the poor + what appears to us to be willing blindness to the crises facing this nation at the present.

All we can say is good luck + thank you for standing up for what you believe is right—when young people do the same thing—people call them hippies or communists or silly idealists but when a man of your reputation stands up to be counted people have to reexamine their own thinking.

L. & K. S. [female and male]

II. Calls for Action

IF THE previous group of letters offered evidence of discouragement at the prospects for peace, this next set conveys a similar sense of frustration and anger. Most of the writers, however, are not content to merely express their solidarity with Spock during and after his trial; instead, they offer varied solutions ranging from legal action directed against the president or the Selective Service to strategies for electoral politics (in which bad leadership would be replaced with good) to calls for more draft resistance or other activism in support of resistance; one letter, for example, mentions Another Mother for Peace, one of the most important peace organizations of the period. Another invokes the name of the recently slain Martin Luther King, Jr., in advocating support for draft resistance, while one writer almost wishes the government will prosecute everyone who supports draft resistance—perhaps assuming that a "fill the jails" strategy would effect political change as it had at times during the civil rights movement.

157. Our youth is a challenging breed who respect authority but want respect in return. . . . They don't like inconsistencies in laws, inequities and our blindness to inhumanity at home and abroad.

Buffalo, New York
June 14, 1968

Dear Dr. Spock,

This is a friendly letter from a former Army Nurse of WWII and a present elementary school teacher. I am a mother of two Spock-reared children, one serving his country. I consider myself a very patriotic American and for this reason I want to come to your defense. I am concerned with the injustice the government has done to you by charging you for violation of the Selective Service Act. I read that the government contends you were counseling, aiding and abetting young men to evade the draft, that you were a part of an alleged conspiracy which supports a nationwide program of resistance to the draft. This character assassination, and accusation may have caused you to lose faith in American justice. Unless our Justice Department is politically motivated to consider an undeclared war as legal violation of the Universal Military Training Act, take heart that American Justice will Prevail. Charges and accusations in the press have portrayed you as a semi-traitor. This sort of thing

Business Executives Move for Peace, picketing the White House, 1969. More of the mainstream face of the antiwar movement. (U.S. News & World Report, Library of Congress)

causes people to sympathize with the government. People may wonder why a man of your learning and calliber would allow himself to become involved in defending our youth who refuse to be drafted. This defense is not unpatriotic as I understand it, but a means of saving lives of sons and husbands. The public seems to have forgotten that you had a part in rearing these sons to better our country. They can't seem to realize that this is the best crop of Americans that the country has ever had—better health, better education, better citizens, better people in every way. The public can't seem to understand that we need our youth to carry on our American tradition of freedom.

Our leaders don't understand our youth and have imposed a homicidal philosophy upon them without considering their feelings, convictions and beliefs about war. Our leaders seem to think American lives are expendable—easily replaced by raising the immigration quota to countries long denied entry. Our youth is a challenging breed who respect authority but want respect in return. Our youth are honest and responsible and more mature in their thinking. Their honesty and true expression must not be confused with disloyalty or irresponsibility. They have a tendency to evaluate and critically analyze the times they are living in because they have taken the study of history and social studies seriously. They don't like inconsistencies in laws, inequities and our blindness to inhumanity at home and abroad.

Youth today resents remaining silent about issues. They don't like to be identified with youth minority groups who are aimless and who escape reality. They complain about news media playing up degenerates of their times—the irresponsible peers who tarnish the image of American youth.

Dr. Spock, your book on Child Care has helped Americans to produce this new generation which we can look upon with pride. This responsible youth likes challenges and likes to challenge. Thank you for trying to save this generation from slaughter. This youth turned to you because they want to be saved and they want to save America. They were not forced but led by their conscience.

You, Dr. Spock, have presented a challenge to our government when you aided the young men who were seeking help. These free-willed dissenters joined your ranks because your philosophy came closest to their convictions and beliefs. These youths have been seeking someone, somewhere—consciously or unconsciously for aid in their dilemma. For those who received no help—they chose to desert after induction and live out their days in exile, others have set themselves afire in protest. This undeclared war must be settled once and for all by the voice of the people. This war must come to a halt—<u>soon</u>.

Our only hope today is in responsible leadership. This we must do at the polls. We need rid of the bluffers and procrastinators in Washington. We want responsible leaders.

Good luck. My prayers are with you.

Sincerely,

M. N. [female]

158. As one insignificant signer of the "Resistance" supporters, I shall view it as an honor if they persecute and imprison each of us.

June 14, 1968
[address unknown]

Dear Dr. Spock,

As one insignificant signer of the "Resistance" supporters, I shall view it as an honor if they persecute and imprison each of us; if they imprison the very best of our people—which I consider you to be. If men like you are imprisoned, there is no other place for <u>any</u> person of conscience.

Thank you so much for giving so many of us a reason being able to hold our heads up in these times of despair and shame.

Sincerely,
[Female]

159. I heard Brother King also say that this Viet Nam War was cruel, immoral, and illegal, and that Boys should resist the draft in order to stop this War.

June 15, 1968

Honorable Dr. Spock—

It was a shock to hear of the conviction of you and two other workers of Peace and Justice.

Dr. King preached the love of Christ and acceptance of Christ's laws would bring Peace On Earth. I heard Brother King also say that this Viet Nam War was cruel, immoral, and illegal, and that Boys should resist the draft in order to stop this War.

When Dr. King was silenced by the cruel blow President Johnson eulogized his greatness and had our American Flag flown at half mast all over the World while American Men and Boys bled and died under this our American Flag at this very time.

How can President Johnson now consent to you and the others being found guilty of crime against your country? I would like to personally ask President Johnson this question but since I can't I hope someone else can and will.

Jesus bless you, your family, the other Workers and their families, and give you all faith and courage, is our prayer.

Thank you.

Sincerely,
Mrs. R. H.
Memphis, Tenn.

160. In my judgement President Johnson is personally liable for damages caused by the death of boys in this illegal war because he had no authority to send them into it.

Pleasant Ridge, Michigan

June 24, 1968

Dr. Spock:

. . . I greatly admire your courage and public spirit in taking the position you have with respect to the War and the draft. As a lawyer I am satisfied that you did not receive a fair trial. The draft should be abolished.

In my judgement President Johnson is personally liable for damages caused by the death of boys in this illegal war because he had no authority to send them into it. His acts were "ultra vires" — beyond his legal power as President. I have always hoped that some such suit would be brought by a family who lost a husband or son in Viet Nam. This might go a long way to stop the tyranny we suffer under. I have no doubt such a cause of action would be denied by the Courts holding that the actions of the President cannot be questioned in the Courts just as they have done in your case but it would be very difficult to convince any fair-minded person that this is not legal tyranny. Men who swear they will support and defend the Constitution must be held accountable for the injuries they cause by violating their oath of office.

If there is no other way to contribute to your defence than to forward a contribution to you directly, I shall be glad to do so.

Very truly yours,

G. W. [male]

[EDITOR's NOTE: At their post-sentencing press conference, Spock and his convicted co-defendants continued to characterize the war as immoral and senseless, and Spock, in particular, showed flashes of emotion. As camera flashes popped and television crews zoomed in, Spock shouted, "I say to the American people, 'Wake up!' Get out there and do something before it's too late! Do something now!" The following letter is a direct response to Spock's pleas.]

161. Tonight on television I heard you say, "America, wake up!" and I want you to know that there is a segment of this population that is awake.

July 10, 1968

Dear Doctor Spock,

Tonight on television I heard you say, "America, wake up!" and I want you to know that there is a segment of this population that is awake.

My two boys "Spock babies" are now ages 10 and 11; not many years from draft age and I fear for them. This useless and horrifying war must stop.

In conversation I "politic" for McCarthy to democrats and for Rockefeller to republicans. Nixon and Humphrey are bad news for our country.

There are many of us that back you all of the way. The same wisdom you used to help me raise my sons is shown in your actions of today. I admire you greatly.

Please realize there are many of us who believe in you and are hoping for the best for you.

What can I do to help?

> Yours truly,
> Mrs. P. K.
> Normal, ILL

162. I never really knew what napalm was or what it did. It's hard to believe the horrible things human beings do to each other.

[undated]

Dear Dr. Spock,

I just finished your book on Vietnam.

I learned many things I never knew. For instance, I never really knew what napalm was or what it did. It's hard to believe the horrible things human beings do to each other.

I have a 6 year old girl and a 5 year old boy. I love them very much and I don't want them growing up in a world of war. I don't want my son to have to fight in a senseless war such as Vietnam. This is the reason I joined Another Mother for Peace. I have written to the other members to let them know about your fine book.

I pray we will see peace soon.
>   Sincerely,
>   Mrs. L. G.
>   San Clemente, Calif.

PS. My parents raised me with the help of your baby + child care book. Thank you.

163. If you are truly interested in equal treatment for all American youth —privileged and underprivileged—then have a test case presented to the Supreme Court.

August 7, 1968

Dear Dr. Spock:

With reference to your conviction for counseling young men to evade the draft, it is my honest opinion that had this case been approached in the right manner, the entire draft law in its present form would have to be declared illegal by the Supreme Court of the U.S., because the law is so written as to allow "legal" draft evasion by the privileged in our society and rampant discrimination against the underprivileged.

If you are truly interested in equal treatment for all American youth —privileged and underprivileged—then have a test case presented to the Supreme Court, i.e., an underprivileged youth who feels that he is being unfairly drafted into military service under a biased, discriminatory method of selection. If the Supreme Court decided in this youth's favor, then the decision in your case would have to be reversed.

Please note attached sent to all the Republican presidential hopefuls and others attending the Republican National Convention at Miami Beach.

>   Very truly yours,
>   M. G. [female]
>   Bronx, N.Y.

III. Staying the Course

IN CONTRAST to the previous letters of support and solidarity, the next set of letters come from Americans angered by Spock's support of draft resistance. For them, Spock deserved to be prosecuted, convicted, and imprisoned (with some thinking his sentence was too light). At issue, primarily, is respect for the rule of law and, in particular, instilling that respect in children. Several writers make reference to their own philosophies of child rearing, indicating that they teach their children a respect for the president and the law; as one notes, if the draft sent her son to Vietnam, she wouldn't want him to go, but "if that's the way it is, that's it." To resist it, or to encourage resistance of the law, is completely out of the question. Another writer cites the Bible (not unlike an opponent of the war in a letter above) in asserting that "the authorities are ministers of God," and therefore must be obeyed. For the parents, it is also apparent that teaching their sons to obey the law is a way of teaching them how to behave as men. Thus, Spock's open advocacy of draft resistance—violating the law and challenging elected authority—is anathema to everything they believe as Americans and as parents. That such advocacy comes from the author of the child-rearing book that some of them used could only make them feel betrayed.

164. We mothers don't want our sons in wars either, BUT . . . if the law ORDERS them to go and fight, they should obey the laws of the country.

[undated, ca. June 1968]
[point of origin unknown]

DR SPOCK—

Besides me, (I have 4 children under 8 yrs.) there are DOZENS of women I know who are throwing your book in the ashcan.

We don't want our children to grow up to be traitors, lawbreakers, hippies, etc. We mothers don't want our sons in wars either, BUT . . . if the law ORDERS them to go and fight, they should obey the laws of the country. And this means that the law applies to ALL young men, not just mine.

The time to fight the WAR is AT THE BEGINNING, not after it is an established fact.

Where were your protests, Dr. Spock, when the former president Kennedy BEGAN THE WHOLE MESS BY HIS DIEM COUP? WHY DIDN'T YOU FIGHT IT THEN, WHEN WE WERE SENDING OUR TROOPS IN AS "ADVISERS", SO JFK SAID, BUT ANY FOOL COULD SEE THAT OUR TROOPS WERE DOING THE FIGHTING THEN, AS NOW? WHY DIDN'T YOU SPEAK OUT THEN, DR. SPOCK?

Perhaps it's a matter of politics with you,—depending on WHO is president, is the determining factor in the quality of your patriotism to this country; if you sincerely cared about the young men going to war, you would urge ALL OF THEM TO DO SO,—and help ease the burden on those already there and also bring a quicker end to it.

I have an intelligent, excellent pediatrician; he does not IMAGINE himself a political authority and an omnipotent adviser to the young people after they pass the age limit of his physical authority over them. Why don't YOU govern yourself accordingly?

A DISGUSTED YOUNG MOTHER

165. I am ashamed to say that I raised my son according to your baby books. My son is now in the U.S. Air-Force, and I am an Air-Force mother, and proud of it.

July 10 68

Dr. and Mrs. (Communist) Spock,

Shame on you both.

You are no doubt receiving a large check from Hanoi.

Thank God you got what was coming to you, only it was <u>too light</u> a sentence.

I am ashamed to say that I raised my son according to your baby books. My son is now in the U.S. Air-Force, and I am an Air-Force mother, and proud of it.

I also lost a nephew two years ago, flying an F 4 C Phantom Jet, over Vietnam, he is still missing in action, but that still does not make us want to blame our country and join up with <u>reds like you</u> and many others.

Thank God our courts are still able to take care of your kind, and the Rap Browns and others, you are all alike, and should be sent to Russia or China where you belong.

I hope you never get out of jail alive.

An Air-Force Mother.

166. My son is 18. I certainly don't want him to have to go—but if that's the way it is, that's it. What you have done, along with others turns my stomach.

July 10, 1968

Dear Dr. Spock:

Let me first say that your book was almost a "Bible" with me in raising my children Barbara, age 20, and Charles, age 18. The pages are torn —the cover is gone and for a long time it's stayed together with a rubber band around it. It was a great help and your word was law and much appreciated.

Now let me say that I just heard the news that you have been sentenced to 2 years plus a fine. I think you were lucky. A fine—what's that, money which I'm sure you can afford—the other—the sentence—that can you afford? It's your life and it was your choice.

My son is 18. I certainly don't want him to have to go—but if that's the way it is, that's it. What you have done, along with others turns my stomach. The sentence is light. All the love and understanding you showed to us mothers in your work and your book doesn't hold true. We teach our boys to be men and you're now tearing that down.

Mrs. J. R.
Endicott, N.Y.

167. The answer to <u>your</u> problem re draft card burning and even to hippies who rebel to our customs can be found in St. Paul's letter to the Romans.

Monday eve
August 12, 1968

Dear Dr. Spock and the rest of your "Boston Five,"

Our two oldest (18 + 16 years old) boys of our four were raised on your "permissive" methods. We've lived to regret it and we've cracked down on them, teaching them to be more responsible and we feel sure, that should their country call upon them now, they would not hesitate to go.

The answer to <u>your</u> problem re draft card burning and even to hippies who rebel to our customs can be found in St. Paul's letter to the Romans. It is applicable today and to this country because we are a Christian nation under God: Romans 13—Let every person be subject to the governing authorities. For there is no authority except from God and those that exist have been instituted by God. Therefore, he who resists the authorities resists what God has appointed and those who resist will incur judgement. For rulers are not a terror to good conduct, but to bad. Would you have no fear of him who is in authority? Then do what is good, and you will receive his approval . . . for he does not bear the sword in vain; he is the servant of God to execute his wrath on the wrongdoer.

Therefore, one must be subject, not only to avoid God's wrath, but also for the sake of conscience. For the same reason you also must pay taxes, for the authorities are ministers of God, attending to this very thing. Pay all of them their dues, taxes to whom taxes are due . . . respect to whom respect is due, <u>custom to whom custom is due</u>, honor to whom honor is due.

> Sincerely,
> Mrs. J. D.
> Greeley, Colorado

IV. Perseverance

ALMOST AS if in response to the preceding group of letters, some people wrote to Spock and explicitly denied the validity of law-and-order arguments in favor of "higher laws," conscience, and moral judgment. The following letters came to Spock following his conviction and offer support, but, unlike the earlier group of sympathetic but exasperated letters, these urge Spock to carry on as though on a spiritual crusade. "Keep faith," one man wrote, invoking biblical passages not unlike some of Spock's critics. In another familiar refrain, one writer suggests Nazis were hanged after the Second World War for not obeying their consciences and, presumably, resisting evil. Many Americans opposed to U.S. policy in Vietnam drew such parallels by the summer of 1968.

168. The normal man cannot sit in judgement of the selfless, the glow surrounding him is too bright and the temptation to bring him down too great.

> June 16, 1968
> Brooklyn, N.Y.

Dear Dr. and Mrs. Spock,

The people gave Pontius Pilate his verdict and condemned Jesus and now 12 men in Boston ruled that morality, conscience and righteousness cannot stand in the way of force and power. And again, nothing has changed and history repeats itself, leaving us with many crosses and so few to carry them. The normal man cannot sit in judgement of the selfless, the glow surrounding him is too bright and the temptation to bring him down too great.

We are devastated but proud to be counted among those who honor, respect and love you.

> Sincerely,
> S. + S. L. [male and female]

169. I hope you are set free

[EDITOR's NOTE: This letter was written in the hand of a child on wide-ruled stationery featuring the images of three clowns. The point of origin is not noted, but Spock responded to an address in Tenafly, New Jersey.]

[undated]

Dear Dr. Spock,

me and my Sister and Brother Were all Raised ON your booK.

I hope you are set free

From,

D. G. [male]

[EDITOR's NOTE: Spock replied, saying, "the government won't put me in prison at least until I have two more trials and that will take two more years." He noted that if he won either trial, he wouldn't have to go to jail at all, and concluded by saying, "so don't get discouraged yet."]

170. President Johnson says that we should obey law and order, but what about higher laws and order?

Hemet, Calif.

July 12, 1968

Dear Dr. Spock:

I don't know whether my letter will reach you or not, but it should since you are so well-known.

The reason I'm writing is to inquire whether you have considered fighting your case on the legality that the U.S. has never declared war and that, therefore, you are not guilty of the crime with which you are charged?

Perhaps my reasoning is not the way the law looks at it, but I look at things from the moral point of view, and I think you did right to follow your conscience the way God led you.

President Johnson says that we should obey law and order, but what about higher laws and order? God says, "Thou shall not kill," yet he sends our boys to do that very thing and he, therefore, disobey's God's laws. If he is so insistent, that the people follow civil laws, then why doesn't he set an example and follow God's laws? How can he expect the public to respect civil laws when he shows no respect for God's laws?

You were merely counseling according to higher laws, the way I see it, and since there has been no declared war, I cannot see that what you did could be interpreted as a crime.

The President, on the other hand, has sent thousands of boys to kill and be killed. This is not justifiable no matter what the consequences when we consider that if we follow God's commandments we let him work out our salvation and he takes the responsibility. "Vengeance is mine, sayeth the Lord."

We have been commanded to love our enemies and do good to them that persecute us,—to turn the other cheek, etc.

Keep courage! If injustice must be served, keep faith and keep in contact with God through prayer, for you will benefit in the end.

Sincerely,

D. H. [male]

171. Counseling young men to avoid the killing and being killed is a crime and a moral obligation. What will become of a country where law has lost touch with morality?

July 12, 1968
[address unknown,
postmarked St. Paul, Minn.]

Dr. Benjamin Spock, Mitchell Goodman, et al

Boston, Massachusetts

Dear Sirs,

You have been convicted and I am saddened and afraid. Counseling young men to avoid the killing and being killed is a crime and a moral obligation. What will become of a country where law has lost touch with morality?

I wish America were free—of fear of freedom. I wish men who try to save lives were honored here. I wish the collective were less important. I wish that I could help you but I have no money and cannot pray. I tell people you are right and war is wrong, but that is nothing. I tell my students not to go to war but they are brainwashed before I meet them. I wish they were free to make a choice.

You must win so that both sides can speak equally to young men. You must win so I will not be afraid to have a son in America. You must win so that I can sign my name—

[unsigned]

172. I am the head of a family of six, Wife, three sons in college and an eleven year old daughter. So you can see that I have personal reasons for being against the draft and war.

July 14, 1968

Dr. Spock,

You will be remembered. Your work in helping mothers to rear their children will insure that. However, I believe that your efforts to save the young men from war and allied stupidities is more important. My wife and I are completely in agreement with what you are doing, and we hope that you are left free to continue.

I know that men of conscience do not need, or rather do not require, letters from people to have them do what they must do. Still I think that you will be cheered to know that many people approve of your actions, and this is my way of telling you so.

I am the head of a family of six, Wife, three sons in college and an eleven year old daughter. So you can see that I have personal reasons for being against the draft and war. I am forty-nine years old, and I have come to believe that in a sense all of these young men of both sides are my sons.

(Incidentally, our sons are in college on scholarships and by their own efforts. I certainly do not make enough money to send them.)

I should think that you might be too busy to answer this letter but I would like to know for sure that you have read it.

Sincerely,
P. W. [male]
Marion, Illinois

173. It is a sad commentary on our system of justice that you must pay a penalty for obeying conscience when Nazi leaders were hanged for <u>not</u> obeying conscience.

July 15, 1968

Dear Sir,

I would like to take this opportunity to commend you on your courageous stand against the illegal and immoral war the current administration is waging against the Vietnamese people.

Although people may consider your stand un-American and unpatriotic, I do not feel this way. You have struck me as a person who truly loves America and believes the nation can lead by magnanimity and justice, not by intimidation and indiscriminate bombing of innocent people. I believe, sir, that like millions of other Americans, you truly love your country, but are appalled by the way the Johnson administration is prostituting its greatness before the world.

I feel that most Americans are on your side, that since the current conflict is illegal and immoral, young men should have the right of conscientious objection on the grounds of the war's illegality, if on no other grounds. It is a sad commentary on our system of justice that you must pay a penalty for obeying conscience when Nazi leaders were hanged for not obeying conscience.

And so, sir, I hope your splendid example of courage in the face of a powerful Establishment will shake the rest of us out of our criminal silence, which implies consent to the crimes of the Johnson administration. When men like yourself, who have nothing to gain, but a lot to lose by dissent, are not afraid to buck the Organization, then there is hope that America can once again be a just and magnanimous nation.

Sincerely yours,
T. R. [male]
Lititz, Pa.

174. But if you are guilty, so are all of us who prefer love to hatred, and value life over death. Therefore, the cause you are fighting for is our common cause.

El Cerrito, Calif.
Sept. 20, 1968

Dear Dr. Spock,

I am one of a multitude of mothers of "Dr. Spock's babies", and I owe you a debt of gratitude for coming to the aid of mothers like myself who are trying to raise our children in the confusion of today's world.

I first came across "Baby and Child Care" in a college psychology class where it was used as assigned reading material. Its practical side proved invaluable in my baby-sitting experience during the rest of my college years.

Between that time and the present, I wore out two paperback copies of the book on my three children, (now 11, 9 and 6) and had to buy a hard cover edition to use in my work as a psychiatric social worker in working with mothers of young children. Every time I use it, I marvel at its eternal timeliness and at the wonderful depth of understanding and love that must have gone into creating it.

Dr. Spock, since you had helped me and countless mothers like myself, to give our children sound beginnings in life, it seems only natural that you would go on to try to provide a better and more peaceful world for them to live in. I was not surprised, therefore, when you changed your emphasis for I saw one as an outgrowth of the other, but I did admire you so much more for it. You could have easily rested on your well deserved laurels, but you chose a much harder road. In working for a world without war, you have demonstrated a real depth of feeling and concern for all the world's children, and have shown yourself a great humanitarian hero in addition to being a great pediatrician.

I now read the "Common Sense Book of Baby and Child Care" with an added reverence. The judges found you "guilty". But if you are guilty, so are all of us who prefer love to hatred, and value life over death. Therefore, the cause you are fighting for is our common cause.

Since I firmly believe with other "Mothers-for Peace" that "War is not healthy for children or other living things", please show me how I can help. I am but one mother with limited resources but I am willing to do all I can to help you in this struggle. And I am sure I speak for many, many others.

 Sincerely yours,
 Mrs. A. H.

President Nixon smiling behind stacks of supportive telegrams, following his "silent majority" speech, November 1969. The implication is that, in spite of the massive Moratorium protests, most Americans supported Nixon's handling of the war. (U.S. News & World Report, Library of Congress)

7 Toward Nixon's War,
September 1968–December 1969

As THE presidential election came and went in the fall of 1968, the flow of letters to Dr. Spock dropped off noticeably for the first time in three years. One explanation is burnout. By September, the year's events—culminating in the dramatic confrontations between police and antiwar protesters at the Democratic National Convention in Chicago—had exhausted many Americans, especially those opposed to the war. Moreover, the election of Richard Nixon, who had campaigned on a promise to achieve "peace with honor" in Vietnam, undercut the impulse for immediate protest.

As a result, it is interesting to note the changed tenor in many of the letters Spock received in late 1968 and throughout 1969. Although the representative anticommunist letters remain (as well as those accusing Spock of disloyalty), the letters expressing frustration over how to end the war, or articulating various concerns about children, or suggesting new antiwar strategies—all of which were so much more common in earlier years—largely fade out of view (though there are exceptions). Instead, the vast majority of the letters that came to Spock in 1969 tell personal stories of young men facing induction or men already serving in the armed forces. Sometimes the letters came from parents seeking Spock's advice on how to protect these men, while other letters came from the young men themselves.

This shift suggests a changing view of Spock and perhaps a changing view of the state of the war. While earlier letters spoke to Spock as an antiwar leader, and may have thanked him for saying what ordinary people felt they could not say or suggested new antiwar strategies, the posttrial letters spoke to him almost as though he had reverted back to the role of a pediatrician only. The letters are, indeed, not unlike the thousands of letters Spock received in the 1940s and 1950s from concerned parents asking specific questions about a child's health and safety; but instead of seeking counsel on an ailment or behavioral issue, these parents sought assistance in insulating their sons from the draft and the war. Why the debates over the war subside for a time is less clear, though the passing of the Johnson presidency—the one targeted by Spock for four years—may explain it.

For Spock, though, the war remained his primary concern. Beginning in the months after his trial, he committed himself to a rigorous schedule of public speaking that lasted for the next several years. He often had speaking engagements lined up for twenty-five days a month and donated almost all of the honoraria to draft resistance and other antiwar organizations. Some of the letters in this chapter came in response to one or another of those speaking engagements.

Finally, it is important to note that the U.S. Court of Appeals in Boston overturned Spock's conviction in July 1969. The Court found that the evidence against Spock and Michael Ferber, in particular, had not been sufficient to convict for conspiracy. In the cases of William Sloane Coffin and Mitchell Goodman, the court overturned the verdicts on a technicality and left the possibility of reprosecution open, but the Nixon administration chose not to try the two again. The court's decision prompted letters from supporters and critics alike.

I. "If You Don't Like Our Way of Life—Pack Your Bag and Get Out"

IN SPITE of the decline in letters sent to Spock, he did continue to receive angry letters from Americans who continued to support fighting North Vietnam and the Viet Cong as part of a larger campaign against international communism. A key difference between the next set of letters and the hundreds of anticommunist messages Spock received over the last several years is that a number of these letters came from family members of men killed or serving in Vietnam. In addition to the usual suggestions that Spock was a traitor or a communist dupe, a number of these letters express as their primary concern the morale of American troops still fighting the war. For these writers, it is an outrage that so many American men fight in Vietnam only to see news reports of Spock's and others' "aid, comfort, and encouragement" to the enemy through their protest.

175. I do not understand how you can refer to the government of the Republic of Vietnam as a "puppet," of the U.S. especially in view of that government's intransigence about getting the peace talks going.

Portland, Maine
February 10, 1969

Dear Dr. Spock,

Just read of your press interview on February 5th. I do not understand how you can refer to the government of the Republic of Vietnam as a "puppet," of the U.S. especially in view of that government's intransigence about getting the peace talks going. You know very well that both Clark Clifford and L.B.J. became exasperated but President Thieu resisted the pressure of their open declarations about ending the boycott. The fact is that you adduced not a scintilla or iota of proof to support your baseless charge.

Actually you are a stooge of Ho Chi Minh, who is in turn a puppet of the Russians, who supply 4/5 of all his explosives, 80% of all the bullets, mine bombs and shells of all kinds which are used to kill innocent South Vietnamese children, while Russians still live in shacks in Siberia and elsewhere. . . .

Sincerely,
G. G. [male]

[EDITOR'S NOTE: The following letter, from a serviceman just returned from Vietnam, "congratulates" Spock for having his conviction overturned.]

176. If you don't like our way of life—pack your bag and get out.

Los Angeles, California . . .
7 12 69

Dr. Spock:

Congratulations! TRAITOR!

You ought to be ashamed of yourself. How long do you think you'd last counseling youth in Russia or China??? They'd execute you in ten minutes—without a trial.

If you don't like our way of life—pack your bag and get out.

I just got home from Vietnam. The morale is high and believe me; the boys know what they're fighting for. I am sure you do not.

I Love My Country,

J. B. [male]

177. How do you think this disgusting publicity your interviews promote effect those loyal men who are fighting in Vietnam? I can see no shame, only pride, in fighting for this country.

Whippany, N.J.

July 14, 1969

Dear Dr. Spock:

I have just finished watching your television interview in oposition to the Vietnam War and the way it is being handled. I personally think that you are causing more harm than good.

You justified those who refuse to accept the draft. You apparently see nothing wrong in ignoring this law. What possible good can this do?

How do you think this disgusting publicity your interviews promote effect those loyal men who are fighting in Vietnam? I can see no shame, only pride, in fighting for this country.

Don't you realize that by the Communists winning this war we could face the same critical situation we did in the beginning of World War 2. We have to stop this aggression now! People are born to be free and should remain that way. If we don't help this country and many others, who will?

You have a lot of influenze with those who have raised their children by your books, and with teenagers, and also with those who are confused about the war. You should use this influenze by cooperating with the federal government instead of promoting radical aggitation.

My brother has enlisted in the Navy and leaves in September. He is proud that he can fight for his country and help keep the world free. I am very proud of him!

This letter probably won't change your attitude, but I think it's important that you know how I feel. I'm sure I have expressed this opinion for many other citizens in this great country.

Sincerely,

Miss C. D.

Student of Whippany Park High School

178. It is clear to me that the purpose of World Communism is to take over the world. Never at anytime in their history have they shown to deviate from this proclaimation.

South Hamilton, Mass.

July 15, 1969

Dear Mr. Spock,

It was with great disappointment that I heard the comments you made at Martha's Vineyard at an interview with a reporter from WHDH-TV. The one comment that stuck in my mind was your reference to "American Imperialism". Apparently you are vehemently opposed to the American intervention in the Vietnam conflict.

As a twenty-five year old wife and mother of two children I too hate to see my contemporaries slaughtered out on the battlefield. But I would not hesitate to allow my husband as precious as he is to me to serve his country in Vietnam if his country needed him. He has already served six years in the Air Force.

I believe you and the other peaceniks are the victims of fuzzy thinking. It is clear to me that the purpose of World Communism is to take over the world. Never at anytime in their history have they shown to deviate from this proclaimation. It is also true that China needs the fertile lands of Vietnam to feed its large population. Another fact you have forgotten is that the Communists started this war. Also to be considered is the outcome for the Vietnamese people if the Americans leave Vietnam. There is an abundance of documented evidence describing the inhumanities that the Communists have ravaged upon the Vietnamese that do not agree with them. Unless the South Vietnamese are in a position to defend themselves the Communists will cause a bloodbath unlike any in human history. Another fact you probably have not considered is the affect that people like you have at the Paris Peace talks. Apparently you have given the National Liberation Front hope that if they continue to stall talks the Americans and the Thieu government will settle for less than victory. What about the precious lives that have already been lost on Vietnam's soil? Their great sacrifice for freedom must be honored or are you more concerned for the draft dodgers in jail?

After listening to people such as yourself spouting such words as "American Imperialism", I cannot help but associate you with the cause of the enemy. The Communists do not allow such opinions to be expressed against them on their soil. This is common knowledge. If America lays down its arms, puts its head in the sand and looks the other way when Communists continue to rape nation after nation what hope will we have? What meaning will our alliances have to the nations we have pledged to support if they are attacked? If our answer is that our freedoms as guaranteed in the constitution are not worth the fight to keep, then perhaps we do not belong on this soil enjoying what others have died to help us keep, only so we can say it was useless. Think again Mr. Spock. Everyday I pray for the continuance of this nation under our present constitution. I pray that God will not allow your voice to matter. I pray that the sacrifices the American soldiers have made will not be to no avail. I pray that people such as you will continue to have the right to say what you say even though I disagree with you with all my being.

Yours truly,

Mrs. G. G.

179. You're riding high now, Doc, but don't forget that Benedict Arnold, Hitler Mussolini and others did well for a while.

7/22/69

[postmarked Brooklyn, N.Y.]

You're riding high now, Doc, but don't forget that Benedict Arnold, Hitler Mussolini and others did well for a while.

The American people will wake up to the doings of skunks like you sooner or later.

G.G. [male]

[EDITOR'S NOTE: In November, following the success of the October 15 Moratorium demonstrations, the antiwar movement staged another two-day moratorium and a mass demonstration in Washington. The latter included a "March Against Death" in which each participant marched with a sign carrying the name of an individual American GI slain in Vietnam; at the end of the march, the names were dropped into coffins. Advance publicity for this event obviously caught the attention of the following letter writer.]

180. You don't need to drop my son's name into the container you mentioned in the newspaper during your protest. He was hoping, before he was killed aiding a wounded man, that you would be given a prison sentence.

1969 Oct 8

Dr. Benjamin Spock

What the president really needs is someone to help him out of the "Fulbright and his ilk morass." It is disgraceful, unAmerican, treasonable and frustrating to millions of Americans who carry the real burden of this war to constantly listen and read of your aid, comfort, and encouragement to our enemy to hold on, that eventually you will deliver, if they will just be patient. Of course we all want the war to end. And it just might if it could be fought. Whether it was the best originally is a moot question now. No wonder the youth of America wonder what is really right concerning moral integrity and such things as duty, honor, country.

You don't need to drop my son's name into the container you mentioned in the newspaper during your protest. He was hoping, before he was killed aiding a wounded man, that you would be given a prison sentence for what you were doing to the thinking of America's youth.

Mrs. R. S., Gold Star Mother

Lamesa, Texas

181. If you enjoy protesting why not protest against Viet Nam Communists who refuse to tell us whether fliers shot down are living! Some 1400 mothers do not know whether they are wives or widows!

New York, N.Y.
November 5th 1969

My dear Dr. Spock:

I recently took a poll, covering a wide variety of individuals, as to what they think of the insolent and ignorant protestors—particularly those who, like yourself, have <u>no</u> 1st hand observations, as to conditions in Vietnam, and how absolutely necessary it is <u>not</u> to flee, or give in to the herd of wishiwashi thinkers! The minute we draw out completely, there would be a massacre by the Viet Cong of vast numbers of innocent people! We all heartily agree with Vice President Agnew!

If you enjoy protesting why not protest against Viet Nam Communists who refuse to tell us whether fliers shot down are living! Some 1400 mothers do not know whether they are wives or widows! Neighbors keep asking a little boy of 4 1/2 why his "daddy" is so wicked as to be in prison so long! You are contributing as much as Bertrand Russell to the extra burden our troops have to bear!

Very truly yours

W. S. [male]

II. Sons in the Cross Hairs: The Agony of War

DR. SPOCK's dual role as pediatrician and peace activist is never more apparent than in the following group of emotional letters. Almost all of the letters in this group came from parents deeply concerned about their sons. Some wrote of sons already stationed in Vietnam, others of sons recently drafted and anticipating service in Vietnam. Still others wrote about sons who had deserted or resisted the draft. Each is concerned about how their wartime experience will affect these young men—either the combat experience, the basic training experience, or the prison experience. The personal parental anguish comes through in their desperate tone, in their pleas for help, and in the way they sometimes blame themselves. Turning to the doctor who helped them raise these boys seems like a logical, familiar step.

182. I did not raise my sons with truth and honor for this—they shall <u>not</u> go—if they cannot find the strength to resist we shall all have to leave, but we raised them for life, and this they should have—and freedom!

9/20/68

Dear Dr. Spock,

I thought it appropriate to write you on note paper made by one of my five children, all of whom were raised from your book. The children are now 15, 13, 11, 8, 6 years old and all well and happy, all of which was made easier and less anxious by your advise.

I want to commend you on your courageous stand to help the same mothers from losing their sons to an immoral war which if it does not murder them will make murderers of them.

You are setting a good example of courage and integrity for our sons. Maybe because of your stand our younger boys will be spared the terrible decision now facing so many. I did not raise my sons with truth

The March Against Death in which participants carried the names of American war dead and deposited them into caskets in front of the White House, November 15, 1969. (Bettmann/CORBIS)

and honor for this—they shall <u>not</u> go—if they cannot find the strength to resist we shall all have to leave, but we raised them for life, and this they should have—and freedom! If all the mothers you helped could be at your side at the jailhouse would that help? If so I shall be there. Thank you.

N. D. [female]
Malibu, Calif.

183. The youngster I once held in one arm while I held your book in the other is now in Viet Nam much against his will and good conscience.

September 20, 1968

Dear Doctor Spock:

The youngster I once held in one arm while I held your book in the other is now in Viet Nam much against his will and good conscience. And what hurts even more is that we, his parents, didn't have the guts and courage to stand up and fight right here on the home front before he was yanked away unwillingly.

However, it's never too late to make amends and so herewith enclosed is a token of our support and appreciation for the stand you have so courageously taken.

We wish it could be far more but every little bit helps—and you undoubtedly need all the help you can get with the costly legal fees ahead of you.

With all good wishes.

ANOTHER MOTHER FOR PEACE[1]
Mrs. F. S.
North Hollywood, California

184. Although I endeavored to get my son to go to jail rather than to Vietnam, he felt that he did not want the stigma of a jail sentence on his record.

[EDITOR'S NOTE: The author of this letter is the same as that of letter 107.]

January 28, 1969
Calgary 44, Alberta
Canada

Dear Dr. Spock,

A year or so ago, I wrote to you requesting your advice regarding means by which I could keep my sons from being inducted into the U.S. Army. I had spent several years studying and analyzing the Vietnam issue, including the history of Vietnam and its problems, and had come to the conclusion that the United States should never have interfered in the affairs of that Asiatic country. You advised that I contact the American Civil Liberties Union in Los Angeles (my birthplace and former residence). Upon contacting the ACLU, I was informed they would be unable to help because of the heavy volume of work facing them.

Both of my oldest sons were drafted. One is in the Reserves in California (putting himself through college); and the other has been in Vietnam for the past six months. Although I endeavored to get my son to go to jail rather than to Vietnam, he felt that he did not want the stigma of a jail sentence on his record. Had it been my choice, I would have gone to jail. However, he is young and his concern for "what people think," rather than "what is right" is often a characteristic of the immature.

It has been my intention for many months to write and thank you for all you have done for the young men of America. Your courageous stand in behalf of draft-age boys was commendable. My family of five, (two girls and three boys), and I are of the opinion that it is your effort of the past several years which will prove to be the instigation of changes in the unjust compulsory military draft laws of the United States.

I have followed the progress of your case in the newspapers, but have seen nothing for several months. I hope that everything is going well for you. Many millions of Americans are grateful to you, although most people are so busy earning a living they seldom have time to write.

With kindest regards and our sincere thanks for your tremendous contribution on behalf of conscionable young Americans!

Sincerely yours,

M. G. [female]

185. My son is in the Army (Infantry) and is scheduled to go to South Vietnam in about another month. I don't want him to go but whether I can talk him into going to jail for five years is another problem.

February 10, 1969

Dear Sir:

I want to commend you for the great effort you have put forth to try and help those who are against this war.

My son is in the Army (Infantry) and is scheduled to go to South Vietnam in about another month. I don't want him to go but whether I can talk him into going to jail for five years is another problem. He has had two years of college and is very anxious to return to school. Three of his best friends were killed in this war (two at the same funeral parlor) which was the reason he couldn't return to the February term last year and allowed himself to be drafted.

Before he comes home I would like to get one thing straightened out. According to the Treaty of 1954 no Americans were to do any of the fighting. I want to know why our allies (Australia, New Zealand, and the rest except S.V) have not been allowed to do any of the fighting by their governments? Do they adhere strictly to the Treaty? They have had no casualties for the last four years so I would like to know why our government doesn't demand that they replace all of our boys who are doing the fighting for the length of time it takes to terminate the negotiations. I am in hopes I'll have something to go on before he gets back. I have written the President for this information but he seems to be too busy "praying for [illegible] he has time to "wait and see."

Any information you can send me will be greatly appreciated.
Respectfully,
Mrs. K. T.
Dearborn, Michigan

186. All his young life he had been against killing. He is presently "doing time."

3-8-69

Dear Dr. Spock

I just happen to have this piece of paper with me. I am having a "hair-do" and so have time and I like to use my spare moments writing to my friends in the Peace Movement. Do you know whether Nixon is still a Quaker? Or has he rejected his faith? If I thought he was I would write and appeal to him on this terrible war. . . .

I have been listening to and comforting a little mother—one of our secretaries, Eleanor—whose young son has been going through holy hell because of his objection to combat duty. All his young life he had been against killing. He is presently "doing time." The sentence was fairly light but the damage done to his soul caused by all the trauma he went through may damage his life. He feels that people will discriminate against him for the rest of his life and Eleanor finds few associates who understand.

If you have time, you might write him—through me. I don't have permission to give his name, but will see that he gets your message. Best wishes and love to you and Mrs. Spock. What is happening in your case at present? Please let me know.

C. A. [female]
Pacific Palisades, Calif

187. I've lost my only son in the war.

7/17/69
Dundee, Florida

Dear Dr. Spock,

Even though they do not write, I'm sure most people in our country share your views expressed on the "To-Day" show, a few days ago.

I thank you for your courage and ability to speak out, what so many of us believe and are saying to each other tho we do not write, or have the courage to say it on T.V. I've lost my only son in the war. God bless you and guide you in your efforts to right the world, and our society.

Sincerely,

Mrs. C. G.

188. I had called the draft board before moving from Illinois and was assured there would be no problem in his changing schools.

July 30, 1969

Dear Dr. Spock:

Thank you for having the courage to stand up and fight for both our boys and for our country. Many, many people appreciate the sacrifices you have made to follow the dictates of your conscience. We won't forget.

This letter is written as an appeal for advice since we do not know where to turn.

Last year, my husband was transferred to Denver, and for financial reasons (in-state vs out-of-state tuition) our son subsequently transferred in the fall of 1968 from Northern Illinois University to Colorado University. In this process, he lost several credits and was four short to qualify as a sophomore here. In March of 1969, he received a reclassification to 1-A, and in contacting the draft board, we learned it was for the reason given above. I had called the draft board before moving from Illinois and was assured there would be no problem in his changing schools. Had we known, he easily could have made up those credits last summer —he is now doing so by taking a course at summer school. Our argument is that he was a full-time student in good standing at NIU and that he should not be penalized for losing some credits in transferring, since he is obligated to make them up.

An appeal is pending. In the interim, he is to report for his physical on August 11. We know there are other avenues for further appeal should this one be denied but we are ignorant of the procedure. I understand there are lawyers here in Denver who will accept cases to fight the draft board without fee, but we do not know who they are.

My husband and I are again being transferred—to Atlanta. Since our son will be staying here, we will need this information before we leave in three weeks so he will know where to turn if his appeal is turned down. Can you help us? Not so incidentally, we have another son who is currently stationed in a combat area in Viet Nam. I know you can understand the anguish of parents in these circumstances.

Please tell us what to do. God bless you.
> Sincerely,
> Mrs. H. M.
> Denver, Colorado

189. He has been taught kindness and gentleness all his life, and on the 3rd. day of basic training, they told him to thrust with a bayonet and yell Kill! This he refused to do.

> Napa, Calif.
> Aug. 12,

Dear Dr. Spock:

May we congratulate you on your recent victory in the courts!! We are for you a 100%! We are hoping that Mr. Coffin and Mr. Goodman will do as well. We have followed your case with great interest. It seems in our country, today, that we are losing the freedom of speech and expression, in many ways. Maybe we should spread some of the Freedom in this country that we're supposed to be securing for the Vietnamese people.

We have always conducted ourselves as good Americans and taxpayers should. We are both employed and have worked to give our two sons the benefit of a good education. As a result, one is just a few units from his Master's in Educating the Emotionally and Physically Handicapped Child. He has three tots of his own, and a little foster child that is a Rubella baby, that we all adore. His wife is getting her degree in Speech Therapy.

Our younger son, is 25, has his B.A. in Radio and Television; he has had 2 acting awards, and a scholarship or two along the way. Now, here is where the story gets bitter! This young man was drafted in Nov. and sent to Ft. Lewis, Wash. He has been taught kindness and gentleness all his life, and on the 3rd. day of basic training, they told him to thrust with a bayonet and yell Kill! This he refused to do. He was humiliated and threatened—all of the choice little things they try—and he still refused. Finally, he was allowed to use his talents as a company clerk, and given time to get some more statements from friends that he was a conscientious objector on Moral grounds rather than religious ones. He had tried to establish this before he was inducted, but the draft board refused to recognize his claim. This strung out until he was home for a week in May, to get some more documents. Upon his return, he was put back into basic, and on the 31 of May, he went to Canada. He called us from there to tell us what he'd done, and what he needed to stay out of the country. With the help of a contact, we made arrangements for finances and his belongings to reach him. At the end of a week, he called us, to let his decision be known. He had decided that it was better to return and face the music like a man than to spend his life running. He turned himself in and asked to be put in the Stockade until his fate was decided. The outcome was 6 mos. hard labor and 2/3's forfeiture of pay! He was sentenced June 25th, and as yet the Army has told us nothing of their own volition. We had to call the Judge-Advocate to find that out. He has met some fine young men who are in the same boat that he's in. Their principles just will not let them do something they consider immoral. And many of these kids, are just like ours, with a good education and something to offer their country, but not to bear arms.

As a matter of fact, one of these chaps, 22 and a fine young fellow, came to see us, yesterday. He had been in the Stockade several months, and finally got out with a bad discharge! With him was another young man, who had just gotten out of Leavenworth (!) for being A.W.O.L. Isn't that a fine commentary on our military? Many of these boys are being sent to Leavenworth and given a dishonorable discharge. We were also told that the punishments are very inconsistent.

Our son, [name deleted] has never even had a traffic ticket!! He would walk around the block to avoid a fight, and is a very peace-loving individual. He is a big husky blond with the typical "Kennedy" mop of hair, and anything but a Momma's boy—Just about now, I wouldn't see anything wrong with that!! He loves contact sports and broke his shoulder playing football.

[He] was on a 9 wk. tour of Europe while he was in College, and is vitally interested in people and the world around him. He has offered to do anything they want him to do except take basic and war means kill to him. In his language, that word is spelled Kill! and no one, but no one, is going to change his way of thinking. He will just continue to return to the Stockade until somebody gets tired of the game, or they kill him.

Their mail is censored and confiscated if the censor is so inclined. [He] discovered they had opened some material he'd sent for from a photography shop and never even told him it had come. They said it was a mistake, but he is most upset about it. Any games or books that are sent must be donated to the library. This is a small thing as we keep telling him, but when you are accustomed to complete freedom and privacy of your own person and belongings this is pretty rough. Any goodies that are sent are also taken; cookies, etc.

We were also told, yesterday, that physical violence is sometimes used on reluctant prisoners. Then tonight, I got the Sept. Pageant and read the article on page 26, and it made my blood boil! After all, all people are not made in the same mold, and it is a crime to try to bend their will or brand them as criminals because they have principles to live by. As his mother, I would like to tell you that I work in a State Mental Hospital, and have seen the results of many round pegs pushed into square openings, and the results are more than sad!

If you could find time to write to our son, we would appreciate it, and to know that someone of your caliber cares about him, might help change the Army's narrow mind. We know this is a lot to ask of you, but we are taking the chance.

Both of us had ancestors who fought in the Revolution and a few more wars besides; so somewhere along the line there was probably another rebel with principles. Anyway, they helped to found this country, and I'll bet they wouldn't appreciate what has come to pass.

We are enclosing a stamped addressed envelope in case you can grant our request. Thank you again. . . .

Sincerely,

Mrs. K. K.

190. They've put him in the infantry, and are teaching him to murder.

[undated]

Dear Dr. Spock,

What can I do as an ordinary citizen, a mother of a fine boy, age 20, who was drafted in June—what can I do to help stop this carnage in Vietnam?

They've put him in the infantry, and are teaching him to murder. He was not raised to be a soldier. He is being penalized because he couldn't keep up 15 credit hours a semester and keep a full time job, nights, supporting himself.

Please, what can I do to help you?

Yours sincerely,

Mrs. A. L.

Warson Woods, Missouri

191. I am in school now and am facing induction into the U.S. armed forces because of poor progression in school (Northeastern University).

Sept. 2, 1969

Dear Dr. Spock,

We have never met so it seems awkward to ask you for help, but I must. My name is [name deleted]. I know of you by reputation from the newspapers and radio commentators. I am in school now and am facing induction into the U.S. armed forces because of poor progression in school (Northeastern University). I have lost my 2-S deferment and have had my pre-induction physical last December (which I passed). I should be inducted within the next 2 or 3 months. I need help and am unable to help myself. I realize the difficulty and hardships which were placed upon you for counseling people to avoid the draft and do not wish to have this happen again. However I would appreciate whatever you might be able to do. Please answer this letter.

Thank you for the time spent reading this letter, I appreciate it.

Yours very truly,
G. K. [male]
Watertown, Mass.

192. In three of the four cases mentioned above, I feel that the action of the local draft board was punitive in assigning a 1A classification and proceeding with the induction process.

Thousand Oaks, California
November 11, 1969

Dear Dr. Spock:

On one of your public appearances on television recently, I heard you make the statement that your public protest of our involvement in Vietnam would include an effort to stand behind those young men who had been indicted for their resistance to the draft.

I am the mother of such a young man, and in our town of approximately 30,000 people there are three other young men who have recently been indicted. I know each of these three other men very well and can vouch for the integrity of their positions and for their idealism. It seems to me, though, that they are rather like lonely prophets crying in the wilderness; there are not many people who support them actively, and fewer who are willing or able to help them. I find a ray of hope in the fact that you support the concept of amnesty, and am, therefore, writing in the hope that you might be able to give me some information. In three of the four cases mentioned above, I feel that the action of the local draft board was punitive in assigning a 1A classification and proceeding with the induction process: the boys had turned in their draft cards though previously they had had exemptions. In making their statement with respect to the ethics of our involvement in Vietnam, they apparently incurred the wrath of the military mind. They expected this to happen and are prepared to pay the price for their dissent but I feel morally obligated to do what I can to see that justice is done. I can find no justification for their being imprisoned for their ideals.

Can you give me any idea about what I could do to help them, or put me in touch with anyone locally to whom I could turn?

Also, on NBC television recently, I saw an interview with a man who represented an international (?) group called Amnesty International. He stated that their concern was with political prisoners of the left and the right, and made some kind of statement with respect to draft resistance. I didn't quite catch it so I can't quote him, but I wonder if you know of such an organization. He specifically mentioned 100,000 people in the Soviet Union imprisoned for religious belief or other dissent, some 80,000 in Indonesia, and a few thousand in Greece. I think I am quoting him accurately "Human rights is a form of universal conscience." This statement intrigued me and I felt perhaps I could get direction from people whose values are reflected in such a statement.

Finally, could you give me any indication of the direction and thrust of your own support of the resistance to the draft? Is there any way that I can be of help?

Thank you very much for your attention to this letter.

Sincerely,

Mrs. M. W.

III. Trying to Stop a War without End

IN ADDITION to the emotional appeals for help and the accusatory letters from critics, Spock continued to receive supportive mail. By late 1969, most of this took the form of suggesting strategies for the antiwar movement or highlighting specific concerns, from issues that should be emphasized to tactical concerns about a handful of "revolutionaries" derailing a mass protest. Such letters should not be considered completely separately from those in the preceding section or in Section IV, for each group represents a side of complicated, interrelated set of concerns.

193. We must stop the worker from going into a War factory and producing a single unit of a murderous War weapon.

August 26, 1969

Dear Doctor:

I would sincerely like to thank you for helping me bring up two healthy, strong, normal (spoiled brat) teenagers, who are now in college. You book was my guiding light.

I am writing you today, to applaud you on your strong anti-war feelings, these past few years. Your voice was loud and clear.

But since talk will not stop a War, positive action must be taken!! We must stop the worker from going into a War factory and producing a single unit of a murderous War weapon. We must start making it a shame to be War-worker, a war-monger or a War-profiteer!! Pickets must be set up outside war factories pleading with working people not to enter.

Do you <u>dare</u> do such a thing? Will you be the first in your area to start a picket line outside a war plant? If enough good decent individuals see the light, all present and future wars can be stopped permanently from the home front.

We can do this on a world-wide scale. In fact, we must, if humanity is to survive!

Respectfully yours,
Mrs. B. L.
Brooklyn, New York

194. I am a world war veteran as are also my two brothers, one of whom was nearly killed while serving in the Marine Corps. We are against this war and this draft 100 percent.

Largo, Fla.
September 22, 1969

Dear Dr. Spock:

I have nothing but the highest admiration for you and your courage in trying to bring this big blunder of our Vietnam involvement to a quick end. If we had more men like you, William Coffin, Fulbright, McGovern,

Hatfield, Kennedy, Church and others, we could put an end soon to this tragic mistake. Keep up the good work. I hope that you have the 500,000 people in your Washington march on November 15th, and hope that the 400 protests on the college campuses are a great success.

I am a world war veteran as are also my two brothers, one of whom was nearly killed while serving in the Marine Corps. We are against this war and this draft 100 percent.

Opposition to the war and the draft are steadily mounting.

Sincerely,

Rev. J. S. [male]

[EDITOR'S NOTE: In the fall of 1969, President Nixon's honeymoon on the question of Vietnam came to an end. Although he had announced the first troop reductions since escalation and had taken measures to move the draft to a lottery system by December, the war continued seemingly unabated. As a result, a number of major protests took place in October 1969, including the nationwide October 15 Moratorium and the November March Against Death in Washington. The culmination of the latter protest included musical performances before a crowd of more than 500,000 around the Washington Monument. As folksinger Pete Seeger led the massive gathering, singing "All we are saying is . . . give peace a chance," Spock shouted into the microphone, "Are you listening, Nixon? . . . Are you listening?" Spock now became as much identified with his criticism of the new president as he had been with Johnson.]

195. We have seen them in action. In public rallys, while preaching personal freedom on one hand, they grab microphones from speakers who oppose them (S.D.S.) and they throw out reporters.

September 23, 1969

Dear Dr. Benjamin Spock,

My husband and I are college students in Michigan and we wish to write you on what we believe to be a very important matter. We have heard that you will be participating in the demonstration in Chicago, October 8–11. Because of you and the reason behind this demonstration (the Vietnam War) we have become interested in participating too. We respect you and everything you have done for this cause. However we are also greatly alarmed when we read papers such as the enclosed. We are quite well aquainted with M.S.U's local S.D.S. chapter, its members and their tactics. We have seen them in action. In public rallys, while preaching personal freedom on one hand, they grab microphones from speakers who oppose them (S.D.S.) and they throw out reporters. I certainly disagree with many laws and practices in the U.S., but I am afraid that groups like the Lansing S.D.S. are even more harmful to the good of the cause that you and others have fought for. Our point is that we are afraid students like those who printed the enclosed will turn your "peaceful march against U.S. participation in V.N." into their "war at home, pro-economic-communistic revolution."

Because of this, my husband, myself and many other students are wary of going to Chicago. It isn't so much that we are frightened of meeting violence, but if we must meet it, let it be for the <u>right</u> cause and not the idiocy you see on the paper I am sending you.

Please, sir, what we ask is that if you know of any way of letting not only young people but also the older citizens of this country and the city officials of Chicago know that the majority of youth (no matter what they look like) want to end war, retain as much peace as possible, and make right the wrongs of our democracy, perhaps October 8–11, 1969 won't turn into a revolution afterall. However, we also realize that a few revolutionaries among a large gathering can start mob violence. How can we see that they, and any other group or official body, do not instigate violence and death for their own purpose?

If it weren't that hope is rapidly dwindling for young people, we would not be so concerned about this peaceful demonstration. But it is and we are.

Please help us, in any way possible.

    Sincerely,
    J & C. R. [female and male]
    Lansing, Michigan

196. I believe the war can now be ended. Nixon is running scared, and the whole anti-war movement is quite beyond his power to contain.

September 27, 1969

Dear Dr. Spock:

You are an honored member of our household (middle-class and suburban, if such labels are appropos) in two significant ways: Through your baby book and through your heroic efforts toward ending the war.

I believe the war can now be ended. Nixon is running scared, and the whole anti-war movement is quite beyond his power to contain. Foremost, it will require a full-scale revolt on the part of the majority of the people in Congress (after all, Congress appropriated the uncountable and unaccountable sums of money for all this barbarism). Second, I doubt that Nixon is as stubborn as Lyndon Johnson, and he certainly does not have the fortitude to withstand even a minor avalanche of protest.

Thus, I regard your forthcoming demonstration in Washington as especially significant and potentially fruitful. I hope it will have the broadest possible base in terms of participants.

It will be impossible for me to attend, but I would offer an idea: In addition to placing the names of Americans killed into a coffin, how about including the names of war victims representing Saigon, the Viet Cong, and Hanoi? Their lives, too, are to be reverenced, and none is my enemy. If their names are not available, their cards could contain appropriate flags or some other symbol (but not numbers, please).

All good wishes,
E. G. [male]
Toledo

197. I am for abolition of the draft by any effective means. I am not unequivocally for pulling out of Viet Nam.

November 27, 1969
New York, New York

Dear Dr. Spock:

Although I sympathize with what appears to be Fascist persecution of you and others by the government I am not convinced that ignominious withdrawal from the Vietnam War is the best course of action for this country at the moment.

Much as I deplore the War, there is a case to be made of abandoning our ally, regardless of how distasteful support of him may be.

Of one thing I am convinced and will support you or any individual who vigorously opposes it—military conscription. In my opinion, this is what has made the atrocity of Viet Nam possible and, no doubt, will create other Viet Nams unless it is abolished, not reformed. You cannot reform Fascism, which is what military conscription is. In my book it was unconstitutional when a running-scared cripple foisted it on the American public and, 28 years later, is still unconstitutional.

I am not opposed to war, per se. I am for killing or injuring in defense of me or my loved ones. I am an agnostic about an after life. I am a believer in <u>this</u> life.

Without the draft, Viet Nam I believe would be impossible. With the draft, the U.S. is turning, or has been turned, into another Nazi Germany, that is to say a military nation. Militarily-oriented nations search for and find wars. This is what they are trained and brainwashed to do.

Sorry I can't make this letter longer. I am <u>for</u> abolition of the draft by <u>any effective means</u>. I am <u>not</u> unequivocally for pulling out of Viet Nam. I will contribute time and/or money to the former goal. I cannot sincerely devote my energies to the latter.

Best wishes,

T. H. [male]

IV. (Anti)War Stories of the Young

THIS LAST grouping of letters from 1969 could easily have fit with the second group in this chapter. They, too, convey the "agony of war" to an extent. The difference is that while the first set of letters came mostly from parents concerned about their sons, this group comes from the sons themselves (in two letters) or close observers of the young people currently affected by the war—or likely to be.

President Nixon, well aware of the anxiety that the war and the draft produced in so many families, moved fairly quickly to reduce draft calls, and in December 1969, the Selective Service held its first random selection draft lottery. Though this, too, produced no small amount of anxiety and tension, it created the appearance of fairness. That may be one explanation for the relative absence of the following kind of letters—the kind detailing the experience of a young man trapped in a system from which there seems no escape—in Spock's mail after 1969.

198. I know that all incidents involving this division are thoroughly investigated but it's obvious that if we left, our mortars would never land in hamlets.

Phou Vinh

28 July [1969]

Dear Dr. Spock,

I have just finished your book on Vietnam.[2] I bought it at the PX here at the 1st Cavalry Base Camp, surprisingly enough. Coincidentally, just a few days ago I read excerpts from the decision of the court that set aside your conviction. For the book and for the court I say—Bravo!

Certainly, you and Mr. Zimmerman wrote a tract; but so did Thomas Paine. There is a time for cool scholarship and a time for hyperbole—you left evidence enough of your familiarity with the former to excuse the latter.

I am here, I was not prepared to go to jail rather than fulfill my ROTC incurred obligation when called to active duty last year, nor was I willing to do so when ordered to Vietnam. I haven't seen much of the war, but from what I have seen, I believe the worst. I hope it's more than a rationalization to say that I'm lucky to be in a position where I can help some people in trouble, the average GI who doesn't want to be here either. Just last week I won a not guilty finding for a Special Court-Martial for a soldier who told an officer to 'get fucked!' There is a new Military Justice Act in effect, it should have a salutary effect on the quality of military justice.

In fairness, I believe the period since you wrote the book has seen significant reduction in the kinds of ruthless raids and artillery bombardments which you so vividly described. That they ever happened is a disgrace to America. I know that all incidents involving this division are thoroughly investigated but it's obvious that if we left, our mortars would never land in hamlets.

I'm sure many officers are cold blooded killers, as you quoted. Many are disgusted by the whole thing. Too many seem to have suspended their own judgement out of deference to their careers.

Surely, you and I would have to respect each other's position. My own opposition to the war came a year after I had foreclosed all but the most extreme and damaging alternative to service for a lawyer to contemplate. I hope that my actions after next June will justify my compromise and that I can continue here to ameliorate the problems of our men. As I said to a friend on the Harvard faculty—don't worry if you are 'not supporting us,' we've got plenty of support, but you have much to say.

Yours for peace,

J. G. [male]

Officer of the Staff Judge Advocate, [Division deleted]

APO San Francisco

199. It seemed to me a real joke that I could better serve as a private (with a bachelor's degree) in the Army than in a well-digging program in Dahomey, West Africa.

Gainesville, Florida
July 29, 1969

Dear Dr. Spock:

I am writing chiefly to express hearty approval of what you are doing to bring about an end to the despicable Vietnam war. However, I also want to congratulate you on your victory in the U.S. Court of Appeals. To those of us who keep up with current events and the mood in America, I must say, it looked grim since the conservative swing (including appointment of Warren Burger) seemed all-pervasive. It's encouraging to think that civil liberties still find some protection in America. Who could doubt that you and Rev. Coffin were simply voicing your opinions as provided for, and protected by, the First Amendment's freedom of speech section.

Personally, I know your feelings well. On April 3, 1969, I had to refuse induction into the Army in Jacksonville, Fla., because of conscience. I had just finished four years at the University of Florida, gaining a B.S. in journalism. I had been in the Peace Corps but got drafted and had to return home. It seemed to me a real joke that I could better serve as a private (with a bachelor's degree) in the Army than in a well-digging program in Dahomey, West Africa. Our priorities were all messed up. Under-developed nations have so much more need than we do; especially constructive need as opposed to destructive need we seem to manifest.

The Surgeon, US Army Recruiting Command, accepted my appeal and medically disqualified me because of high blood pressure. I received a I-Y (national emergency only) classification only a month ago. It was a hard struggle to avoid prosecution, but I did it. Las month, also, I submitted my conscientious objector claim. I feel confident that, without the knowledge that I had refused induction, the Surgeon would not have acted as he did.

Now that I have the best desirable situation—free from immediate worry about the draft—I want to concentrate on helping others express their consciences and end this war. I am 23 years old and have lots of time to do it in. Let me know how I can help you, specifically. And again, congratulations!

Sincerely,

J. S. [male]

200. Being a Roman Catholic, I know I've no leg to stand on concerning any official stand taken by the Church forbidding its members to serve in the Armed Forces.

Balboa, Calif.
8/19/69

Dear Dr. Spock:

Forgive me for laying my troubles before you, since you've incurred many of your own by simply following your conscience.

Last June I graduated from California State College at Fullerton with a Bachelor's Degree in English. Last Friday, August 15, I received my I-A draft classification and an induction notice. The former was dated August 5, the latter August <u>6</u>. I am getting a postponement in my induction date—August 20—because of the delay in receiving my notice (It had to go through two address changes—no fault of mine since the draft board had my change of address.); because my father had a heart attack July 27 and is still recuperating; and because I've a birthday coming up September 13. I haven't received my induction date notice yet, but should by tomorrow or the next day.

I am also applying for an I-O classification as a conscientious objector. Being a Roman Catholic, I know I've no leg to stand on concerning any official stand taken by the Church forbidding its members to serve in the Armed Forces. I am basing my appeal simply upon my conscience as influenced by my religious training (eleven years of Catholic School) and the attitudes I've developed in the last few years through college, discussions (and arguments) with others, and the reading of writers of esteem—writers whose greatness and art stem primarily from their compassion for their fellow man, good and evil.

My appeal form is due no later than August 29, ten days from today. Therefore, I ask you, Dr. Spock, for any advice you can give me concerning my appeal. I am prepared to scrub floors at a mental hospital—any kind of work, no matter how demeaning, as long as I can be of some service to my fellow man rather than bear arms or contribute to the bearing of arms against him. Thank you.

Respectfully,
B. H. [male]

201. They looked so young and vulnerable that my heart ached and I thought, will they be next.

October 21, 1969

Dear Dr. Spock:

You not only have love for babies first opening their eyes to life, but you also have a heart full of compassion for some of those same babies who are now growing up and opening their eyes for life ahead. But they cannot plan ahead and are suffering a breakdown, etc., because of the fear of being sent out to die or a living death in Vietnam for <u>nothing</u> and you are doing your utmost to help them.

When France, who was and is a proud country, was fighting in Indochina, now Vietnam, I have heard that she did not draft one soldier, but fought with paid Volunteers and her Officers. But she lost the flower of her Officers. We are losing the <u>flower of our Youth</u>. But she got out and did not led losing face deter her.

I have read that we have about 250,000 wounded. Some have no arms, no legs, no eyes. Are they not our <u>living dead</u>? Could you call attention to them to the people like you do for the dead. Some will be in mental institutions, for the rest of their lives if not wounded or killed. Could you also have leaflets made to be given our to the people.

Nixon says give him 3 years more, at the rate he is going it will be 6 or more. Could the parents of 14, 15, and so on who will be then drafted be alerted. Nixon says he will take them at 19.

I went to the candlelit parade in Flushing on the 15th. While listening to the speakers, I noticed 4 young boys about 17 or thereabouts, taking a few minutes off from listening, playing that string game that you transfer from one hand to another. They looked so young and vulnerable that my heart ached and I thought, will they be next. . . .

God Bless you and keep you for many years to come. We need you. And I know you will, like the old saying, "strike while the iron is hot. . . ."

Sincerely yours,
Miss J. B.
Flushing, Queens, N.Y.

202. I will tell him that the shrillest rantings of hysterical super-patriots and the uncomfortable rumblings of the clutchers-at-conformity failed to silence or intimidate the voices of conscientious objection.

[EDITOR'S NOTE: This letter came handwritten on a "Joyous Christmas Greetings" card.]

[undated]

Dear Dr. Spock:

It has taken the gentle contagion of seasonal spirit to impel my wife and me to do this small but—to us—most important thing, which has been put off far too long: to express to you our deepest gratitude for all you have done—and continue to do—in defense of conscience and humanity, in a time when far too many Americans shun such values as being not quite "respectable," or (therefore?) unpatriotic. When our son David, not yet two, reaches the age at which one reads and thinks and looks about and begins to question some of the eternal "verities" of American virtue, as put forward in some self-righteous history book—if he ponders Vietnam and asks me, Why? How could they? and where were goodness, fairness and bravery all those years? I will tell him that neither Americans nor any other people have exclusive patents on virtue or on vice, but that all the Colonel Rheaults and the Lieutenant Calleys,[3] and all their fear—and hate-ridden—and thoughtless—fellow citizens whose support permitted their deeds and their deaths, all of these were in the end no match for the courage of thousands of young men who put their bodies and their social "standing" on the line in support of their deep opposition to the mad, cruel course which America was following. I will tell him that the shrillest rantings of hysterical super-patriots and the uncomfortable rumblings of the clutchers-at-conformity failed to silence or intimidate the voices of conscientious objection, of protest by students, teachers, clergymen, doctors, their wives and children, youngsters and oldsters—and that their numbers grew until even the great "silent majority" acknowledged the rightness of their cause. And I will tell him—or perhaps that history book will tell him—that among the braves and finest Americans in that time when it took guts to express even <u>doubts</u> as to the rightness of our course, a man with much to lose stepped forward and proclaimed with gentle firmness that our leaders and policies and the laws which they were using were wrong, and must be opposed and disobeyed—and he was right, and even the great power of his government failed to silence him and others like him, until their truths won out. A dashing John Wayne–type here, asks our David? No, David, a kind, sincere and thoughtful man, whose medical and human wisdom brought needed patience and understanding to your parents in many a crisis of fever and tantrums and diet and growth pains.

We thank you from the bottom of our hearts. May peace and love be with you and your family in this holiday season, and throughout the year to come.

G. and S. G. [male and female]
Los Angeles, Calif.

Competing images of men during wartime. *Top*: A crowd of "hard hats" (New York construction workers) demonstrate in support of the war, May 1970. (Bettmann/CORBIS) *Bottom*: A crowd of Vietnam Veterans Against the War, gathered on the Mall in Washington, DC, April 1971. (U.S. News & World Report, Library of Congress)

8 The End of the Tunnel, 1970–1972

As RESISTANCE to President Nixon's handling of the war grew in late 1969 and early 1970, the themes of letters to Dr. Spock reverted to a more evenly distributed set of core topics not unlike those appearing in the mail he received in 1966 and 1967. There are letters that suggest new strategies for the antiwar movement, and others that again emphasize the impact of war on children, and others expressing frustration over their apparent inability to end the war. The anticommunist supporters of the war continued to write, but in smaller numbers. In fact, the number of letters to Spock about the war declined significantly after 1969. This may have been due in part to Nixon's continuing public assertions that he was deescalating the war (despite secretly escalating the air war) and perhaps in part thanks to reforms in the draft system.

When Nixon announced on April 30, 1970, that he had ordered American and South Vietnamese ground troops into Cambodia to destroy enemy staging areas just inside the Cambodian border, the nation erupted in protest. More than 350 college campuses closed down or went on strike, including Kent State University in Ohio, where, on May 4, National Guard troops killed four students and wounded another eleven. Many of the letters in this chapter respond to these events—if not directly, then indirectly—as they express concern for American men still subject to the draft, currently fighting in Vietnam, or the children of Americans and Vietnamese.

I. Trying to End America's Longest War

BY 1970, the full-scale American combat operations in Vietnam were entering their seventh year (though, depending on how one dated the origins of American intervention in Vietnam, the number of years could be said to be much higher). The antiwar movement could claim some victories in that period, but it had not stopped the war; nothing made that clearer than the late April invasion of Cambodia. Thus, the following selection of letters came from Americans still trying to find just the right recipe to end the war. The suggestions range from economic boycotts, to giving young people the vote (and, in 1972, getting them to vote for George McGovern), to protest strategies that demonstrate widespread unity in favor of withdrawal from Vietnam. The United States ultimately withdrew in 1973 following the signing of the Paris Peace Accords. Saigon and the South Vietnamese government fell in 1975, thirty years after Ho Chi Minh declared Vietnamese independence.

203. In the next peace march, we can make a dramatic impact if <u>all</u> the marchers carry the flag, with a liberal dose of peace symbols of course as well.

Champaign, Ill
Feb 25, 1970

Dear Dr. Spock,

At yesterday's coffee-discussion at the Univ. of Illinois, you brought out a point of fundamental importance: our society is becoming conditioned to peace marches; for future marches to be effective, we peaceniks must be inventive, colorful, never stale.

May I please offer a suggestion for the next march on Washington? Recall the Veterans Day Parade, when thousands marched with small replicas of the American flag, waving them proudly. In the next peace march, we can make a dramatic impact if <u>all</u> the marchers carry the flag, with a liberal dose of peace symbols of course as well. Some of the benificent effects will be:

1) the U.S. flag speaks better to middle class America than the Viet Cong flag.
2) the peace movement will begin to associate itself with patriotism (not anarchy, Communism, or whatever) in the minds of the people.
3) this will counteract the mindless conservatives who wave the flag as a repudiation of the peace demonstrations.

Dr. Spock, the local peace movement lacks drive, stamina, forcefulness. We need the impetus of a successful national demonstration which will make page 1, not as you say be "buried on page 33." I think this (new?) idea can give our movement the push it needs. If you agree, please use your influence to implement the idea, so there will be enough flags for all of us when it is time for the next mass rally. . . .

R. + S. E. [male and female]

204. It is our leaders and our generation who have turned our youth into hippies and dissenters, shoving them up against a wall and telling them to go and make war, or else go to prison.

May 9, 1970
Minneapolis, Minnesota

Dear Dr. Spock:

I am taking the liberty of writing to you, because I have felt pretty dependent upon you since my son was a baby. He is now 22. . . .

I have watched your activities with much interest, and even wrote to the judge, at the time you were convicted, hoping to be of some help to you. I know you are sincerely interested in our young people so am sending you a copy of this letter which I am also sending to the Mpls Tribune, Richard Nixon, Donald Fraser, and George McGovern, hoping to help in some small way. It is as follows:

It is pretty plain to see why our "boys" under twenty-one are too young to vote in this country but are old enough to go and die like "men" for it.

I'm over forty, but can still see the hypocirsy of others elders who look down upon college students who dissent over the pitiful state of affairs our leaders have put our great country in. Even the hippie, who is sneered at, with his long hair and bearded appearance, is only choosing a peaceful way of rebelling against our phony values.

Personally, I, for one, am proud of our young people today. They are much smarter than our generation ever was. It is our leaders and our generation who have turned our youth into hippies and dissenters, shoving them up against a wall and telling them to go and make war, or else go to prison.

Today we have the most informed voters in history, due to the mass news media available to everyone, through radio, television, newspapers, etc. However most people over twenty-one are too busy making a living to pay enough attention to political affairs. It is our young people between sixteen and twenty-one who are sincerely interested in these affairs, particularly as their very lived depend upon them.

I would like to see everyone from the sixteen to twenty-one age bracket given the vote and I'll wager we'll find a more peaceful way of getting along with our neighbors through-out the world, than shedding American blood all over the face of the earth. . . .

Very sincerely,
Mrs. M. M.

205. I would like to suggest that all those who are for ending the Viet Nam War cease to be consumers from the American economy, except for essentials such as food and shelter.

New York, N.Y.

May 14, 1970

Dear Dr. Spock:

In the weeks since I read <u>Decent and Indecent</u>,[1] I have spent many hours trying to figure out what I could do to express some of the idealism which your book has inspired in me. I think I have found a way and I would like to ask your support of it.

I would like to suggest that all those who are for ending the Viet Nam War cease to be consumers from the American economy, except for essentials such as food and shelter. My idea is to copy Chavez' grape strike, only the target would be all American businesses.

I discussed with an economist at Columbia, how many people would have to participate in such a joint effort in order to threaten the economy with collapse. In summary, it appears that if 27 million people in America who are either students or in other capacities connected with the academic community, were to diminish their expenditures by a mere 20%, that the GNP, due to the economic multiplier effect, would decrease substantially. Were this to occur, the stock market, already shakey, would be in a precarious position indeed. If people outside the academic community participate the impact would be greater still. In such circumstances the war machine could not function.

The mere threat of this would, I believe, put more pressure on Mr. Nixon than all the demonstrations we could possibly mount. Dr. Kissinger, my professor at Radcliffe, constantly advises Nixon that public opinion is so ephemeral that it's hardly worth considering in policy decisions; therefore he should ignore it. But an economic boycott is something no president could ignore. Nixon would have to act, rather than face a 1929. Nixon would have to end the war—at once.

Such a boycott would have the advantage of being legal and nonviolent. It would answer the question of housewives at home with their babies of "What can I do?" (You can stop buying Saran Wrap and Sara Lee cakes and your spring wardrobe, etc. etc.) Further, it's publicity potential would be phenomenal. The media would recognize that such a move is not the mosquito bite of selected boycotts—no, this is attacking the guts of the economy. All such publicity should be valuable for its educational effect.

Dr. Spock, I know you are an incredibly busy man, and it embarrasses me, a housewife, to make such a request of you, but I wonder if I could hear from you or a member of your staff whether you think my idea has potential.

If you do think so, I would like to enlist your support in any way that you see fit. It seems to me that the most effective way to get the idea across to the greatest audience and with the greatest impact, would be for you to speak out on it. If this is not possible, I would like to be able to use your name in writing to other figures in the peace movement, to Senators and Congressmen, in press releases and so on.

Sincerely,

Mrs. M. A.

[EDITOR'S NOTE: Spock responded that he is "totally absorbed in speaking at universities and raising money for the defense of draft resisters and resisters in the armed services."]

206. Like millions of others I daily experience the terrible frustration of being absolutely helpless to do anything that will have any effect whatsoever in stopping the war.

Mamaroneck, New York
May 22, 1970

Dear Dr. Spock:

I believe I have an idea to stop the war in its tracks but it demands leadership by someone with courage and a national respect for his antiwar beliefs. More than anyone else, you fulfill these qualifications and therefore I am appealing to you to give the idea your prayerful consideration.

All of the protests, marches, jailings and prayers by those who despise the war have lead to nothing but failure and even death at the hands of our own militia. Like millions of others I daily experience the terrible frustration of being absolutely helpless to do anything that will have any effect whatsoever in stopping the war. I am sorry to admit to myself that money is a greater motivating force to politicians than blood. How then can the silent majority exploit this fact of our capitalistic nation, I asked myself? A steel boycott could do it! Steel is basic to our national economy we have always been told. Therefore let every man and women—especially all the parents of the students who are wasting their lives and efforts by protesting—who despise the war, stop buying anything made of steel—automobiles, washing machines, refrigerators, lawn mowers . . . down to steel kitchen knives. It would cause a minor depression—the desired effect! But the difference would be that it could be instantly stopped the day the last American left Viet Nam. No war-hating American would object to driving his car a year longer or using a substitute for steel where possible.

A boycott would not be as dramatic as a parade, window-smashing or rock-throwing, but it would be far more effective in a non-violent way which is how Mr. Nixon says he likes to have us protest. No one gets hurt. It is completely legal.

If you would spark the idea by presenting it on a national TV hook-up, a miracle could happen in a few weeks. I do not want any credit for the idea—it would be all yours and you would deserve all the credit for starting the steel boycott that stopped the war.

If for any reason you would prefer not to use my suggestion, please let me know as soon as possible for I will continue to seek someone who will try.

> Very truly yours,
> T. G. [male]

207. I recognize the value of civil disobedience at critical times, but in this case it is the war we want to stop—not the government.

> Greenwich, Connecticut
> May 6, 1971

Dear Dr. Spock:

I have always considered your advice on baby care as the most sensible available and would still recommend it to my daughter when she needs it, but I find it absolutely incredible that you would participate in the demonstrations in Washington this past week. What possible good can this kind of activity do?

I recognize the value of civil disobedience at critical times, but in this case it is the war we want to stop—not the government. This kind of misdirected energy only alienates the average citizen from the important objective when actually it is the average citizen whom we need to come and join the effort.

I wish you could organize a nation-wide demonstration of unity of the national will for peace to take place within all communities which have any kind of peace group. (There is one here in Greenwich.) This demonstration would last only a short time, perhaps an hour, but all over the country on the same day and at the same time. It would be a chance for everyone who believes we should leave Vietnam completely, all men and planes, within let us say 6 months, to stand up and be counted. Most of us after all cannot go to Washington and if we did try to, it would be chaotic. (Think of the pollution from all those buses tied up in traffic.)

No, the demonstrations should be close to home, short and simple so that Mr. and Mrs. Average Citizen can take part. It could take place in the middle of September when everyone is back from vacation. It might consist of a short address in each community by an appropriate leader, the signing of a scroll or petition to be sent to President Nixon and the mass singing of "America the Beautiful." It is important that there be a patriotic song. People who are for peace do not want to be branded as unpatriotic. Perhaps they love there country more than the hawks and they want to be able to show it. And somebody must tell the kids that carrying the Vietcong flag around will not win any friends or influence anybody in the cause of peace. They are using bad psychology.

The proposterous actions this week in Washington are repellant to most of us. Let us have a demonstration at home in which parents can join. After all most communities have parents with college-age kids. Lets see how many will turn out to sing together. Then Mr. Agnew will not be able to say that only a very small number of all Americans took part.

Most sincerely,
Mrs. H. A.

[EDITOR'S NOTE: Letters to Dr. Spock about the Vietnam War dropped off considerably in the second half of 1971, but picked up again in the spring of 1972 after Spock became a formal candidate for president on the People's Party ticket. In addition to his steady speaking schedule on college campuses and before civic organizations, Spock now added campaign events on the third party's modest budget. Such occasions gave Spock the opportunity to continue blasting Nixon and his failure to end the war within three years of taking office. As a result, many of the last letters he received on the war came in response to campaign appearances. Note that some writers asked him to throw his support behind Democratic candidate

George McGovern, himself an outspoken opponent of the war. Spock never had any chance of winning the election and he knew it. Then, as now, the obstacles to getting third party candidates on ballots in all fifty states proved insurmountable, and debates with the major party candidates were out of the question. On election day, he received 78,000 votes.]

208. I urge you to formally endorse Senator McGovern for the nomination for President.

May 12, 1972

Dear Dr. Spock,

I urge you to formally endorse Senator McGovern for the nomination for President.

Your fourth party is paving the way for the future and I am in favor of its ideals and aspirations. At this time of crisis we cannot afford another four years with the possibility of Richard Nixon. He, as you know, deceived the Americans by bringing the men home little by little from Saigon while at the same time extending the war into Cambodia and Laos with plane and men, the loss of which is never accounted for fully. And now his latest sinister move in mining the North Vietnamese waters.

You must know as well as I do that McGovern has been an outspoken critic of our involvement in Vietnam from the very beginning + that he is a man of wisdom and intelligence.

I do not believe as you stated recently on a T.V. program that he will be manipulated. We should give him a chance to lead America in the right direction. A statement from you <u>now</u> would greatly assist. Is there any better contender?

Yours sincerely,
W. M. [female]
Santa Barbara, Ca.

209. I have a son in Canada so that some emotion is involved in our consideration but even if we didn't, I would vote for a change in November.

Auburn, CA
September 1, 1972

Dear Dr. Spock:

You are a brave man to aspire to the Presidency. Now I am pleased to reflect on my presence at the AAP when you were given a standing ovation and when I shook your hand and chatted with you & Mrs. Spock at the nice reception for you in San Francisco.

It does seem to me that you should consider combining your strengths with those of Senator McGovern. From what I hear your platforms are very similar. Some Democrats may think McGovern would appropriately be a leader of the Peace & Freedom Party! Have you conferred with him? He needs all the support he can get to defeat President Nixon in November. You might be offered a post in HEW.

You would have the satisfaction of being a force in the much needed change in our political leadership. It is likely that I'm not alone in this opinion of those professional people who are realistically concerned.

I have a son in Canada so that some emotion is involved in our consideration but even if we didn't, I would vote for a change in November.

Now that I've expressed myself, I can keep my mind on my patients. If you are in or near Sacramento, we hope you may visit us.

Sincerely,

G. B., M.D. [male]

II. The Last Gasps of Hostility

UNTIL THE end of the war, Dr. Spock continued to receive mail from those who found him and his political views repugnant. The usual accusations of Spock as a communist and traitor, of blaming him for the immoral and disloyal American youth, and for effectively causing the deaths of American servicemen in Vietnam all persist. Although the proportion of such letters dropped significantly, the following sample shows that the passion with which the authors wrote did not.

210. Our poor boys are getting killed in Vietnam and by your lectures you are living off their suffering and misery. Shame on you.

Sir:

I would suggest you see a psychiatrist. You sound like a paranoid person. Your remarks are very unreasonable and you now apparently live of your lectures. Our poor boys are getting killed in Vietnam and by your lectures you are living off their suffering and misery. Shame on you.

Your angry attacks only make you sound stupid. Perhaps you have become senile, embittered. As far as we are concerned the courts made a mistake and you belong in prison with the other criminals.

You may appeal to some because you recommend draft dodging but by an large majority of American public hates you.

W. M. [male]
Lancaster, Penna
Sept 29 [1970]

211. So in spite of you and your pot smokers, long hairs, slackers, Black Panthers and other riffraff, we are going to save our Democracy and Free Enterprise in the way our Government thinks best.

Long Beach, Ca.
May 25, 1971

Dear Dr. Spock:

. . . Do you recall the Loud mouth Father Coughlin of the Hitler era. Well you put me in mind of him. You dont realize that you cant talk peace with a Hitlerite or a Communist. Their talk for peace is a talk for your surrender. However, Father Coughlin did not crawl under fences and in windows, and stop traffic in the highways to put his idea over. In his mad rush for power Hitler would not talk peace he would only talk for your surrender. And this is the way of Communist.

To my notion you are only a poor blind Blithering fool like your friend Dr. Coffin of Yale. Just exactly what you two birds think we should do to save our U.S.A. from the march of Communism, I could never decipher. If you guys think Communism is O.K. you know you can buy a ticket to Moscow or Peking. So in spite of you and your pot smokers, long hairs, slackers, Black Panthers and other riffraff, we are going to save our Democracy and Free Enterprise in the way our Government thinks best.

To classify you and Dr. Coffin is not very difficult. You are the Father Coughlin and the Gerald K. Smith of the Vietnam War.

Yours truly,
J. H. [male]
Long Beach, Ca.

212. For years you have been preaching disloyalty, treachery and violence in the disobedience of the law.

> Pittsburgh, PA
> May tenth, 1972

Sir:

Your comments on President Nixon's announcement on policy in Vietnam are typically Spock . . . . lying, disgusting, thoroughly treasonable. In my eighty years it has been my fortune to know an unusually large number of all kinds of people, and I have never met a more thoroughgoing bastard.

One of the greatest misfortunes this country ever experienced was the acceptance by so many parents of the teachings you disseminated. They are largely responsible for the presence today of so many young people who refuse all responsibility, have no sense of obligation, are totally self-centered, in many cases cowardly and in many utterly lacking in morality. I think you knew that would be the outcome of your teaching, and meant to do your country a vast injury.

For years you have been preaching disloyalty, treachery and violence in the disobedience of the law. There is no way in which a man could injure the country which should have his allegiance that you have not employed.

What a pleasure it would be to have my hands on one end of a rope with the other slipnoosed around your neck, you vicious traitor! There has to be a hell . . . . if only for you.

C. K. [male]

III. Personal Appeals

THIS BOOK'S final group of letters reinforces the public's sense of Spock as inhabiting two roles—political leader and trusted adviser on children. All of these letters come from parents. Some write of their sons in Vietnam (including one who died there), while others write in desperation, hoping to find a way to keep a son from being sent to Vietnam. Another worries that children growing up watching the war on television will become desensitized to the violence. The final letter dwells on the fate of Americans missing in action in Vietnam—this before the war ended and the issue took on additional meaning. The unsettled nature of this correspondence predicts the restless effect the war continued to have on the larger public in the years after the war. Like a fever that spikes and drops and feels always just beyond one's control, the Vietnam War and what to make of it, continued to torment Americans for decades after its end.

213. My son like many other boys are pushed beyond human endurance —I believe this is murder and should be investigated as was the My Lai massacre.

[EDITOR'S NOTE: This letter from a Detroit mother of a soldier killed in action was written, first, on the bottom of a letter from the Army's Office of the Adjutant General, indicating that her son had been posthumously awarded several medals, and, second, in the margins and between the lines of a copy of a letter written by her son on the day before he died. Excerpts from the Adjutant General's letter and the son's letter are included below; the mother's handwriting is indicated in underlined text.]

Department of the Army
Office of the Adjutant General
Washington, D.C.
17 Apr 1970

Dear Mrs. [Name Deleted]:

I have the honor to inform you that your son has been awarded posthumously the Bronze Star Medal, Army Commendation Medal, Purple Heart, and the Good Conduct Medal. . . .

Arrangements are being made to have these awards presented to you in the near future by a representative of the Commanding General, Fifth United States Army. . . .

My continued sympathy is with you.

Sincerely,
K. G. W.
Major General, USA
The Adjutant General

<u>What more did they want? If the army didn't push him beyond human endurance and gave him a little rest, he could have continued fighting— and lived to receive his own medals and awards.</u>

Second page, on son's letter:

<u>My son was told being a Sgt. he would have to spend 6 mos. in the front lines. After more than 6 mos. and two requests to be sent to a safer place —he was told there were no replacements and was sent to this danger-</u>

ous TET mission. [My son] wrote this letter one day before he was killed. I typed the letter so it would fit on one page.

15 February 1970

Dear Mom,

Just a short note to say hello and to let you know I'm alright.

I was talking to a couple of people that just came back from the rear and they said that it is now almost impossible for people to get rear jobs, that is people in the infantry—there aren't any replacements. If you are unable to get those letters or whatever you want to call it let me know. I'm starting to get sick and tired of beating around the bush. As of the 29th of this month, I'll have less than five months left in the Army. That means that if I break an arm or ankle or something, I could get ETS. If your way won't work, then I may do something drastic. We have been in the field now for over 20 days.

Sec. of Def. Laird had to rest in Florida for several days after spending only TWO days in Vietnam.

It's bad enough being here, but once we do get a chance to go in to the rear, they just harrass us to death. It's stupid. My hatred for the Army is fantastic. My hatred for the U.S. just grows and grows. Maybe the latter will change when I come home. I hope it does. How sad—to die for something that forced you to hate it so. Will this hatred last thru eternity?

People in the infantry are treated like dirt. Everybody has it better than an Infantryman.

As you can see I'm very depressed, tired, and perturbed. I'm about at wits end with the army. To be pushed so far, I doubt if any body could survive a field of booby traps.

You remember the mustache I had when I left. Well, I had to shave it off when I got in ACO. When we got a different CO, he said we could grow them again. Then we switched CO's, then we couldn't have them. Now we can again—pure frustration. If I'm told to shave it off, I will go berserk. War is deadly. Men lives are at stake, to treat them like boy scouts is cruel and unforgivable.

In the rear, they say that the War's over. But people are still being killed. What foolish games these people play (act).

Well, I guess that's about it.

Love,

J. [male]

My son like many other boys are pushed beyond human endurance—I believe this is murder and should be investigated as was the My Lai massacre. From a bitter and saddened mother.

Mrs. J. B. [female]

214. I did not rear 3 sons to fight a stupid war in Vietnam. I am totally against this war.

[undated, ca. May 1970]

My dear Dr. Spock,

I have meant to express my sincerest gratitude for all you have accomplished to Bring about Peace. Long ago I learned to warmly respect you for your sensitive knowledge in encouraging mothers to grow into a deeper and more sensible state of motherhood. This country and indeed parents all over this world owe you a Mountain of respect and love for the great chance you've taught us to take as we become mothers. Our love for you is warm and deep and forever real.

I do not use this means to express how I feel about how you have helped us to become reasonable mothers.

I am writing to relate my sense of total feeling of futility about this Vietnam War. There is something so terribly, horribly wrong with this Nation Because we have failed our young men and women and ourselves in the process. We have advanced into an area that almost seems impossible to comprehend, yet we cant' give ourselves Peace. We go to the moon, but we're still in Vietnam, now Cambodia; no telling where else. We can't spend funds to Eliminate illness, mental and physical, for our babies and teen aged men and women, but we'll spend unheard of funds to get to the moon, the A.B.M., others like programs.

Now Cambodia. It is a far more frightening word than Vietnam ever was because who knows where any of it will Ever End. I think the implications are far more reaching than any of us admit just now. I am very frightened, and it seems reasonable for this feeling after considering Nixon's little talk last evening. How he expects the young men and women in this nation to continue, year after year, to take War—War—War—all in Easy stride, I can never imagine.

I have three sons. One was forced to enlist or get drafted because he was attending a "2 year college" and he simply got fed up with the local Selective Service Board on his Back every few weeks. This son served for 2 years as a Specialist Aide to the Commanding General of the 3rd

Armd. Division in Europe. I did not really enjoy and encourage this servitude; there seemed nothing I could do. Another son suffered a leg injury on a Honda when he was Engaged in an accident. My third, youngest son was drafted and finally after three months honorably discharged on hardship basis.

I did not rear 3 sons to fight a stupid war in Vietnam. I am totally against this war. Like you, I was ashamed and shocked by L.B.J.'s turn about in Vietnam.

You and the dear Robert F. Kennedy made me realize a concrete value of Peace. My sons came in the late '40s and I recall the fear of the Second World War.

My youngest son who could be called for service if matters continue declares that he'd go to Sweden if it Ever comes to the draft forcing him thing again. I would personally march and do anything within my power to help against war and another young man leaving to fight this war.

This is what I wanted to tell you. That I am very willing to help in any way I can to protest this war. I am sick to death of it and there is no end in sight. You stand ten feet tall in my mind and heart for all you are doing and have done to promote peace. . . .

> Sincerely
> M. S. [female]
> Suffolk, Virginia

215. Our son has looked into the Reserves without success and I asked why if Athletes and sons of prominent people can find a haven in the Reserves, why can't my son?

May 11, 1970

Dear Sir:

My son is classified 1-A has just passed his physical examination and is 123 in the draft, and will be 23 yrs old in Nov. We fear his induction will be coming up soon. He has four years of college, majoring in Industrial management and at the present time is working for Wycoff steel in Newark, N.J. He is registered with the Pittsburgh draft board who stated last week that anyone with no.s 1 to 145 could be called in the month of May. His father and I are deeply concerned about our <u>only childs</u> welfare and strongly oppose the Vietnam War as does our son. We know the hour is late, I have procrastinated too long in trying to do something to delay our son's induction or prevent it entirely, but concern for him impels me to look for advice and I feel you are the one who can possibly help.

Our son has looked into the Reserves without success and I asked why if Athletes and sons of prominent people can find a haven in the Reserves, why can't my son? Also why are so many boys rejected because they have fake injuries or by a stroke of luck are rejected by their draft physicals when they are just as healthy as our son who has a deviated septum which makes it impossible to breathe thru his nose, not much of a handicap but just as legit as those of his buddies who have been reject-ed on a letter from their Dr. We weren't smart enough, or too honest up until now to look for a way out but now we are desperate and need help. Any advice you can give us will be more than welcome. May we expect a prompt answer, the time is late.

Sincerely,

Mrs. W. H.

Pgh., Pa.

216. We are both deeply opposed to war in any form; besides which, we are very close to each other and our two-year-old daughter and cannot let ourselves be separated in any way.

5-23-70

Dear Dr. Spock,

My husband is currently applying for a III-A (Hardship) deferment from the draft. He is graduating from Fordham University and thus los-ing his student deferment. We are both deeply opposed to war in any form; besides which, we are very close to each other and our two-year-old daughter and cannot let ourselves be separated in any way. The only alternative for us to his deferment is Canada together.

I feel (and passages in Baby and Child Care support the feeling) that for any child our daughter's age the father's absence would cause emo-tional damage. For our child, I believe this would be magnified by the fact that she is accustomed to a greater amount of her father's presence than most children. During the past year, I have had to work part-time, and we have arranged our schedules so that one of us was always home with [our daughter]. She is accustomed to being with her father six mornings a week until 2:00.

It seems to me that a letter from a doctor or child psychiatrist that emotional damage would be caused to [our daughter] by her father's prolonged absence, would be a decided help in our application. We are desperately poor.

Could you possibly give me some advice on finding a doctor who might see us, and might write such a statement, without charging an extremely high fee? I don't ask <u>you</u> to do this, because I don't suppose you have much time for individual cases, besides which I don't suppose you are very popular with Selective Service officials. I hate to bother you at all, but you are the only person I know of who is deeply concerned with both children and the draft. I hope you can give us some advice, even the name of an agency.

Yours in peace,

A. S. [female]

NY, NY

217. I feel there is more than a possibility that the children will grow to be complacent and learn that violence is a standard occurrence in their lives.

June 17, 1970

Dear Dr. Spock,

This morning I finished reading "Decent & Indecent." Not by nature a writer of "fan-letters," I am nonetheless moved to write you. I cannot say it was an enjoyable book to read, but I was deeply impressed by your ideas and the clarity with which they were expressed.

As a young mother I feel very much worry and genuine fear for my children and all children in these times. Perhaps my main fear, overriding the ever present threat of nuclear annihilation, is that it may be impossible to teach the little ones to be loving adults. My fears for our country and the world are the same as yours although I view it on a more local level. The brutality and senselessness of our Asian policy and internal policies concerning blacks & the young are ripping apart country and family. Children witness the body count each evening on the news and although my children are too young to pay attention to television, I fear for the older ones. I feel there is more than a possibility that the children will grow to be complacent and learn that violence is a standard occurrence in their lives. The bodies shown maimed and murdered on the news are presented much as un-real people and the video-suffering takes on the aspects of some grisly cowboy & indian film.

Our country is falling apart and I can see little hope to save it. Our major cities may soon become battlefields with small children watching the violence outside their homes with no more horror than they view the evening news.

I truly yearn to help the radicals in their efforts buy my first duty is to my children. I must try to raise them in a way to encourage them in growing up as sane, peaceful adults.

For these reasons, my hopes and fears as a mother, radical and one who yearns for a day of peace, I write you.

I feel fortunate to raise my children under your written guidance and am proud of you as one of the few truly loving Americans. My thoughts and hopes are with you in all your attempts at restoring sanity and advocating peace.

Mrs. L. A.
San Francisco, Calif

218. This letter is not intended to speak for me alone, but for all the families of American Prisoners and Missing in Southeast Asia, who wait, day by day, for some word of their loved ones.

Los Angeles, California
October 23, 1970

Dear Dr. Spock,

First, may I introduce myself: I am [name deleted], wife of Lt. Col. [name deleted], U.S.A.F., who bailed out of his burning aircraft over North Vietnam on November 11, 1966, and is listed missing in action. Since that day, neither I nor my two small girls have received any official information about his fate.

This letter is not intended to speak for me alone, but for all the families of American Prisoners and Missing in Southeast Asia, who wait, day by day, for some word of their loved ones. Many of us have waited years.

During the past year, we wives and families have become active in campaigns of writing letters to Hanoi to show American concern for these some 1,500 men. Some of us have traveled to Paris and around the world to many foreign capitals in search of the truth about our loved ones. We have learned very little.; however, we do know that Hanoi watches, with great interest, American public opinion.

The reason I turn to you is because of your eminence in humanitarian work. In conversations I have had with the North Vietnamese Peace Delegation, they have lauded your work, as well as we Americans, in the peace movement. I know the would listen to you if you appealed to them for word about the fate of those American Prisoners and Missing in Southeast Asia.

If you could find it in your heart to help these families who wait in agony for news of their men, I would appreciate a personal interview with you to discuss the situation.

Thank you for your time and interest in my letter.

Sincerely,

P. M. [female]

Unscientific sample of three hundred communities from which letters to Spock were sent, 1967–1969.

Alabama
  Anniston
Alaska
  Anchorage
Arizona
  Phoenix 2
  Tucson
Arkansas
California
  Anaheim 2
  Berkeley
  Beverly Hills
  Coronado
  El Cerrito
  Garden Grove
  Granada Hills
  Huntington Park
  Inglewood
  LeGrand
  Long Beach
  Los Angeles 6
  Los Gatos
  Malibu 2
  Modesto
  Mohegan Lake
  Monterey
  Monte Sereno
  Napa 2

  North Hollywood
  Pacific Palisades
  San Clemente
  San Diego 2
  San Francisco 5
  San Jose
  San Raphael
  Santa Maria
  Santa Rosa
  Selma
  Thousand Oaks
  Ventura
Colorado
  Boulder
  Colorado Springs
  Denver
  Englewood
  Greeley
  Palisade
Connecticut
  Danbury
  Groton
  Ledyard
  Old Lyme
  Stamford 2
Delaware
Florida
  Clearwater

  Dundee
  Ft. Pierce
  Gainesville
  Marathon
  Merritt Island
  Miami 2
  Miami Beach 2
  Punta Gorda
  Sarasota
  Tampa
  West Palm Beach
  Winter Park
Georgia
  Athens
  Atlanta
  Savannah
Hawaii
  Honolulu
  Kaialua
Idaho
  Boise
Illinois
  Champaign 2
  Chicago 3
  Decatur
  Maywood
  Normal
  Oak Park

Park Forest
Peoria
Rockford
Urbana
Westmont
Indiana
  Ft. Wayne
  Indianapolis
  Peru
  Remington
Iowa
  Davenport
  Des Moines
Kansas
  Leavenworth
Kentucky
  Louisville
Louisiana
Maine
  Bethel
  Lewiston
  Portland
Maryland
  Baltimore
  Hagerstown
  Silver Spring
  Suitland
Massachusetts
  Arlington
  Boston 2
  Brookline
  East Falmouth
  Fall River
  Greenfield
  Hamilton
  Marblehead
  Milton
  Newtonville
  Pembroke

Somerville
Stoneham
Watertown
Michigan
  Ann Arbor 2
  Bloomfield Hills
  Dearborn
  Detroit 2
  Grand Rapids 2
  Lansing
  St. Joseph
  Ypsilanti
Minnesota
  Minneapolis 2
  Stillwater
  Wheaton
Mississippi
Missouri
  Clayton
  St. Louis 2
  Warson Woods
  Webster Groves
Montana
  Butte
  Conrad
Nebraska
  Omaha
Nevada
New Hampshire
  Fitzwilliam
  W. Chesterfield
New Jersey
  Glen Rock 2
  Morristown
  Newark
  Plainfield
  Pompton Plains
  Ridgewood
  Trenton 2

  Whippany
New Mexico
New York
  Albertson
  Aurora
  Bronx 3
  Brooklyn 6
  Buffalo
  East Northport
  Ellenville
  Elmira
  Endicott
  Forest Hills 2
  Greenlawn
  Hastings-on-
    Hudson
  Ithaca
  Mamaroneck
  New City
  New York 17
  Oswego
  Plattsburgh
  Pomona
  Queens
  Schenectady
  Southold
  Suffern
  Syracuse
  White Plains
  Yonkers
North Carolina
  Asheville
  Washington
North Dakota
Ohio
  Akron
  Cleveland 4
  Lakewood
  Stow

Toledo
Wooster
Oklahoma
  Tulsa 3
Oregon
  North Bend
  Salem
Pennsylvania
  Devon
  Lancaster
  Lititz
  McKeesport
  Norristown
  Philadelphia 6
  Pittsburgh 3
  Sewickley 2
  Swarthmore
Rhode Island
  Providence 2
  W. Warwick

South Carolina
South Dakota
Tennessee
  Memphis 2
Texas
  Dallas
  Denton
  El Campo
  Houston 2
  Lamesa
  Waco
Utah
Vermont
  Burlington
  Lyndonville
Virginia
  Alexandria 2
  Danville
  Luray
Washington

Johnston
Lynnwood
Olympia
  Pullman
  Seattle 4
  Tacoma
  Walla Walla
Washington, DC 5
West Virginia
  Huntington
Wisconsin
  Brookfield
  Hazel Green
  Madison 2
  Milwaukee
  Whitehall
Wyoming

Vietnam 1

Unknown 15

NOTES

Notes to the Introduction

1. For national studies on the antiwar movement, see Charles DeBenedetti, *An American Ordeal: The Antiwar Movement of the Vietnam Era* (Syracuse, NY: Syracuse University Press, 1990); Adam Garfinkle, *Telltale Hearts: The Origins and Impact of the Vietnam Antiwar Movement* (New York: St. Martin's, 1995); Rhodri Jeffreys-Jones, *Peace Now! American Society and the Ending of the Vietnam War* (New Haven, CT: Yale University Press, 1999); Thomas Powers, *Vietnam: The War at Home* (New York: Grossman, 1973); Melvin Small, *Johnson, Nixon, and the Doves* (New Brunswick, NJ: Rutgers University Press, 1988); Melvin Small, *Antiwarriors: The Vietnam War and the Battle for America's Hearts and Minds* (Wilmington, DE: SR Books, 2002); Tom Wells, *The War Within: America's Battle over Vietnam* (Berkeley: University of California Press, 1994); Lawrence Wittner, *Rebels against War: The American Peace Movement, 1933–1983* (Philadelphia: Temple University Press, 1984); Nancy Zaroulis and Gerald Sullivan, *Who Spoke Up? American Protest against the War in Vietnam, 1963–1975* (Garden City, NY: Doubleday, 1984). For more localized studies and studies of more narrow subsets of the movement, see James Dickerson, *North to Canada: Men and Women against the Vietnam War* (Westport, CT: Praeger, 1999); Michael Ferber and Staughton Lynd, *The Resistance* (Boston: Beacon Press, 1971); Michael S. Foley, *Confronting the War Machine: Draft Resistance during the Vietnam War* (Chapel Hill: University of North Carolina Press, 2003); Michael S. Foley, "Sanctuary! A Bridge between Civilian and GI Protest against the Vietnam War," in Robert Buzzanco and Marilyn Young, eds., *A Companion to the Vietnam War* (Boston: Blackwell, 2002); John Hagan, *Northern Passage: American Vietnam War Resisters in Canada* (Cambridge, MA: Harvard University Press, 2001); Mitchell K. Hall, *Because of Their Faith: CALCAV and Religious Opposition to the Vietnam War* (New York: Columbia University Press, 1990); Kenneth J. Heineman, *Campus Wars: The Peace Movement at American State Universities in the Vietnam Era* (New York: New York University Press, 1993); Mary Hershberger, *Traveling to Vietnam: American Peace Activists and the War* (Syracuse, NY: Syracuse University Press, 1998); Andrew Hunt, *The Turning: A History of Vietnam Veterans against the War* (New York: Columbia University Press, 1999); Richard Moser, *The New Winter*

Soldiers: GI and Veteran Dissent during the Vietnam Era (New Brunswick, NJ: Rutgers University Press, 1996); Amy Swerdlow, *Women Strike for Peace: Traditional Motherhood and Radical Politics in the 1960s* (Chicago: University of Chicago Press, 1993).

2. For example, see Lawrence Baskir and William Strauss, *Chance and Circumstance: The Draft, the War and the Vietnam Generation* (New York: Knopf, 1978); James Fallows, "What Did You Do in the Class War, Daddy," *Washington Monthly,* October 1975; H. Bruce Franklin, *M.I.A.: Or Mythmaking in America* (New Brunswick, NJ: Rutgers University Press, 1993); Arnold Isaacs, *Vietnam Shadows: The War, Its Ghosts, and Its Legacy* (Baltimore: Johns Hopkins University Press, 1997); Jerry Lembcke, *The Spitting Image: Myth, Memory, and the Legacy of Vietnam* (New York: New York University Press, 1998); Myra MacPherson, *Long Time Passing: Vietnam and the Haunted Generation* (New York: Doubleday, 1984); D. Michael Shafer, *The Legacy: The Vietnam War in the American Imagination* (Boston: Beacon Press, 1990); Fred Turner, *Echoes of Combat: The Vietnam War in American Memory* (New York: Doubleday, 1996).

3. Thomas Maier, *Dr. Spock: An American Life* (New York: Harcourt Brace, 1998), 202.

4. Robert McElvaine, ed., *Down and Out in the Great Depression: Letters from the Forgotten Man* (Chapel Hill: University of North Carolina Press, 1983), 7.

5. For interesting insights on the language of these justifications, see Christina Klein, "Family Ties and Political Obligation: The Discourse of Adoption and the Cold War Commitment to Asia," and Jonathan Nashel, "The Road to Vietnam: Modernization Theory in Fact and Fiction," in Christian G. Appy, ed., *Cold War Constructions: The Political Culture of United States Imperialism, 1945–1966* (Amherst: University of Massachusetts Press, 2000). See also Tom Engelhardt, *The End of Victory Culture: Cold War America and the Disillusioning of a Generation* (New York: Basic Books, 1995).

6. Stephen Whitfield, *The Culture of the Cold War,* 2nd ed. (Baltimore: Johns Hopkins University Press, 1991); see Peter J. Kuznick and James Gilbert, "Introduction: U.S. Culture and the Cold War," in Kuznick and Gilbert, eds., *Rethinking Cold War Culture* (Washington, DC: Smithsonian Institution Press, 2001), 1–13.

7. Alan Brinkley, "The Illusion of Unity in Cold War Culture," and Peter Filene, "Cold War Culture Doesn't Say It All," in Kuznick and Gilbert, eds., *Rethinking Cold War Culture.* Filene, who treats the Cold War as fought primarily by elites, apparently does not find Richard Gid Powers's evidence of a grassroots anticommunist movement persuasive; see Powers, *Not without Honor: American Anticommunism* (New Haven, CT: Yale University Press, 1997).

8. Betty Friedan, *The Feminine Mystique* (New York: Norton, 2001); Elaine Tyler May, *Homeward Bound: American Families in the Cold War Era* (New York: Basic Books, 1988); Jane Sherron DeHart, "Containment at Home: Gender, Sexuality, and National Identity in Cold War America," in Kuznick and Gilbert, eds., *Rethinking Cold War Culture*, 132.

9. See, for example, Harriet Hyman Alonso, *Peace as a Women's Issue: A History of the U.S. Movement for World Peace and Women's Rights* (Syracuse, NY: Syracuse University Press, 1993); and Swerdlow, *Women Strike for Peace.*

Notes to Chapter 1

1. The Yalu River separates North Korea from China. During the Korean War, some called for bombing Chinese territory in Manchuria, across the Yalu River. President Truman thought such action would further provoke the Chinese into a further protracted war and rejected the idea.

2. *The Cleveland Plain Dealer* is a daily newspaper to which Spock often wrote letters when he lived in the city and was associated with Western Reserve University.

3. Southeast Asia Treaty Organization.

4. Huntley was a television news anchorman on NBC's nightly *Huntley-Brinkley Report.*

5. Longtime journalist for CBS, in the mid-1960s, Sevareid appeared regularly on the *CBS Evening News.*

Notes to Chapter 2

1. *New York Times* columnist James Reston.

2. Presumably referring to historian and antiwar activist Staughton Lynd who had recently made a trip to North Vietnam with historian Herbert Aptheker and Students for a Democratic Society leader, Tom Hayden.

3. Civil rights leader Martin Luther King, Jr., had to this date been publicly silent on the issue of the war, though by early 1967 he came out strongly against the war.

4. Island in the Marianas and site of fierce fighting between American and Japanese forces during World War II.

5. Heavyweight champion Muhammad Ali (né Cassius Clay) had, by the spring of 1966, publicly pledged to resist the draft.

6. Spock did not, in fact, run for the Senate, though he publicly mused about the possibility.

7. At the time this letter was written, a presidential commission was in the process of reviewing the fairness of the Selective Service System which provided

draft deferments for, among others, undergraduate students. Many Americans expected the undergraduate deferments to be eliminated in 1967, but they were not.

Notes to Chapter 3

1. Attu is the westernmost island in the Aleutian chain and was occupied by the Japanese from June 1942 to June 1943.

2. Nguyen Cao Ky, South Vietnamese prime minister, 1965–1967, and vice president, 1967–1971.

3. Floyd McKissick, director of Congress of Racial Equality (CORE), 1966–1968. Stokely Carmichael, chairman of the Student Nonviolent Coordinating Committee, 1966–1967. Departing from a strict adherence to nonviolent direct action, McKissick and Carmichael aligned these two civil rights organizations with the more militant—and growing—Black Power movement.

4. The Sheep Meadow is a large open space in the southern half of Central Park. On April 15, 1967, preceding the march to the United Nations, a number of draft-age men burned their draft cards in a well-organized and well-publicized ceremony.

5. Co-host, with Chet Huntley, of the nightly news program, *The Huntley-Brinkley Report.*

Notes to Chapter 4

1. The writer refers to civil rights leader Martin Luther King, Jr.; Yale University chaplain William Sloane Coffin, Jr.; MIT professor of linguistics Noam Chomsky; and longtime Socialist Party leader and pacifist, Norman Thomas.

2. The Dow Chemical Company manufactured napalm, a jellied gasoline incendiary weapon delivered mostly in bombs dropped from American aircraft all over South Vietnam. Napalm kills by asphyxiation and burning, but most Americans associated it with shocking images of Vietnamese civilians disfigured by napalm burns. By 1967, antiwar protesters frequently demonstrated outside Dow offices and manufacturing plants, as well as against Dow's college recruiters on many campuses.

3. Founding editor of conservative magazine *The National Review,* Buckley hosted his own syndicated television show, *Firing Line,* beginning in 1966.

4. Robert McAfee Brown, professor of religious studies, Stanford University, and co-founder of Clergy and Laity Concerned About Vietnam.

5. James Gavin retired from the army in 1957 at the rank of lieutenant general, and used his credentials as a World War II hero to bolster his outspoken criticism of the Johnson administration's prosecution of the Vietnam War.

6. Senator from Minnesota and a Democrat, McCarthy ran on a peace plat-

form against incumbent Lyndon Johnson for his party's presidential nomination in 1968. McCarthy nearly defeated Johnson in the New Hampshire primary in March 1968, and Johnson soon quit the race.

7. Dr. Tom Dooley, a young naval medical intern, participated in the transfer of Vietnamese Catholics from North Vietnam to South Vietnam in 1954—the subject of his book *Deliver Us from Evil* (1955). From 1956 to 1961, he established several hospitals in Laos. He died from cancer in 1961. Years later it came out that he had served as a CIA informant while in Laos.

8. H. Rap Brown and Stokely Carmichael, leaders of the Student Nonviolent Coordinating Committee which, by 1968, had renounced nonviolence and made itself a leading organization in calling for Black Power.

9. Coffin, in particular, had been floating the idea of churches granting symbolic sanctuary to draft resisters and AWOL GIs as a new protest tactic.

Notes to Chapter 7

1. In September and October, the antiwar organization Another Mother for Peace organized a letter-writing campaign to Spock in which it encouraged women to clip out the title page of their copies of *Baby and Child Care* and mail it to him. Presumably, this was intended to show Spock how many women who had first relied on him for his child-rearing advice also supported his peace work. Over these two months, Spock received 142 letters that either included the title page or made reference to the Another Mother for Peace appeal. The next letter came from that group.

2. Benjamin Spock and Mitchell Zimmerman, *Dr. Spock on Vietnam* (New York: Dell, 1968).

3. Robert Rheault and William Calley were accused of ordering executions in two separate incidents that came to light in 1969. Rheault ultimately resigned (though his case was dropped because the CIA refused to declassify information critical to his case) after being accused of having a suspected Viet Cong double agent (who worked with the American Special Forces) killed. Calley, a second lieutenant, was one of the officers who led the March 1968 massacre of roughly five hundred unarmed civilians at My Lai.

Notes to Chapter 8

1. Benjamin Spock, *Decent and Indecent: Our Personal and Political Behavior* (New York: McCall, 1969).

INDEX

ABOUT THE EDITOR

MICHAEL S. FOLEY is Associate Professor of History at the City University of New York's Graduate Center and the College of Staten Island. He is author of *Confronting the War Machine: Draft Resistance During the Vietnam War* (2003).